The Alternative Comprehensive Spending Review 2007

The Alternative Comprehensive Spending Review 2007

Edited by
Colin Talbot and **Matt Baker**

Manchester University Press

Manchester and New York

Distributed exclusively in the USA by Palgrave

Published in association with The Herbert Simon Institute, University of Manchester

Published by Manchester University Press
Oxford Road, Manchester M13 9NR, UK
and Room 400, 175 Fifth Avenue, New York, NY 10010, USA
www.manchesteruniversitypress.co.uk

Distributed exclusively in the USA by
Palgrave, 175 Fifth Avenue, New York,
NY 10010, USA

Distributed exclusively in Canada by
UBC Press, University of British Columbia, 2029 West Mall,
Vancouver, BC, Canada V6T 1Z2

British Library Cataloguing-in-Publication Data
A catalogue record for this book is available from the British Library

Library of Congress Cataloging-in-Publication Data applied for

ISBN 978 0 7190 7807 1 *paperback*

First published 2007

16 15 14 13 12 11 10 09 08 07   10 9 8 7 6 5 4 3 2 1

Printed in Great Britain by The Cromwell Press, Trowbridge

Contents

Tables

Figures

Boxes

Contributors

Tim Ambler is a Senior Fellow at London Business School. His main research covers dynamic marketing capabilities, how advertising works and the evaluation of marketing performance. He is currently also researching narrative disclosures in company annual reports as well as regulation and deregulation by the EU and UK governments. His books include *Marketing and the Bottom Line* (2000, 2003), *Doing Business in China* (2000, 2003), *The SILK Road to International Marketing* (2000) and *Marketing from Advertising to Zen* (1996).

Claire Annesley is Lecturer in European Politics at the University of Manchester. Her research is in the areas of comparative politics, political economy and welfare capitalism with a focus on gender. Claire is the current convener of the Women and Politics Standing Group of the European Consortium for Political Research (ECPR) and is founder and convener of the Gender Research Network (GRN) in the School of Social Sciences at the University of Manchester. She presently co-leads the Network's project on 'Women and New Labour'.

Matt Baker is the Editorial Executive for the Herbert Simon Institute at the University of Manchester. He is a former editor of The Big Issue in the North and is a regular contributor to The Times Higher Education Supplement. His work has appeared in The Daily Telegraph, The Financial Times and The Independent among other publications.

Stephen Brookes is currently the Home Office Director for the Government Office for the East Midlands and combines this role alongside that of Visiting Senior Fellow in the Centre for Public Policy and Management (CPPM) at Manchester Business School. His research includes information exchange and analysis between partnerships, developing a process for assessing the effectiveness of partnership working and in researching links between crime and drugs.

Francis Chittenden is Chairman of the UK Small Business Committee of the Association of Chartered Certified Accountants. He lectures, publishes and consults internationally on taxation, regulation and financial management of small and medium-sized enterprises (SMEs). He has been involved in research projects with the Leverhulme Trust, the Institute of Chartered Accountants in England and Wales, the Cabinet Office, the DTI Small Business Service and the British Chambers of Commerce.

Robert Chote was appointed director of IFS in October 2002. He was formerly an adviser and speechwriter to the First Deputy Managing Director of the International Monetary Fund since 1999, working first for Stanley Fischer and then for Anne Krueger. Between 1995 and 1999, he was Economics Editor of the Financial Times.

Previously, he served as Economics Correspondent of the Independent and a columnist on the Independent on Sunday, where he was named Young Financial Journalist of the Year by the Wincott Foundation.

Alan Dyson is Professor of Education in the University of Manchester where he co-directs the Centre for Equity in Education (with Mel Ainscow). His research and teaching interests are in the relationship between social and educational inclusion and, particularly, in the relationship between education and other areas of public policy in urban contexts and he is currently leading the national evaluation of full service schools.

Francesca Gains is a Senior Lecturer in the Politics Division of the Faculty of Social Sciences at the University of Manchester. She is the Research Co-ordinator for the Evaluating Local Governance project and Senior Research Fellow of the Institute for Political and Economic Governance (IPEG). Her research includes the introduction of new constitutions in local government and the introduction of new political management arrangements in central government through the establishment of executive agencies.

Ian Greener is a Senior Lecturer in the Centre for Public Policy and Management (CPPM) at Manchester Business School. His teaching interests include: health policy; the politics of policymaking; understanding the governance of the public sector and research methods. His research interests are in theoretical explanations of continuity and change in public services, philosophy of research and in gender in management.

Damian Grimshaw is a Reader in Employment Studies at Manchester Business School and co-directs the European Work and Employment Research Centre (EWERC). He runs undergraduate and postgraduate courses on International Employment Policy and Practice and International Human Resource Management. His research covers several areas of employment policy and practice, involving both case-study research in small and large organisations and cross-national comparisons of employment systems.

Carole Johnson is a Lecturer in the Centre for Public Policy and Management (CPPM) at Manchester Business School. Her research is in public management reform, in particular joined-up government, public sector performance policy and management, the role of Parliament in scrutiny, local economic development and local, regional and European governance.

Peter Kawalek is a Lecturer in Information Systems at Manchester Business School. He has contributed to a number of UK and European research projects in the areas of adaptive systems, software engineering and business process modelling. He has undertaken research and consultancy engagements across a number of sectors including insurance, telecommunications, manufacturing, rail and software development.

Ann Mahon is a Senior Fellow and Director of Postgraduate Programmes at the Centre for Public Policy and Management at Manchester Business School (MBS). She directs and contributes to a range of postgraduate and executive education programmes and directs the public health and healthcare management course unit on the MSc Healthcare Management at MBS.

Willy McCourt is a Senior Lecturer in Human Resource Management in the Institute for Development Policy and Management at the University of Manchester. He has carried out research and consultancy in Africa and Asia for national governments and development agencies. His research interests cover governance and public policy, management and reform; human resource management; training and development and organisational behaviour.

Ray Oakey is Professor in Business Development at Manchester Business School. His research interests include the problems of innovation and growth in high technology industry in general, and high technology small firms in particular at both national and international scales. He is the founder of the international annual High Technology Small Firms Conference (begun in 1993) and the associated edited book series.

Rob Paton is Professor of Social Enterprise, and Head of the Centre for Public Leadership and Social Enterprise (PuLSE), in the Open University Business School. He has had a long-standing interest in how value-based organisations can sustain both their social commitments and effective, enterprising forms of management and organization. His recent research has centred on the performance agenda being promoted to not-for-profit organisations by governments and funders.

Joe Ravetz is a Research Fellow in Planning and Landscape in the School of Environment & Development at The University of Manchester. He is a chartered architect with interests and experience in regional planning, economic development, environmental management and community regeneration. He is also working on the Economic and Social Research Council's 'Global Sustainability' programme and has been actively involved in the European Commission's DG12 Integrated Visions project.

Jill Rubery is Professor of Comparative Employment Systems at Manchester Business School and co-directs the European Work and Employment Research Centre (EWERC). Her research work and publications have covered labour market regulation policies and the role of minimum wages; new forms of work and flexibility; women's employment and women's pay; employers' working-time policies and international comparative labour market analyses.

Kirstein Rummery is a Senior Lecturer in Social Policy at The University of Manchester. She is a member of the editorial board of *Policy and Politics*, the *Understanding Welfare* series and *Policy World,* and the forthcoming co-editor of *Social Policy Review*. She is an active member of the Gender Research Network. Her main research interests are in the field of citizenship and disability rights, health and community care policy, and partnership working and the governance of health and social care.

Jean Shaoul is Professor of Public Accountability at Manchester Business School. Her research interests cover the broad area of public policy, focusing on the use of private finance and market mechanisms in public infrastructure and service delivery, particularly in transport and healthcare.

David Steven is managing director of River Path Associates, a British knowledge consultancy. He is an associate researcher for the London Institute's SmartLab, and has affiliations with the Department of Population and International Health at the Harvard School of Public Health. Over the past few years, he has worked on a range of global issues, including international relations, environment policy, the AIDS epidemic, globalisation, access to pharmaceuticals, the impact of new technologies, governance, entrepreneurship, higher education and governance. David is editor of the website www.globaldashboard.org

Colin Talbot is co-director of the Centre for Public Policy and Management and the director of the Herbert Simon Institute at Manchester Business School. He has advised Parliamentary Committees on performance and public spending issues for the Treasury, Public Administration and Welsh Affairs Committees. His current research projects are on 'performance regimes' – the complex context of performance 'steering' in public services and how public services delivery bodies cope with competing demands.

Kieran Walshe is Professor of Health Policy and Management at Manchester Business School where he also co-directs the Centre for Public Policy and Management. He is also research director of the NHS service delivery and organisation research programme and deputy editor of the International Journal for Quality in Health Care. His research interests concern quality and performance in public services, regulation and inspection, organisational failure and turnaround and policy evaluation and learning.

Jay Wiggan is a Research Associate in the Centre for Public Policy and Management at Manchester Business School. His current research interests include the nature and impact of performance policy, management and regulation within the public services, governance and the central executive and the development of employment and social security policy.

Foreword

This is the first 'alternative' Spending Review to be produced under the auspices of the Herbert Simon Institute at University of Manchester.

Manchester – both the City and the University – of course has a long history as a centre of 'edgy' ideas and critical actions. We are very much, to use an Americanism, 'outside of the Beltway'. We are near enough to the nation's capital to be fully informed, without being so close as to be absorbed. The role of the new Herbert Simon Institute is to promote critical and serious thinking about the public policy and management issues which confront us regionally, nationally and internationally.

This alternative Spending Review gives many of our academics an unusual licence to state a case and make an argument, rather than report on often dry research outputs. We hope this will bring something to the debates around the CSR due to be announced in October.

This is especially so because the current Government promised a full national debate, involving Parliament and the people, about our national priorities in the run-up to CSR07. There has been precious little evidence of that. The Government and civil service have largely continued their time-worn tradition of keeping all the debates about priorities and policies firmly within the Whitehall Village.

Perhaps Mr Brown, as Prime Minister, will change all that. It would be a welcome breath of fresh air. But given that he has presided over the secretive nature of the five spending reviews since 1998, it seems rather unlikely. Hopefully this publication will help in some small way to prise the door just a little more open.

Colin Talbot
Director of the Herbert Simon Institute
University of Manchester

Acknowledgements

Thank you to Gillian Appleby for editorial assistance.

Section I: The context

1. Overview: a milestone for progress

Matt Baker

"Life is beautiful, death is peaceful," observed the science fiction writer Isaac Asimov, "it's the transition that's troublesome."

As Gordon Brown settles into his new role as Prime Minister to lead "a new government with new priorities" only time will tell whether his appointment marks a smooth and orderly transition or the beginning of an uncomfortable ride that sees his administration bumping through the rapids of change.

There is perhaps no more eagerly awaited portent to mark this crucial transition period for the government than the 2007 Comprehensive Spending Review (CSR).

Covering the spending period to 2011, it provides Gordon Brown with an ideal opportunity to stamp his authority on a new Premiership. By demonstrating long-term priorities his aim will be not only to reach out to a post-Blair Britain but also connect with deeper cultural trends.

In doing so, Brown's hand will finally be declared, duly setting out the Government's outlook for the next election and mapping Britain's course through demographic and socio-economic change, globalisation, international terrorism, climate and technological change.

That this will be done in a tight fiscal context raises the stakes even higher.

What, then, should we expect a decade on from the first CSR? What reforms are urgently needed and how should the Government release the resources needed to address the key challenges of our age?

In this 'alternative' CSR a disparate and distinguished group of authors answer these and other questions, offering their views on what direction should be taken to meet the government's goals of sustainable growth and employment, fairness and opportunity, a secure and fair world and modern and efficient public services.

What emerges in their analysis, especially in the touchstone issues of health, crime, education and now the environment, is a picture of progress being undone by poor performance management, targets undermining achievements and confusing reforms.

If the government is to regain credibility with an increasingly disgruntled electorate, our authors argue that the gulf between targets and aims must be addressed to establish coherent policies which show real improvements. Confusion cannot and should not exist between meeting government-set targets and genuine standards of achievement.

Our National Health Service, as Prof Kieran Walshe rightly points out, has long held enormous totemic significance. Under a New Labour mantra of modernisation and renewal, this has arguably increased, with the central tenet of their plan being the radical overhaul of a service deemed unsuitable for the 21st century.

Consequently this has driven up public expectations to the point where the NHS is judged more critically than ever before.

Success has, in part, been achieved, with the most sustained increase in tax funded resources for healthcare in 30-years providing waiting list cuts, more hospitals and increased numbers of staff.

But this has been deeply clouded by other failures, particularly financial mismanagement, which has sent the NHS spiraling into crisis. The reality now facing Brown is, as Prof Walshe explains:

"…that during a period of resource largesse, a whole series of uncosted and poorly thought through policy commitments were made, with little thought to their financial consequences. The NHS remains in financial intensive care – the overspend has been brought under control through the traditional finessing of NHS accounts, but the underlying position remains highly problematic."

Underlining this imbroglio is a recurring malaise of "tighter performance management – its [the Department of Health] response to each problem or difficulty in the NHS is to intervene, and to institute more intrusive and controlling systems of measurement and monitoring."

All of which, Prof Walshe notes, has taken place "at a time of growing policy incoherence and repeated re-organisation within the NHS – again, led by the Department of Health. The Department's programme of reform has been often ill-considered, and its implementation has been rushed, with predictable consequences. Having reorganised the NHS in 2001 creating 28 strategic health authorities and about 315 primary care trusts, the Department reorganised it again in 2005 and further reorganisation seems likely. The substantial financial costs of reorganisation have never been measured, and the transitional and long-term impacts on service delivery are almost always deleterious."

A similar pattern can be seen in education, where an initial wave of success has subsequently crashed on a shoreline of intractable problems.

In the years immediately following 1997 the education system appeared to be buoyed by an interventionist, target driven approach and results suggested that Tony Blair's much vaunted commitment to this department was raising standards to hitherto unknown levels.

But, as Prof Alan Dyson points out, such a target-driven culture has encouraged a widespread practice of 'gaming the system'.

"Cases where targets have been met while the underlying aims of policy have not been realised are not isolated instances in education. One reason seems to be that departmental targets are themselves translated into sub-targets at different levels of the system – for instance, at the level of local authorities or schools. Meeting these targets then becomes a high stakes affair. At the extreme, local authorities can find their services privatised, head teachers can lose their jobs, and schools can be closed down if targets are not met. In this situation, meeting the target by any means possible becomes the priority, even if that involves practices that are incompatible with the underlying aims of policy. So, for instance, the apparently dramatic rise in primary school standards since 1997 appears, at best, to be much less than government accounts would suggest, and may be largely illusory. Performance has become confused with genuine standards of achievement. As a result, teaching to the test, and even downright cheating, has been substituted for the more complex activity of enabling children to learn valued knowledge and skills."

Of all the criticisms to dog Labour's difficult third term, the phrase 'not fit for purpose' could well inflict the most damage and haunt the Home Office for many years. Facing a tough transition of hard reforms, the Home Office further demonstrates the problems that arise when performance management is unable to keep track of policy delivery.

With mistakes including a failure to archive DNA evidence properly, subsequently ensuring that hundreds of crimes went undetected, the 'disappearance' of 500 serious offenders after the Home Office failed to pass on details of offences committed by Britons in other countries and releasing thousands of foreign prisoners who should have been deported, serious questions need to be posed about increasingly centralised performance regimes.

"Do the measures take account of public value?" wonders Dr Stephen Brookes. "The challenge is to ensure consistent standards of performance but to do so in a way that minimises the burdens on frontline services and resists any further attempts at what frontline leaders would describe as 'micromanagement'."

Shackling frontline leaders with more of the same confusing reforms and interventionist policies from the school of Swiftian detachment runs the risk of making meeting targets become an end in itself. It also threatens to make the Government's real achievements recede like chimeras as an unforgiving picture of failed delivery and unfulfilled promise emerges.

No issue perhaps throws up more challenges that demonstrate the gap between aspiration and action as the environment does.

Joe Ravetz sums up this dichotomy in explaining that Defra's core mission of sustainable development "cuts right across the pro-growth assumptions of almost every other department of government, creating a fundamental policy dilemma."

If the government is truly serious about developing the idea of an 'environmental contract', which Environment Minister David Milliband recently argued is needed to set out the rights and responsibilities of citizens, businesses and government in achieving environmental goals, then a clear and coherent line of thought needs to be unravelled from the skein of confusion surrounding the notion of sustainable living.

"In practice," explains Ravetz, "there is often confusion with carbon accounts and carbon footprint, and there are many gaps between the evidence, the policy levers to respond to it, and the institutions with the capacity for action. For instance the DCLG has set a target that all new dwellings should be 'carbon neutral' by 2016, but the implications for the industry and the householder are only now being explored.

Overall there is a kind of discontinuity, faced with the uncomfortable challenge that 'business as usual' is leading rapidly and visibly towards global collapse. This suggests that a more radical transformation of the economy is called for."

This discontinuity or undefined policy areas is precisely the territory that needs to be mapped out comprehensively if a coherent understanding of the challenges that will shape our next decade is to be established.

Whether Brown will rise to calls for radical action, though, remains very much in the balance. With the Conservatives currently proclaiming themselves as the natural "heirs to Tony Blair" any radical action by Brown may well be seized upon as evidence of a 'lurch to the left'. As long as debate remains mired in talk of who owns the 'middle ground' small changes at the margins may be all that is to be expected.

But as Labour's majority continues to be whittled away by a resurgent opposition and the scale of global challenges facing Britain continues to expand, there may ultimately be no hiding place on the fringe.

The raft of reforms contained in these pages is a blueprint for building a better domestic and international infrastructure, and for demonstrating bold and innovative leadership.

We see, for example, calls for an extended Comprehensive Resource Review setting out a business case and investment portfolio for each sector and government department in transforming towards a one planet economy; a radical redesign of the Department of Health and a dramatic downsizing in its staff, role and function to match; the introduction of 'social mobility' PSA targets; more interventions to influence the actions and behaviour of employers and the introduction of 'gender budgeting'.

There is analysis, too, of cross cutting issues at the heart of change such as E-government and Web 2.0, gender policies and social enterprise. Similarly, there is no hiding from the thorny issues of private finance initiatives (PFIs), public sector pay and the fiscal constraints affecting this year's CSR.

Perhaps as Brown ponders his first few months as PM, his situation will, to borrow an analogy from David Steven's analysis of Tony Blair's early foreign policy, be "a journey into the unknown".

The electorate senses this too, which is why this opening period should operate under the compass of a strong, far-sighted and bold CSR.

A CSR representing a note of caution or a retreat from the frontiers of change will not suffice. Only a milestone for progress will do.

2. Public finances: the constraints

Robert Chote

Introduction

Labour's years of plenty for public spending have come to an end. In his March 2007 Budget, Gordon Brown confirmed that the squeeze that began relatively gently in the 2004 Spending Review is set to become much tighter in the three years to 2010-11 that will be covered by the 2007 Comprehensive Spending Review – a period that is likely to span the date of the next general election. The average real increase in public spending over this period will be half that seen since 1999 and will fail to keep pace with growth in the economy. This requires painful choices, even among those areas that have received the bulk of Mr Brown's largesse in recent years.

This chapter begins by describing why the Chancellor has felt it necessary to squeeze spending at the very time that it could imperil his ambition to win an election as Prime Minister. It then asks how tight the CSR envelope is in historical perspective. Finally, it identifies the winners and losers that have already emerged from the review, as well as assessing some of the trade-offs that still have to be made.

The public finances and the spending squeeze

The Chancellor's tax and spending decisions are constrained by his two fiscal rules:

- The *golden rule* requires him to borrow only to invest on average over the ups and downs of the economic cycle. This means keeping the current budget – revenues minus non-investment spending - in balance or surplus;
- The *sustainable investment rule* requires him to keep public sector net debt below 40% of national income in every year of the current economic cycle.

Five or six years ago, it looked as though both rules would be met by a huge margin over the cycle that the Treasury then expected to span the seven financial years from 1999-2000 to 2005-06 – even though the Chancellor had decided to increase public spending rapidly in its second term. But while spending duly rose significantly as a share of national income, tax revenues weakened suddenly and unexpectedly in 2001-02 and 2002-03 as weak stock market performance hit City profits and bonuses.

In successive Budgets and Pre-Budget Reports, the Chancellor predicted that revenues (particularly corporation tax payments) would rebound. But his forecasts were consistently overoptimistic. Despite the slower spending growth planned for 2006-07 and 2007-08 in the 2004 Spending Review, IFS and other analysts argued in the run-up to the 2005 election that the Treasury's forecasts for government borrowing were likely to be about 1% of national income (£13bn in today's money) too optimistic at the end of its five-year forecasting horizon. We argued that the Chancellor should adopt more cautious revenue forecasts and that some combination of fresh tax increases and reductions in public spending plans would be necessary to bring about the improvement in the public finances that he thought necessary to meet his fiscal rules with an appropriate degree of caution. The Chancellor dismissed any such suggestion during the election campaign:

> "People say that we won't meet our fiscal rules. Once again, with the public finances strong, we will prove them wrong".[1]

But, shortly after the 2005 election, it was clear that government borrowing was once again failing to shrink as quickly as the Treasury had hoped and that Mr Brown was on course to breach the golden rule by a modest amount. Such a breach would have little direct economic impact, but would certainly be embarrassing.

Lo and behold, a month later the Treasury published a paper noting that economic activity had been slightly stronger than previously thought in 1999 and arguing that the current economic cycle had therefore begun in 1997-98 rather than 1999-2000. At a stroke this made the golden rule easier to meet, because the government had run a significant current budget surplus in 1998-99. Even if the disappointing trend early in the year persisted, Mr Brown was back on course to meet the rule again.

The re-dating of the cycle spared the Chancellor the embarrassment of breaching the golden rule, but it did not deal with the fact that his forecasts for the public finances remained too optimistic looking forward. (Whatever the starting point, the Chancellor tends always to predict that the current budget balance will be in surplus by around ¾% of national income in five years' time.) Mr Brown began to address this in the Pre-Budget Report of December 2005, taking the advice that he had so frequently dismissed before the election. He cut his underlying corporation tax revenue forecasts, announced £3bn of tax increases (mostly on North Sea oil companies) and pencilled in a cut in public spending as a share of national income for the period to be covered by the 2007 CSR. For the third parliamentary term running, the Chancellor chose to announce new tax raising measures in the 12 months following an election victory.

The Chancellor continued to announce fresh tax raising measures in the 2006 Budget and 2006 Pre-Budget Report, followed by a broadly revenue-neutral tax and tax credit reform package in the 2007 Budget. The tax measures announced since the election will raise an extra £7bn in 2008-09, helping to offset some of the downward revisions to the Treasury's revenue forecasts. The 2007 Budget also confirmed that total public spending will grow by 2% a year on average over the

---

[1] 'Row over £11bn black hole', *Guardian*, 22 April 2005.

three years of the CSR, after whole economy inflation. It pencilled in the same real growth rate for 2011-12. The Treasury's 'cautious' estimate of economic growth over this period is 2½% a year, so the Treasury expects this to cut public spending as a share of national income.

The Treasury expects the current budget balance to have been in deficit by £9.5bn or 0.7% of national income in 2006-07. At the time of writing, this would leave the golden rule met with £10.5bn to spare over what the Treasury now believes to be a 10-year cycle ending in 2006-07. If the Chancellor had not added two extra years to the beginning of the cycle in 2005, the rule would have been broken by £3.7bn.

Looking forward, the Treasury expects the tax burden (broadly defined) to rise by 0.8% of national income over the next five years. This is to be brought about primarily by a rise of the same amount in income tax and national insurance receipts. But, given that the current budget balance this year is so much weaker than the Treasury anticipated it would be a few years ago, this would not be sufficient on its own to get the current budget balance up to the surplus of ¾% of national income or so in five years' time that the Chancellor looks for. Hence the need to confirm the squeeze on spending during the CSR and to pencil in an additional tightening in 2011-12. This is expected to cut current spending by 0.7% of national income, improving the current budget balance by the same amount. Together the rising tax burden and squeeze on current spending is expected to improve the current budget balance (the difference between the two) from a deficit of 0.7% in 2006-07 to a surplus of 0.8% of national income in 2011-12.

Figure 2.1 Public sector revenues, spending and budget balances

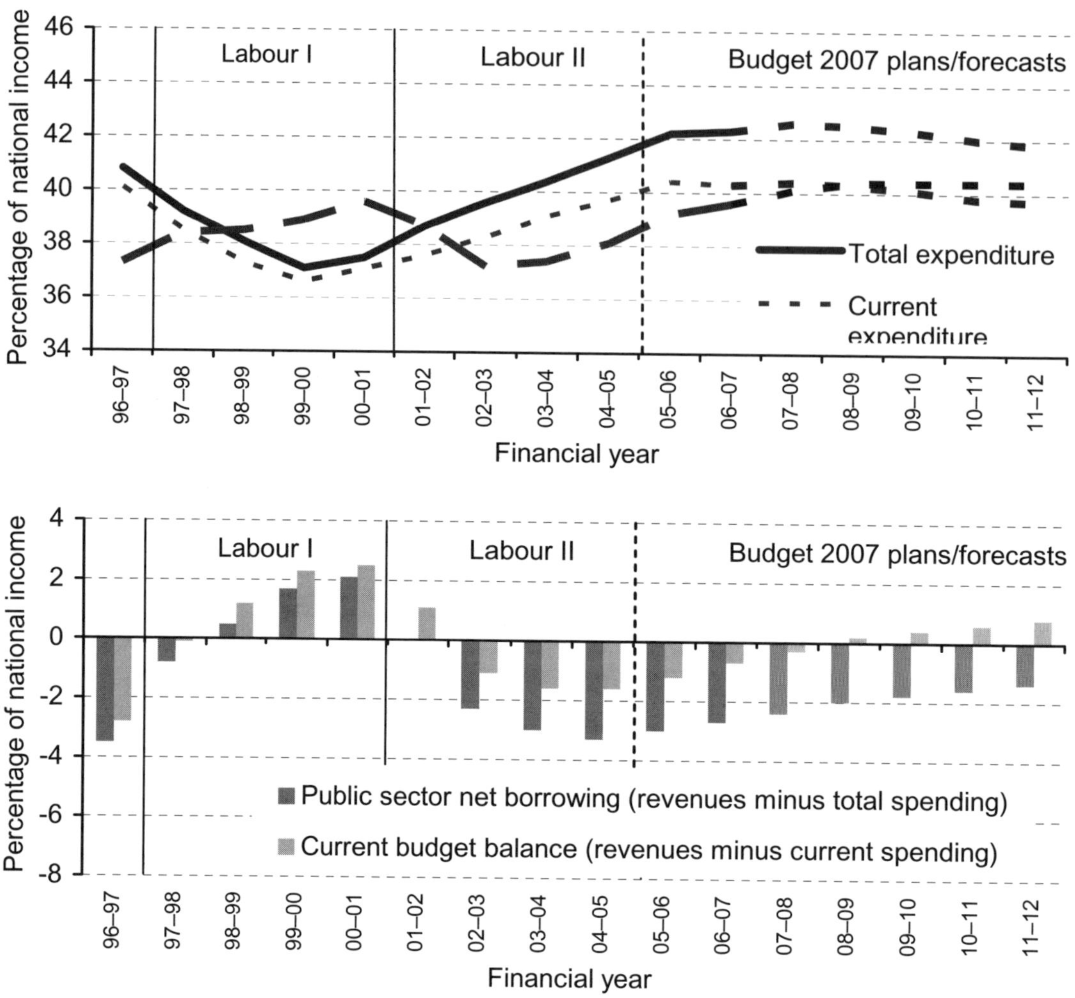

Source: HM Treasury, Budget 2007

The 2007 CSR: how tight is it?

As Figure 2.1 illustrates, Labour's tenure in office began with two years in which total spending fell on average in real terms, as Mr Brown stuck to the plans he inherited from the Conservatives. This was followed by a third year of weak spending growth, partly unintentional as Whitehall departments spent less than they were allocated. Thereafter we had the years of plenty. Spending growth exceeded 4% a year in real terms in each of the next six years, slowing somewhat in 2006-07 and 2007-08, the two final years covered by the 2004 Spending Review. Budget 2007 confirmed that spending will grow by 2% a year on average in real terms in the CSR years and pencilled in the same growth rate for 2011-12. On average over the CSR period capital spending will rise by 3.2% a year and current spending by 1.9% a year.

Figure 2.2 Total public spending

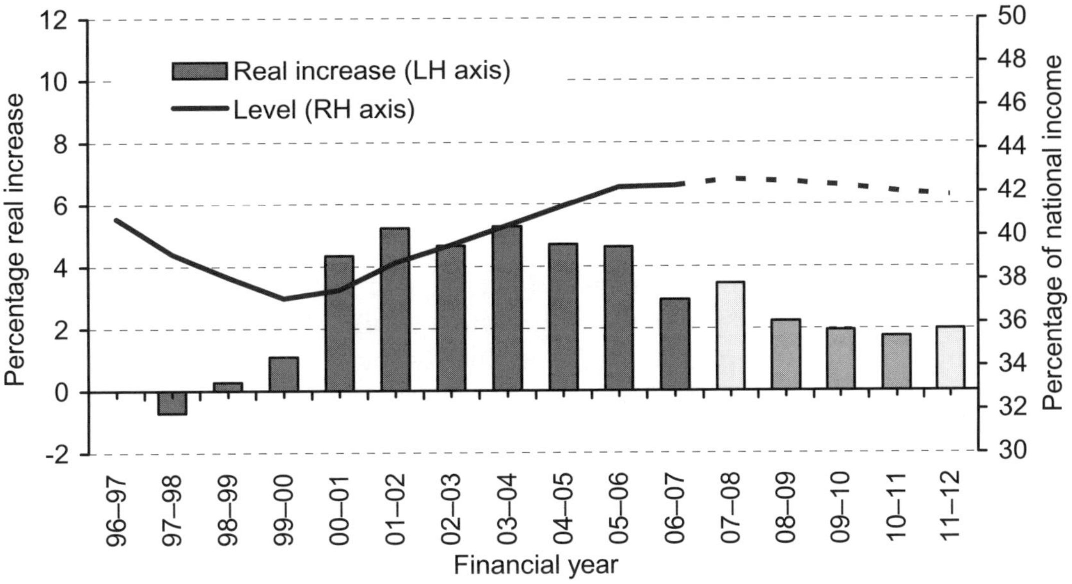

Note: Growth in real spending is calculated by deflating spending by growth in the GDP deflator; while this might not be the appropriate deflator for the increase in the cost of goods and services purchased by public spending, it could be considered the most appropriate deflator when considering the cost to the taxpayer.
Source: HM Treasury, Budget 2007.

How tight is this? The 2% a year planned growth in total spending is half the 4% a year we will have seen during Labour's years of plenty (1999-2000 to 2007-08), but still higher than the 1.5% delivered by the Conservatives (1979-80 to 1996-97). It is also nowhere near as tight a squeeze as the 0.2% real cut in Labour's first two years in office, although it was helped then by falling unemployment and debt interest costs that are unlikely to be replicated in the CSR period. Total spending growth was low during the Conservative era in part because of falling capital spending: stripping that out, the 1.9% a year increase in current spending planned over the CSR is only slightly more generous than the 1.7% a year increase delivered by the Conservatives.

Comparing the size of the state to the size of the economy, Labour inherited a level of total public spending equal to 40.8% of national income in 1996-97. This fell to a trough of 37.1% in 1999-2000 and is expected to peak in 2007-08 at 42.6%. The CSR plans would reduce spending to 42.0% in 2010-11, with the additional year of slow growth pencilled in for 2011-12 bringing it down to 41.8%.

You could argue that having public spending fall as a share of national income is in effect a 'cut' even if spending is rising in real terms. For example, you might expect public spending to have to rise in real terms over time to ensure that public sector wage increases keep up with private sector ones and to ensure that social security payments keep pace with the improving living standards of those in paid work. When the Conservatives proposed increasing spending in real terms, but reducing it by 2 percent of national income over six years in the 2005 election, Mr Brown and his colleagues certainly described it as a cut. To be precise, they described it is a £35bn cut by converting the decline in spending as a share of national income into cash terms using the expected cash value of the economy in 2011-12. On the same basis, Mr Brown's plans to reduce public spending by 0.6 percent of national income over the CSR would be a £9 billion cut, rising to £12 billion if you include his tentative projection for 2011-12. Using the end-period cash value inflates the figure: a more reasonable approach is to use 2007-08 prices, in which case the cut as a share of national income would be worth £8bn over the CSR years and £10bn to 2011-12.

Another way to characterise the tightness of Labour's spending plans is to ask how the expected increase in real national income in the CSR years and the year following would be divided between public and private spending. Labour's plans imply that the "proceeds of growth" would be split 35.5% to public spending and 64.5% to private spending. Interestingly, this is much closer to the split in the Conservative era (31.1% public / 68.9% private) than under Labour to date (48.8% public / 51.2% private).

The 2007 CSR: winners and losers

Somewhat oddly for a Comprehensive Spending Review that is supposed to take a holistic and strategic approach to the Government's spending priorities, allocations for some departments have been dribbled out ahead of the Review proper:

- Budget 2006 announced that the Department for Work and Pensions, HM Treasury, HM revenue and Customs and the Cabinet Office would face cuts of 5% a year in real terms;
- The 2006 Pre-Budget Report announced a real cut of 3.5% a year for the Department for Constitutional Affairs and real cuts of 5% a year for National Savings & Investments, the Food Standards Agency, the Privy Council Office, the Government Actuary's Department and the Central Office of Information;
- Budget 2007 announced a real increase of 2.7% a year for the Department for Education and Skills (corresponding to a 2.4% increase in education spending in the UK), a real cut of 3.5% a year for the Attorney General's Departments and a real cut of 5% a year for the Office of Fair Trading.

These pre-announcements already account for almost 20% of the £674bn that the Treasury forecast in Budget 2007 would spend in total in 2010-11. If we take this information and make some educated guesses about spending growth in other areas, we can focus on what is likely to be the key remaining trade-off: between spending on health (the big winner during the years of plenty) and other politically significant priorities such as defence, transport and environmental protection.

Table 2.1 Possible 2007 CSR allocations by category

	Real average annual growth in spending:	Change as % of GDP in 2007-08 cash terms:
Total envelope		
Total spending (confirmed in Budget 2007)	+2.0%	-£7.7bn
Total spending after refilling AME margin	+1.9%	+£1.6bn
Known allocations as of Budget 2007		
Home Office	0%	-£1.0bn
DCA / Attorney General's	-3.5%	-£3.5bn
10 small departments	-5%	-£0.7bn
Education (UK)	+2.4%	-£0.1bn
Assumptions		
Official Development Assistance	+11.2%	+£1.8bn
Debt interest payments	+3.5%	+£0.9bn
Social security and tax credit expenditure	+1.7%	-£3.1bn
Remaining trade-off		
NHS	+3.4%	+£3.1bn
Other (inc defence, transport, environment)	+1.0%	-£7.1bn

Source: HM Treasury, IFS calculations

Table 2.1 shows average real increases in spending per year over the CSR period and also the change in spending in each area as a share of national income converted into 2007-08 prices. This allows us to identify where the £8bn "cut" in spending as a share of national income over the CSR period, referred to above, may come from.

The table begins by noting that total spending is to rise by 2% a year (falling by £7.7bn as a share of national income in 2007-08 terms). The next Chancellor will presumably wish to refill the Annually Managed Expenditure Margin (a rainy day reserve). This will cut the increase in the spending that remains to 1.9% a year.

In addition to the known allocations described above, we assume that official development assistance will rise by the amount necessary to make steady progress towards the Government's goal of matching the UN target of 0.7% of gross national product by 2013. This implies a very rapid increase of 11.2% a year, but this costs only £1.2bn in national income terms because ODA is a relatively small budget. We also assume that within Annually Managed Expenditure, debt interest costs and social security and tax credit bills rise at the same rate that they are projected to do in 2006-07 and 2007-08. Crucially, this assumes that the Chancellor does not factor in a more rapid increase in the latter to provide resources for tax credit increases to help meet the challenging target to halve child poverty from its 1998-99 level by 2010-11. In the wake of the changes announced in the 2007 Budget, IFS analysis suggests he will need to find another £4bn by 2010-11 to give himself a 50:50 chance of meeting the target for child poverty in that year.

This leaves the key trade-off between health and other spending areas. The table assumes that the Chancellor allocates the NHS a 3.4% real increase each year, equal to the long-term rate seen between 1950 and 1997. This would allow remaining departments (including defence, transport and environmental protection) annual real increases of 1%, the same rate that they are planned to enjoy on average in 2007-08. In terms of shares of national income, this would mean giving the NHS the equivalent of an extra £3.1bn and seeking cuts from other areas worth the equivalent of £7.1bn in 2007-08 prices. But there are an infinite number of possible trade-offs between these categories. For example, Mr Brown could give the NHS the 4.4% minimum recommended by the Wanless Review, leaving the rest just 0.4% a year.

Conclusion

Public spending has moved through three distinct phases under Gordon Brown's Chancellorship: a tight squeeze as he built fiscal credibility by sticking to the plans he inherited from the Conservatives; rapid increases as he pumped money into health, education and tax credits; and now gradual retrenchment as he tries to reduce government borrowing after a succession of overoptimistic fiscal forecasts.

It is clear that the squeeze will require belt-tightening even from the departments that fared best during the years of plenty. Despite a settlement that will see education spending in the UK stop rising as a share of national income – and even if we assume that the Chancellor does not find extra resources to further reduce child poverty – the flow of resources to the NHS will have to slow significantly unless other politically sensitive areas of spending face implausibly severe real cuts.

The Chancellor may of course decide in due course that this pace of spending growth is inconsistent with the Government's aspirations to deliver world class public services and to reduce poverty in the UK and overseas. In which case these aspirations would have to be reined in or more money would have to be found. The fiscal rules make it hard to borrow more, so this may require fresh tax raising measures in future Budgets.

3. Spending Reviews and Public Service Agreements – policy and practice

Colin Talbot

The advent of the Spending Reviews process – and the associated Public Service Agreements (PSAs) – has been hailed by its originators as a radical innovation and seen internationally as part of a trend towards what has variously been called 'outcome based governance'[1] or 'budgeting for outcomes'[2].

Prior to 1998 – when the whole CSR/PSA system was launched – the UK central government had operated for over 30-years with an annualised budgetary system known fondly as 'PES' – for Public Expenditure Survey. PES, ushered in by the Plowden Report (1961), had in its day similarly been hailed as a revolutionary innovation. Plowden however had its sceptics:

> "In some fields the results of … (chopping and changing in resource decisions) … is fairly obvious and new procedure would not make much difference … (but) let us at least have a general pro forma for expenditure over five years, the first year clear, the four later years shading off into impenetrable fog. This will make us all feel better about it."

The author of the above 'translation' of Plowden Report was the veteran public administration academic W. J. M. 'Bill' Mackenzie in an article in The Manchester Guardian (May 1963) in which he mercilessly mocked Plowden. His attack took the form of a very funny 'translation' of the whole Report into language which could have come straight out of the mouth of Sir Humphrey Appleby, talking in private of course, and long before that character was thought of.

Resource Accounting and Budgeting

The last major reform of PES began in the early 1990s with the introduction of 'resource accounting and budgeting' (RAB). On one level RAB seemed unarguable. When public organisation came to account for (and plan) their activities they reported (and planned) only in terms of the amount of cash they would spend over a 12 month period. (PES plans formally extended beyond 12 months, but as noted above no-one took much notice of that).

What was missing from these cash accounts (and plans) were two important elements – capital assets and debtors/creditors and this is what RAB was designed to rectify. The policy drivers behind RAB were multiple – firstly, the

---

[1] Molen, K. v. d., A. v. Rooyen, et al., Eds. (2001). Outcome-based Governance: Assessing the Results. Cape Town, Heinemann.

[2] Osborne, R. and Plastrik (1997). Banishing Bureaucracy. Reading, Mass., Addiuson-Wesley.

public sector had a sorry history of failing to maintain some of its assets (allowing spending on maintenance of schools and hospitals to be the first victim of any budgetary squeeze because these were 'invisible' cuts). Secondly, it simultaneously often kept far too many assets – many of which it didn't even know it owned. One of the features of the big privatisations of the 1980s (gas, telecoms, railways, etc) was that the public corporations turned out to own huge unused or under-utilised buildings and land which they subsequently sold off. If this was true for public corporations it was doubly or triply true for other parts of the public sector – especially Whitehall departments. Thirdly, no-one had any idea from the Whitehall cash accounts of where it was committed to further expenditure (where, for example, a new destroyer or building had been ordered which would have to be paid for next year). Fourthly, at the other end of the spending chain there was no idea of what government was owed – for example in unpaid taxes or to take a more recent example unpaid child maintenance owed to the Child Support Agency.

There was a fifth, usually unstated, policy driver – the whole agenda of contracting out, public-private partnerships, public finance deals and the like. This required some sort of process of making comparisons between public and alternative private (or voluntary) sector suppliers. The use of incompatible accounting policies – with the former using cash accounts and the latter resource or 'accruals' accounts – made such comparisons extremely difficult and RAB was meant to, at least in part, solve this problem, along with the others.

Comprehensive Spending Review

When New Labour came to power in 1997 they had pledged to stick to the (usually purely notional) years two and three spending plans of the outgoing Conservative government. This gave them a breathing space within which to carry out what Gordon Brown announced would be a 'comprehensive spending review' (CSR), which would take a 'zero-based' approach to all spending programmes. The old PES system which had lasted – with modifications – for 30 years - was quietly buried. In the summer of 1998, with much fanfare, the first CSR duly appeared[3]. (Although published in 1998 the CSR covered spending for the three years from 1 April 1999 through to 31 March 2002. The PSAs published in December 1998 covered the same period.) Whilst most of the media coverage and political debate focussed on the shift in New Labour's policies towards the start of what was widely seen as large-scale spending on public services, the CSR 'revolution' was largely ignored. What were the key elements of the new system?

Part of the new system was the so-called Golden rules covering the content of spending (e.g. capital versus current; economic cycles; etc) which have been hotly debated elsewhere. I want to focus here on the new spending system itself.

---

[3] Chancellor of the Exchequer (1998). Modern Public Services for Britain: Investing in Reform - Comprehensive Spending Review: New Public Spending Plans 1999-2002. London, Parliament.

Several new elements were combined in the CSR:

- A split between capital and current spending
- A split between 'annually management expenditure' (AME) and 'departmental expenditure limits' (DELs) – the former only fixed for one year and covering volatile, non-discretionary areas of spending like benefits and contributions to the EU and the latter fixed, supposedly, for three years ahead.
- Both of the above combined to make 'Total Managed Expenditure' (TME) which was also planned, or rather estimated, for three years ahead
- Departments were to be given much greater flexibilities between years (i.e. able to bring spending forward or push it back, so long as they kept within their three year envelope) and also greater in-year flexibility
- And last but not least this was to be the start of a new, three year, type of spending cycle which would revolutionise the management of public spending

This new system was supposed to provide much greater stability in public finances, create opportunities for strategic management within departments, allow for long-term investment planning, and so on. Above all the tyranny of so-called 'annualisation' – only being able to plan one year ahead – was supposed to be ended.

Public Service Agreements

In return for greater stability in medium term finances government departments were going to be held to account through a new system of PSAs. The first batch were published a few months later[4]. This is where the 'outcomes' focus started to emerge. PSAs were supposed to be focussed on the eventual outcomes of policy and hold departments to account for delivery of these outcomes. (Outcomes in this context are the social or personal impacts of government activities – having a hip-operation is an 'output' or service, being able to walk again is an 'outcome'[5]).

It was however from the start a little confusing about how PSAs were supposed to work. They were talked about as 'quasi-contracts' but it was unclear who the contractual partners were. In one set of explanations PSAs were an agreement between HM Treasury and the 'spending departments' about what the latter would deliver in terms of outcomes and modernisation in return for the extra cash which CSR98 allocated them for the 1999-2002 spending years. However the PSAs were also supposed to be a contract between the Government and 'the people and Parliament'[4] about what New Labour would be delivering

---

[4] Chief Secretary to the Treasury (1998). Public Services for the Future: Modernising, Reform, Accountability - Comprehensive Spending Review: Public Service Agreements 1999-2002. London, The Stationary Office.

[5] HM Treasury (2001). Choosing the Right FABRIC - A Framework for Performance Information. London, HM Treasury.

for all the extra public spending. Indeed, the Government duly announced it would start producing an Annual Report setting out how it was doing against the PSAs and other targets which seemed to strengthen the Government to public contractual element.

Policy and Practice

Since 1998 there have been further Spending Reviews in 2000, 2002 and 2004 and the fifth 'Comprehensive' Spending Review is due to be announced this year (2007).

Now the quick-eyed amongst you will have noticed two oddities about the sentence. Firstly, the three year cycle first became a two year cycle (2000, 2002, 2004) and then reverted to three years (2007). Secondly, only the first and fifth Spending Reviews are described as 'Comprehensive'.

Is this mere detail and pedantry? Well, unfortunately not. The two year Spending Reviews may have occurred every two years but they were still three year Spending Reviews – e.g. Spending Review 2000 set out spending plans for the 3 years April 2001 to March 2004. As result year three of each Spending Review from 1998 to 2002 turned out to be meaningless as it was superceded out by the next Spending Review. So the whole process became known – in a classic bit of 'Sir Humphrey' Whitehall-speak – 'a three year spending cycle reviewed every two years'. You could not make it up.

The result was that one of the much vaunted benefits of the whole new process – three year stability in spending plans allowing for more strategic management – was cut back to two years and therefore, it might be reasonable to assume, only two-thirds as 'strategic' as the original policy? Nor was this the only element of instability introduced into the system. The Chancellor of the Exchequer still makes an annual Pre-Budget Review (PBR) statement (usually in December) and a Budget Statement (in March). Both of these have been used to make announcements about changes to spending plans – indeed the PBR has become more and more like a mini-Budget and the Budget more and more like a Spending Review. No-one has done the calculation, but it would be a reasonable guess that spending plans for years two and three under CSR are no more certain now than they were under the old PES system so wonderfully ridiculed by Bill MacKenzie.

What caused these deviations from the original policy? The simple answer is politics. If the original three year cycle had been adhered to the next Comprehensive Spending Review would have appeared in the summer of 2001, but New labour planned to hold a General Election in the spring of 2001. As the new CSR was due to announce important extra resources for public services – especially health and education, two key political battle-grounds – having the announcement several months after the Election would have been a bit fruitless. So CSR2001 became SR200 and the whole process became 'a three year spending cycle reviewed every two years' – until the latest one, which has been a three year process. The reasons may well also be political – CSR2007 will be Gordon

Brown's first one as Prime Minister rather than Chancellor and offers further possible political benefits. If PM Brown is not forced into an early election, then a new two year SR in summer 2009 (with hopefully better public finances and more largesse to dispense by then) would be ideal for an autumn 2009 or spring 2010 election. Far fetched? Possibly, but no more implausible than 'a three year spending cycle reviewed every two years'.

The timing issues have not been the only problems with the new system. It has not introduced quite as much stability at the macro-level as desired – there have been periods of both substantial under-spending – during the period around 2001 - and later of significant overspend (more recently, especially in health but in other areas too). And whilst longer-term budgets may be good for Whitehall departments, there is little evidence this has 'trickled-down' to front-line services, where budgets seem just as volatile as ever.

PSAs have had a similarly rocky history. The aim of the PSAs was supposed to be focussed on 'outcomes' and the government claimed this was the focus of the 1998 batch. However detailed analysis showed they were more about outputs and processes than outcomes[6] [7]. Whilst this has subsequently improved and they are now mostly about outcomes, this has its own set of problems. Firstly, outcomes are difficult to measure and the National Audit Office has found significant problems with the published data[8] [9]. Secondly, despite initial resistance in Whitehall to the whole idea that departments' performance should be measured the focus on outcomes soon won around the Mandarins. Outcomes are generally long-term, and not only difficult to measure but even more difficult to attribute to government action. So outcome focussed PSAs offered enormous scope for the 'smoke and mirrors' so beloved of Whitehall. There have been a few well-publicised casualties of the new system (most notably Education Secretary Estelle Morris over exam results, but in general PSAs have had little impact in the political domain[10].

Where Next?

What happens to the whole CSR/PSA system under a Brown premiership will be very interesting. The chances are it will not be dumped – the present Chancellor

----

[6] Talbot, C. (2000). Memorandum to the Treasury Committee - Spending Review 2000 and Public Service Agreements: 12 Questions for the Chancellor. London, House of Commons.

[7] National Audit Office (2001). Measuring the Performance of Government Departments. London.

[8] Comptroller and Auditor General (2005). Public Service Agreements: Managing Data Quality – Compendium Report (HC 476). London, National Audit Office.

[9] Comptroller and Auditor General (2006). Second Validation Compendium Report - 2003-06 PSA data systems (HC 985). London, National Audit Office.

[10] Johnson, C. and C. Talbot (2007). "The UK Parliament and Performance: Challenging or Challenged?" International Review of Administrative Sciences **73**(1).

has too much invested in the system for that – but we might expect substantial modification.

The first and most important will probably who does CSR and PSAs. They have until now provided HM Treasury and the Chancellor with some very strong levers over the rest of Whitehall. It is doubtful PM Brown will welcome these powers remaining in HM Treasury, so some shift towards No. 10 Downing Street and Cabinet Office seems at least possible, if not likely.

Secondly, we are unlikely to see much change to the structure of the spending system and a probable reversion to two yearly reviews.

Thirdly, we are likely to see some substantial change to PSAs. These are said to be much more 'cross-cutting' and 'whole of government' targets for CSR2007. But underneath that HM Treasury is also supposedly working on a new form of more output and efficiency based controls aimed at departments.

Section II: Departmental reviews

4. Department for Education and Skills

Alan Dyson

DfES and New Labour education policy

When Tony Blair famously declared his three priorities in government to be "education, education and education", he propelled the Department for Education and Skills (DfES) into a central role in the delivery of New Labour's overall policy agenda. It is a department which is charged first and foremost with driving up the quality of educational provision and standards of performance in order to produce a 'world class'[1] system of education and training. However, this imperative has to be understood within an economic context, as a means of developing the human capital on which economic growth depends[2]. As the Prime Minister puts it:

> ...we cannot hope to prosper as a nation if we do not educate all our citizens properly.[3]

In other words, simply driving up levels of accreditation is not itself enough unless those increased levels can be assumed to translate into skills and capacities in the workplace. This means that the department not only has to take responsibility for vocational education and training *per se*, but that it has to bear in mind the broad economic consequences of its overall management of the system.

New Labour has been very clear that what matters is what one Secretary of State called "excellence for the many, not just the few"[4]. Blair's notion of "educating *all* our citizens properly" (my emphasis) is not simply a rhetorical flourish. The country, New Labour argues, has a long history of groups of children and young people who do badly in the education system and subsequently disengage from learning as adults. These groups are at risk of finding themselves 'socially excluded'[5] in the sense that they find good

---

[1] HM Government (2005b) Higher Standards, Better Schools For All: More choice for parents and pupils. Cm6677 (London, HMSO).

[2] Wolf, A. (2002) Does Education Matter? Myths about Education and Economic Growth (London, Penguin Books).

[3] Blair, T. (2005) Education and regeneration. 18 November 2005 (London, 10 Downing Street).

[4] Blunkett, D. (1999a) Excellence for the Many, Not Just the Few: Raising standards and extending opportunities in our schools. The CBI President's Reception Address by the Rt. Hon. David Blunkett MP 19 July 1999 (London, DfEE).

[5] Blunkett, D. (1999b) Social Exclusion and the Politics of Opportunity: A mid-term progress check. A speech by the Rt. Hon David Blunkett MP (London, DfEE).

employment hard to come by, live in relative poverty, have poor health and are concentrated in areas of poor housing and public services. As the DfES drives towards a world class system of education and training, therefore, it has to ensure that these groups are not left behind. Indeed, it has to find ways of closing the gap between these excluded groups and their more advantaged peers. That is why, as the then Secretary of State for Education and Skills, Ruth Kelly, explained:

I see my department as the department for life chances. And that is why I see it as my job to boost social mobility…Our task is to make sure that for everyone involved in learning, excellence and equity become and remain reality.[6]

Not only does this immeasurably complicate the drive for excellence, of course, it also requires the department to become involved in a wide range of issues that affects the lives and life chances of children, young people and adults. So, if DfES is concerned with standards of attainment in secondary mathematics, or with the international competitiveness of UK universities, it is also concerned with promoting healthy eating, reducing teenage pregnancies and ensuring that children are protected from abuse.

The 2004 Spending Review

The scale and complexity of this remit are reflected in the structure of the department and the range of its PSA targets in the 2004 review. Its directorates cover not only schools, higher education and lifelong learning, but also children, young people and families. Its work, therefore, goes beyond state funded education *per se* to embrace issues in workforce preparation and development on the one hand, and social and health policy-related issues around children and families on the other. Its objectives in the 2004 spending review, accordingly, focused on raising standards and tackling the attainment gaps in schools, preparing young people to enter skilled employment or higher education, and raising and widening participation in higher education. However, they also included tackling the adult skills gap and the multi-strand imperative to, "safeguard children and young people, improve their life outcomes and general well-being, and break cycles of deprivation". (2004 Spending Review PSAs: 11-12).

In fact, the department's achievements against the 14 targets set in 2004 have been modest. The 2006 departmental report[7] concludes that, in the case of six targets, largely positive achievements can be reported (for instance, the target has

---

[6] Kelly, R. (2005) Education and social progress. 26 July 2005 (London, DfES).

[7] DfES (2006a) Departmental Report 2006. Cm 6812 in: DfES (Ed) The Stationery Office).

been, or is on course to be, met); for five, achievements are mixed (for instance, one part of the target has been met but another has not, or it is too early to say); and for three there is slippage in achieving the target. There is also slippage in five of the eight targets outstanding from the 2002 Review. This assessment appears more negative when the nature of the targets achieved and missed is taken into account. For instance, while targets for increasing the stock of registered childcare, setting performance targets for further education colleges and increasing the take up of sporting opportunities by school-age children have been achieved, the cornerstone targets for the achievement of pupils in schools have not – or, at least, not in full.

Moreover, there are serious doubts about what 'meeting a target' actually means. For instance, a target for increasing participation in higher education is reported as on course to being achieved. Yet there is growing evidence that participation amongst lower socio-economic groups is static, and that any increase is taking place largely in post-1992 universities and FE colleges offering HE courses[8]. Similarly, the departmental review claims that the target of 60 per cent of 16 year olds achieving 5 'good' GCSEs by 2008 is on course. However, it has had to recognise that some of this apparent success is due to schools' switching their pupils to GCSE-'equivalent' vocational courses, particularly in areas of disadvantage where those pupils would otherwise be low-attaining. As a result, the department is having to redefine its performance benchmark from 2007 onwards as 5 'good' GCSEs *including* English and Maths. On this measure, some 13 per cent fewer pupils currently achieve the target level[9].

In both these cases – and there are many more – targets have been met, but it seems unlikely that the underlying aims of policy have been achieved. The negative aspects of this situation are thrown into stark relief by the apparent successes enjoyed by the department in the years immediately following 1997. For a while, it seemed as though the Government's interventionist, centralising and target-led style was on the point of producing dramatic results in terms both of the performance of the education system and of impacts on underlying problems of social exclusion. However, recent years have shown that intractable problems still remain. The 2005 Schools White Paper (the basis for the Education and Inspections Act 2006) lists these somewhat gloomily:

> Despite the sharp improvement in the number of good schools, there are too many children being let down by schools that are coasting, rather than striving for excellence.[10]

---

[8] Hayward, G., Hodgson, A., Johnson, J., Oancea, A., Pring, R., Spours, K., Wilde, S. & Wright, S. (2006) The Nuffield Review of 14-19 Education and Training: Annual report, 2005-06 (Oxford, University of Oxford Department of Educational Studies).

[9] DfES (2006c) Statistical First Release: GCSE and Equivalent Results in England 2005/06 (Provisional) (London, DfES).

[10] HM Government (2005b) Higher Standards, Better Schools For All: More choice for parents and pupils. Cm 6677 (London, HMSO).

...despite the progress that has been made, at every stage of our education system, parental background still plays too important a role in determining attainment and life chances: those from better-off families do better than those from less well-off families. [10]

Despite all the progress we have made in improving the basics, it is still the case that almost a quarter of children leave primary school without the necessary skills in literacy and numeracy to make a success of the secondary curriculum. [10]

Our participation rate for 17 year-olds in continued education and training is ranked 27th out of 30 industrialised countries. [10]

All of this, of course, comes in the context of a highly critical UNICEF report which suggests that failures in education are part of a wider government failure to provide appropriately for the nation's children. As one senior educationalist has – somewhat tongue-in-cheek – suggested, perhaps the under-performing DfES should be treated in the same way as the department treats others:

I imagine that the same 'fresh start' discipline that has applied to local authorities and schools will be applied to the DfES. So I look forward to seeing the advert seeking tenders from private-sector companies to run the DfES or, perhaps, offering control of the department to a small religious sect in return for a very modest investment, which doesn't even have to be upfront.[11]

Policy and delivery challenges

Not surprisingly, the Government's own analysis of its current situation (not least in the Schools White Paper itself) suggests that what is needed is further – but more determined – reform along lines that have been pursued since 1997. The preferred strategies in this period for the development of a 'world class' system have been characterised as the pursuit of 'standards', the reform of educational structures and practices in the interests of 'effectiveness', the continuing marketisation of the education system and the creation of a culture of performativity[12]. Strategies aimed at what we might call the social inclusion agenda in education – closing attainment gaps, promoting social mobility, and so on – tend to have taken the form of targeted interventions with particular groups and in particular areas. These include, for instance, the Sure Start initiative[13],

[11] Wells, A. (2007) Fresh start, The Guardian, 6 March 2007, available online at: http://education.guardian.co.uk/egweekly/story/0,,2026872,00.html, accessed 9 March 2007.

[12] Phillips, R. & Harper-Jones, G. (2003) Whatever next? Education policy and New Labour: the first four years, 1997-2001, British Educational Research Journal, 29(1), pp. 125-132.

[13] DfEE (1999) Sure Start: Making a difference for children and families (London, DfEE).

aimed at supporting young children and their families in highly disadvantaged areas, those aspects of the work of the Connexions service[14] aimed at enabling disadvantaged young people to make the transition from school to further education, employment or training, and the Widening Participation initiative[15] aimed at encouraging students from 'non-traditional' backgrounds to access higher education.

On the face of it, the methodology of outcomes-based budget-management embodied in the CSA system sits well with these strategies. By setting clear objectives from which measurable performance targets can be derived, the Government is in a position to ensure that funding is linked to service improvement rather than to servicing the ever-increasing costs of maintaining the status quo. However, the DfES's activities within this system have become embroiled in at least three sets of problems:

1.   *The detachment of targets from aims*

The cases I cited earlier, where targets had been met whilst the underlying aims of policy had not been realised, are not isolated instances in education. One reason seems to be that departmental targets are themselves translated into sub-targets at different levels of the system – for instance, at the level of local authorities, or schools. Meeting these targets then becomes a high stakes affair. At the extreme, local authorities can find their services privatised, head teachers can lose their jobs, and schools can be closed down if targets are not met. In this situation, meeting the target by any means possible becomes the priority, even if that involves practices that are incompatible with the underlying aim of policy. So, for instance, the apparently dramatic rise in primary school standards since 1997 appears, at best, to be much less than government accounts would suggest, and may indeed be largely illusory[16] [17]. As one commentator[18] has pointed out, 'performance' – getting children to pass tests – has become confused with genuine standards of achievement. As a result, teaching to the test, and even downright cheating, has been substituted for the more complex activity of enabling children to learn valued knowledge and skills.

---

[14] DfEE (2000) Connexions: The best start in life for every young person (London, DfEE).

[15] DfES (2003b) Widening Participation in Higher education (London, HMSO).

[16] Statistics Commission (2005) Measuring Standards in English Primary Schools. Statistics Commission Report No.23 (London, Statistics Commission).

[17] Tymms, P. (2004) Are standards rising in English primary schools? British Educational Research Journal, 30(4), pp. 477-494.

[18] Richards, C. (2005) Standards in English Primary Schools: Are they rising? (London, ATL).

2. *A focus on parts, not the whole*

In the context of an objective - and target-driven approach - there has been a strong incentive for decision-makers and practitioners at all levels of the system to focus on particular imperatives in isolation from one another. In this way, the interaction between those imperatives is overlooked. So, for instance, the Government has attempted to focus provision for lifelong learning more closely on the important task of raising the vocational skills level of the national workforce. However, as the National Institute of Adult Continuing Education's (NIACE) submission to the 2004 CSR points out[19], an exclusive focus on accredited vocational provision has the effect of reducing or wiping out provision for adult learners functioning below accredited levels, or needing to be eased back into learning, and thus threatens to increase levels of social exclusion.

Even where multiple imperatives exist at a national policy level, they may not be joined up in any convincing way, particularly where such imperatives fall on different sides of the divide between the 'world class system' agenda and the social inclusion agenda. For instance, there are excellent reasons why schools should participate in the Every Child Matters initiative and, in particular, why they should host a range of services for children, families and other adults in their areas. Yet the 2004 Children Act, conscious no doubt of the need to leave schools free to concentrate on standards of attainment, places no obligation on them to collaborate with local implementation of Every Child Matters. It is only latterly that an amendment has been accepted in the Education and Inspections Bill placing a rather vague duty on schools to promote children's 'well being'. Similarly, the recent *volte face* over admissions in faith schools[20] speaks of a Government trying – and failing – to reconcile competing imperatives. It makes sense, in terms of equitable access and the promotion of community cohesion, for faith schools to admit children from other faiths or none. So, the Secretary of State expressed his intention to require that faith schools admit a quarter of the students from outside the faith in question. However, it makes much less sense from the point of view of school autonomy, parental choice and the attempt to develop a diversity of provision, and within a short period of time the requirement was withdrawn in favour of a voluntary agreement of dubious worth.

Not surprisingly, it is difficult for decision-makers at other levels of the system to make sense of such disconnected and contradictory imperatives. As the leader of one of the head teacher associations recently argued, they appear as a constant stream of initiatives and demands that interfere with provider institutions' ability to get on with whatever they define as their core business. In particular, he complained about the requirement that schools offer childcare provision.

---

[19] National Institute of Adult Continuing Education (NIACE) (2004) Lifelong learning and the spending review (Leicester, NIACE).

[20] Meikle, J. (2006) Johnson backtracks in row over faith schools, The Guardian (London)

Although this requirement is important from a social inclusion perspective –
amongst other things, enabling women in disadvantaged areas to re-enter the
labour market - he could not, he argued, see how the imperative to drive up
standards of attainment could be reconciled with a requirement that schools
should take responsibility for "the administration of the national baby sitting
service"[21].

3.   *A mismatch of means and ends*

All of this points to a significant contradiction between the aims of government
policy and the means being used to realise those aims. The education system is
complex and the task of educating learners to high levels is multi-dimensional
and uncertain. Whilst it is relatively easy to get providers in the system to pursue
narrowly-specified targets, improvement in any deeper and longer-lasting sense
seems to require that they share an understanding of policy aims and are able to
exercise their professional judgement in complex situations to find ways of
realising those aims. Yet the strategies available to government are a curious
mixture of centralisation and local autonomy. Providers are set targets, subject to
centrally-driven initiatives, held to account for outcomes and sometimes given
detailed prescriptions for practice, at the same time as they are freed from more
local control, encouraged to diversify, and told to innovate. Nowhere does there
seem to be any strategy for involving decision-makers throughout the system in
understanding policy dilemmas and working with national policy-makers to find
shared solutions.

This situation becomes acute in relation to what we have called the social
inclusion agenda. The relationship between social background and educational
achievement is deeply entrenched and has resisted the efforts of policy-makers in
many countries over many years. It seems likely that any attempt to disturb it
will require co-ordinated and fundamental interventions across a wide range of
policy domains[22]. Although this government might arguably have the range of
interventions about right, they have no means of co-ordinating these in a system
of diverse and quasi-autonomous providers, even if the policy imperatives
themselves were more coherent than appears to be the case.

---

[21] Brookes, M. (2006) Taking control. Speech by Mick Brookes, General Secretary
NAHT, to Annual Conference on Monday 1 May 2006 at 11.30am (Haywards Heath,
NAHT).
[22] Raffo, C., Dyson, A., Gunter, H., Hall, D., Jones, L. & Kalambouka, A. (in press)
Education and Poverty: Mapping the terrain and making the links to educational policy
(York, Joseph Rowntree Foundation).

Where to in 2007?

What this analysis suggests is that the 2007 CSR has to consider not only what objectives and targets need to be set for DfES, but also how they relate to the management of the education system as a whole. It cannot overlook the extent to which the PSA framework itself is implicated in what I would argue are significant policy failures in education. In principle, a set of broadly-articulated aims and objectives, such as those set out in the 2004 review, can usefully set out an agenda for the service as a whole. They can be used to guide imaginative policies and practices at all levels of the system, taking due account of the complexities of that system and the inevitable interactions and trade-offs between different priorities. In practice, however, the PSA framework's translation of aims into objectives, and objectives into targets, is replicated throughout the system. Education providers and decision-makers are faced with a plethora of increasingly disconnected sub-targets, enforced through a mixture of aggressive accountability, high levels of specification, and successive centralised initiatives.

Assuming that the current PSA system is sacrosanct, the task is to break the link between targets at national level and target-driven policies and practices at other levels of the education service. This might be achieved in a number of ways:

1. The stakes associated with meeting targets could be reduced. The meeting of targets is a high-stakes affair for heads, principals and governors, who are at risk of losing their positions if they are seen to fail, while their institutions risk merger or closure. Ministers – at least since the departures of David Blunkett and, particularly, Estelle Morris – seem reluctant to tie their own futures to the meeting of targets, so there is no reason why similar flexibility should not be extended through the system.
2. The dubious trustworthiness of national measures of performance could be acknowledged more openly. DfES's development of 'contextual value added' as a measure of school performance, and its recent insistence that the 5A*-C GCSE measure should include GCSE English and Maths, already constitute implicit acknowledgements that the performance measures in use since 1997 have not been entirely fit for purpose.
3. The current universal system of pupil testing in schools (i.e., one in which very nearly every child is assessed) could be replaced by a sampling system. The curriculum is already sampled for assessment purposes and international programmes of assessment invariably rely on assessing a sample of students rather than the whole cohort.
4. The sophistication of performance measures at lower levels of the system could be acknowledged and celebrated. Schools and other education institutions now have access to a complex range of data (relating to sub-

group attainment, progress, value-added and so on) which gives a much fuller picture of performance than do the rather crude national targets.

It may also be that the formulation of targets in terms of learner attainments has to be rethought, particularly insofar as those targets that take the form of thresholds of attainment which specified proportions of learners are expected to attain. While attainment-based targets fulfil the criterion of transparency, in their current form they sit uneasily with key government agendas that make a greater acknowledgement of the complexities of the education system. For instance, the 'personalisation' agenda[23] places the emphasis not on learners hitting benchmark levels in common assessments by predetermined fixed points, but on individual pathways through numerous learning options, with assessment on different measures as and when learners are 'ready'. The 'Every Child Matters' agenda[24] places the emphasis on a wide range of outcomes for children and families that are not captured in current educational performance data. Likewise, the 'new localism' agenda[25], with the consequent rethinking of the role of the local authority[26], implies a degree of local discretion to set priorities that are not simply handed down from Whitehall.

In this context, it is instructive to consider the sorts of targets that are set in Scotland. There, the Scottish Executive Education Department (SEED) works to targets which focus on quantity and quality of provision ("deliver better quality services…", "provide a modern, high-quality learning environment…", "ensure local authorities set targets…").[27] There is no reason why the emphasis of targets for the DfES should not be framed similarly. In this way, the department becomes accountable for quantity and quality of provision and for the establishment and maintenance of systems to ensure quality, while the monitoring of learner outcomes takes place within that high-quality system, at levels where it can be conducted in the sophisticated and contextualised way that is necessary.

Targets of this kind need not be 'soft'. For instance, inspection and quality assurance processes throughout the education system have become increasingly robust and data-based in recent years. There is an argument to be made for formulating targets in terms of the proportions of institutions achieving good gradings from these processes, particularly since the inspectorates are at arm's length from DfES. Even more interesting, inspection and quality assurance seem

---

[23] Miliband, D. (2004) Personalised learning: building a new relationship with schools. Speech to the North of England Education Conference, Belfast, 8 January 2004 (London, DfES).

[24] DfES (2003a) Every Child Matters. Cm. 5860 (London, The Stationery Office).

[25] Aspden, J. & Birch, D. (2005) New Localism – Citizen Engagement, Neighbourhoods and Public Services: Evidence from Local Government (London, ODPM).

[26] Lyons, S.M. (2006) National prosperity, local choice and civic engagement: A new partnership between central and local government for the 21st century (London, HMSO).

[27] Scottish Executive (2006) Education Department Business Plan, 2006/2007 (Edinburgh, SEED).

to be moving in the direction of an audit system in the sense that institutions report on their own performance and their reports are then audited against a range of evidence. It is a short step from here to enabling institutions to set their own criteria.

Such a development may be particularly important in light of the move towards collaboration between educational providers, and between those providers and other social agencies. For instance, the 14-19 agenda[28] is concerned with the creation of multiple pathways of provision across a range of providers. In this context, the appropriate unit of accountability is not the individual institution, but the local network. Similarly, the Every Child Matters agenda is delivered through collaboratives of education, social care and health providers at local level. In both these cases there is something to be said for allowing local collaboratives to determine their own aims, auditing their performance against these aims, and expressing national targets in terms of the proportion of such collaboratives performing well in their own right. Among other things, this would lessen the likelihood of providers' activities being distorted by national targets transmitted down the line. For instance, if NIACE (2004) is right that the current focus of national targets on level 2 and level 3 accreditation disenfranchises learners working below these levels, an alternative is to allow targets to be developed locally – perhaps particularly in areas of low educational engagement – for the participation of marginalised groups in *any* learning activity.

There is, of course, much that could be done even within the current orthodoxy of attainment-based targets. For instance, the Secretary of State has recently acknowledged that 'threshold' targets (i.e. those set in terms of the proportion of learners achieving specified levels) may lead to the abandonment of those who fall below this level, and chime discordantly with a system committed to 'personalisation'[29]. He argues instead that the focus should be on measures of progress. It is not difficult to see how PSA targets could be formulated in relation to the proportion of learners making progress at a rate appropriate to their starting level, thus making the achievements of low-attaining learners as valuable as those of learners working around current threshold levels. Even if such a target were transmitted down the line in the current crude manner, it ought to have the effect of making education providers accountable for the attainments of *all* learners.

Moreover, there are other alternatives to threshold targets. One of the targets in Scotland, for instance, has a specific purpose of raising the average attainments of the lowest-attaining 10% of learners[27]. In the same vein, the Fabian Society has recently argued that targets should be formulated with a view to 'narrowing the

---

[28] HM Government (2005a) 14-19 Education and Skills. Cm 6476 (London, HMSO).

[29] Johnson, A. (2006) Speech for Rt Hon Alan Johnson MP, Secretary of State for Education and Skills, The National College for School Leadership New Heads Annual Conference, 16 November 2006 (London, DfES).

gap' between groups of learners[30]. There already is (from 2004) one such target, developed in terms of the gap between children in care and their peers. It might be better to focus on attainment gaps between, say, the population as a whole and the lowest-attaining 10%, or between different gender, ethnic and social class groups, or to set a generic target which addresses the maximum permitted gap between any group and the national average. Some of these differences are highly sensitive, but the data exist on which this can be based, and calculations of this kind are often made by schools and other providers. Similarly, the target for widening participation could be strengthened by formulating targets for the participation of learners from less-advantaged backgrounds and, particularly, for their participation in pre-1992 universities.

Some conclusions

The PSA framework, with its transparent aims, objectives and targets is superficially attractive as a means of maintaining a contract with citizens about what they can expect from their government and from the public services overseen by the government on their behalf. However, in education at least, it has become not merely a means of reporting on achievements, but of managing the service. In the context of a fragmented system, comprising a multiplicity of semi-autonomous providers competing against each other in the market place, the conversion of national targets into institutional targets has become a crucial mechanism for aligning the work of providers with national priorities. However, this mechanism has the unfortunate effect of reducing the complexities and contradictions of the education system to a series of disconnected imperatives. In turn, these provoke instrumental behaviour on the part of providers as the meeting of targets becomes an end in itself. In particular, since targets relating to the overall performance of the education system can be achieved while paying little attention to marginalised and low-attaining learners, the framework of targets as currently formulated tends to cut across the Government's avowed concern for social inclusion.

The responses to this situation that have been suggested here – weakening the link between national and local targets, shifting the focus from learner outcomes to the quality and characteristics of provision, and reshaping current targets so that they have a stronger focus on equity – could all help overcome some of the more perverse consequences of the current system. Indeed, there are some indications that government thinking is already moving in this direction. However, there is a more fundamental issue to consider. The balance of powers and responsibilities between central government and individual education providers embodied in the current system could easily be reconfigured. The 'new

---

[30] Fabian Society (Great Britain).Commission on Life Chances and Child Poverty (2006) Narrowing the Gap: The final report of the Fabian Commission on life chances and child poverty. (London, The Fabian Society).

localism' agenda has the potential to offer an alternative, in which local decision-making, the participation of local people, and the professional judgements of local teachers, lecturers and administrators play a more prominent role. While such a system would not obviate the need for a national strategic overview, neither would it require that overview to be exercised through national targets in anything like their current form. It would, in short, involve trusting policy-makers, professionals and citizens at the local level, while engaging them in a critical dialogue with national policy-makers. The 2007 CSR may come too soon for such a fundamental shift to be realised. At the very least, however, it should not stand in its way.

5. Department of Health

Kieran Walshe

Introduction

Health, healthcare, and especially the beloved National Health Service have always necessarily been key political priorities for British governments, for at least four reasons. First, and perhaps most importantly, opinion polls and electoral results show that the public sets great store by the state of the NHS and holds government largely responsible for its performance. It has a totemic significance in Britain, even today, as a concrete representation of enduring societal values and beliefs about our responsibilities for and to each other. Second, the media – both national and local – feed this public interest with a constant diet of stories which are rarely good news for government or the NHS – dirty hospitals, MRSA superbugs, hospital closures, rationed cancer drugs, treatment denials or delays, and so on. The public perception the media engenders is of a badly managed health service, often in crisis and usually failing its users and the taxpayer, and for the majority of electors who make little or no use of the health service beyond seeing their GP once or twice a year, it is these perceptions that matter. Thirdly, the Department of Health is responsible for one of the largest single areas of public spending, with an annual budget of about £80 billion in 2006/07, or 27% of government spending[1], and a seemingly inexhaustible demand for a continuing, ever larger share of available resources. Fourthly, unlike many other public services, central government runs the NHS itself. NHS organisations (NHS trusts and primary care trusts) are the creations of the Department of Health, and though their boards are appointed by the Appointments Commission, the legislative framework makes it clear that they are accountable to and work under the direction of the Secretary of State for Health, their assets and liabilities are the responsibility of the Department of Health, and the Department of Health operates a tight and highly controlled system of performance management through the ten regionally based strategic health authorities which are effectively its regional offices. It is perhaps the most centralised government-run healthcare system in Europe.

But for this government, health and healthcare are perhaps even more important. Since 1997, new Labour has constantly promised to renew and modernise the NHS, and to provide a health service fit for the 21st century. It has set ambitious targets for improved service performance – particularly around access and waiting for treatment – and has provided the most sustained and

---

[1] HM Treasury (2006). Pre budget report 2006. Investing in Britain's potential: building our long term future. London: HM Treasury.

deliberate increase in tax-funded resources for healthcare seen in at least the last 30-years. It has driven up public expectations of the NHS, and as a result finds itself, and the performance of the NHS judged more critically than ever before.

This chapter first sets the scene by outlining the development of Labour policy on the NHS from 1997 to the present, and highlighting how the government's thinking about both purpose and direction has changed. It then goes on to review the Department of Health's performance against the PSA objectives and targets set in the Comprehensive Spending Review in 2004 (and briefly against previous PSA targets set in 2000 and 2002), and explores how useful these measures are in assessing the Department of Health. Finally, it considers the issues and concerns which need to be faced in the current Comprehensive Spending Review round in 2007 and in the future setting of PSA objectives and targets, and calls for a fundamental change in the relationship between the Department of Health and the NHS. The chapter focuses largely on the healthcare responsibilities of the Department of Health, which dominate the Department's own thinking and activities. It does, however, also reflect on the Department's wider role in ensuring and promoting public health, and its somewhat neglected responsibility for social care.

Labour's policy journey from 1997 to 2007

In policy terms, Labour has travelled a long and sometimes difficult road since it came to power in 1997. Having started with few specific policies on health and healthcare beyond a desire to undo some of the effects of 18-years of Conservative administration (the internal market, GP fundholding, NHS trusts, contracting, private finance and privatisation and the like) it has finished a decade in power both by reverting to those policies it once opposed and by implementing them more forcefully and radically than its predecessors in government ever did[2].

Broadly, three key phases in Labour's thinking about the NHS can be identified[3][4]. First, from around 1997 to 2000 we saw a period of strong national direction and a focus on centralised planning and control. Government believed that by managing the NHS more effectively from the Department of Health, by reforming ways of working and systems and processes of care with the engagement of the professions, and by setting clear national targets, frameworks, indicators and plans it could bring about improvement. This period reached its apotheosis in the NHS Plan[5] – a prescriptive, 10-year "vision" for the NHS which embodied this rationalist, centralist, and some would say Stalinist phase in

[2] Walshe K (2005). Health care under new Labour: rebuilding or dismantling the NHS? British Journal of Healthcare Management 2005; 11(3):73-76.

[3] Klein R (2001). Whats happening to Britain's National Health Service? New England Journal of Medicine 345(4):305-308.

[4] Klein R (2004). Britain's National Health Service revisited. New England Journal of Medicine 350(9):937-942.

[5] Department of Health (2000). The NHS Plan. A plan for investment, a plan for reform. London: The Stationery Office.

policymaking. But the perverse incentives and irreducible complexities of performance managing an organisation the size of the NHS from the Department of Health were increasingly evident to ministers, and the limits of what could be achieved through central control quickly became apparent.

Second, from 2000 to 2002 we saw a period in which government became convinced that the low level of spending on healthcare in the UK compared to other developed countries in the OECD was not a strength to be valued (showing how parsimonious, economical and efficient our healthcare system was) but a weakness to be rectified. It recognised that by spending around 7% of GDP on healthcare (compared with an EU average of around 9%, and levels of around 11-12% in countries like France and Germany) we were condemned to live with a second-rate healthcare system which could never match the standards of access and service quality found elsewhere, and it found that as a result we had some of the worst healthcare outcomes (in terms of avoidable mortality from cancer, heart disease and other conditions) in Europe. The Wanless report[6], commissioned by the Treasury (not the Department of Health) provided ample evidence and confirmatory support for this shift in direction, and was the basis for the decision in the Comprehensive Spending Review in 2002 to engage in the most significant deliberate increase in healthcare spending in the history of the NHS. Government committed resources to increase NHS spending by 7.5% pa in real terms over five years, taking the overall budget from £68 billion in 2002/03 to £96 billion in 2008 (at 2002/03 prices). Healthcare spending as a share of GDP would rise from 7% to about 9.4%. Internationally, at a time when governments across the developed world were struggling to contain the inexorable rise in healthcare costs, it was a unique step to take. However, in the general exhilaration this munificence evoked, it was tempting to assume that more resources could or would solve all of the NHS' problems. In fact, countries which were already spending more on healthcare than we planned to spend by 2008 still faced the same problems of managing demand for health services, rationing access to new and expensive therapies, reforming healthcare delivery and the healthcare professions, and dealing with ever rising public expectations.

The third phase in Labour's thinking about the NHS, which started in 2002, has been one of ideological conservatism about healthcare funding – a continuing commitment to a tax-funded healthcare system largely free at the point of use and available according to clinical need – and increasing radicalism about healthcare delivery. In short, it has embarked on the transformation of the NHS into a national health system – funded and regulated by central government, but organised and delivered by a wide range of healthcare provider organisations at a local level. It is a model commonplace in the rest of Europe. Government has set about creating a healthcare market (albeit a heavily regulated one) by promoting diversity and plurality in provision, encouraging the entry of new providers in the independent and not for profit sector, and converting existing

---

[6] Wanless D (2002). Securing our future health: taking a long term view: final report. London: HM Treasury.

NHS providers to "foundation NHS trusts", a new and more autonomous form of public benefit corporation outside the direct control of the Department of Health. It has put in place market mechanisms by reinstating systems of commissioning (including reinventing GP fundholding as practice based commissioning) and by creating new funding arrangements through which providers are only paid for the activity they undertake (so-called Payment by Results). It has started to give patients or users more choice in their selection of healthcare provider, enabling them and their advisors (principally their GP) to choose where, when and how they receive treatment. All of this demands fundamental changes in the role of the Department of Health too – and here government has talked of refocusing the Department on its regulatory, supervisory and funding responsibilities and downsizing it to deal with a much more limited range of functions. It has taken some important steps in this direction (for example, handing responsibility for pay negotiations over to a coalition of NHS Employers, and passing some responsibility for the oversight of performance to the Healthcare Commission and to Monitor, the regulator for foundation NHS trusts). But in practice, the Department of Health remains very much in charge, and continues to try to control the NHS as tightly as it has always done.

The 2004 CSR and PSA objectives and targets

In the Comprehensive Spending Review round in 2004, the Department of Health agreed four objectives, and eight targets, and its progress towards them is summarised in table 5.1 on the next page[7]. In brief, it is a mixed picture. Five of the eight targets look likely to be met, two will not be met, and one is still hard to call. But it is the content of the objectives and the targets, and the connection between them and the real policy and management agenda for the Department of Health which really demands discussion. Are these the right objectives and targets, and do they provide a real and meaningful measure of how the Department of Health is doing?

Arguably, the four main objectives reflect major high level priorities for the Department of Health, but the targets chosen to measure progress are somewhat selective and, in some respects at least, potentially misleading.

Some of the targets – notably those concerned with improving the health of the population – have been appearing in government public health policies for approaching two decades. Targets for reductions in rates of mortality from heart disease, stroke, cancer and suicide were first set by the Conservative administration in the Health of the Nation White Paper in 1992[8]. Then, as now, the targets were set at levels which would be achieved simply as long term epidemiological trends and treatment patterns continued. These are not

---

[7] Department of Health (2006). Autumn performance report 2006. London: Department of Health.

[8] National Audit Office (1996). The health of the nation: a progress report. London: NAO.

ambitious or challenging targets, but more importantly the PSA does not make it clear how DoH policies and actions are meant to affect population level health indicators like this over this kind of timescale. In short, these are not meaningful targets because they cannot be sensibly linked to DoH performance.

Table 5.1 CSR 2004 PSA objectives and targets: progress summary

Objective	Target		Performance
Improve the health of the population	1	Increase life expectancy, reduce mortality from heart disease, cancer and suicide	On course to meet most targets by 2010, though doing so is largely a matter of continuing long term trends
	2	Reduce health inequalities in infant mortality and life expectancy at birth	Not on course – class inequalities in infant mortality and life expectancy are widening, not narrowing
	3	Reduce adult smoking rates and halt the year-on-year rise in childhood obesity; reduce teenage conception rates	Smoking rates declining, but not fast enough; limited data on childhood obesity, but target unlikely to be met; teenage conception rates falling but not fast enough
Improve health outcomes for people with long term conditions	4	Offer personalised care plans and cut emergency bed days through better primary care	Some reduction in use of emergency bed days – but association with better long term conditions are questionable
Improve access to services	5	Ensure that no-one waits more than 18 weeks from GP referral to hospital treatment	Very challenging target requiring major service redesign across the NHS, and much work is ongoing
	6	Increase takeup and success rates of drug treatment programmes	Target met
Improve the patient and user experience	7	Secure sustained improvements in national patient survey ratings	Small improvements in inpatient, primary care and mental health service surveys.
	8	Support more older people to live in their own homes where possible	Limited data suggests a rise in older people staying in their own homes rather than moving to residential/nursing home care

Some of the other targets – like those concerned with infant mortality, childhood obesity, adult smoking and teenage conception rates, and particularly the class differentials in these indicators – are more challenging and have, generally, not been met. Again, some of these targets have been around for a long time – and continuing measurement is no substitute for policy action. In many of these areas, improvement requires wider action by government, not simply by the Department of Health, and that action has not been forthcoming. For example, reducing adult smoking cannot be simply achieved by mounting endless stop smoking campaigns, and by making smoking cessation treatments (nicotine replacement therapies and psychological therapies) available – both of which the Department of Health and the NHS have done. It requires wider action by the Treasury to increase the costs of smoking substantially through taxation; by Revenue and Customs to control and reduce the massive illegal trade in tobacco imported for resale from low tax regimes in other countries of the European Union; by government to increase the minimum age at which tobacco products can be purchased to 18 years and to ban smoking in public places and in the workplace; by local authorities to ensure that retailers observe the law and do not sell cigarettes to children; and so on.

Some of the targets – particularly those concerned with care for those with long term conditions and care for older people – are selective and rather open to interpretation. For example, while improved primary care and continuity of care for those with long term conditions (which is the PSA objective) may well result in a fall in the number of emergency admissions (which is the target), other things – such as competing pressures for emergency beds, a reduction in emergency bed availability, or the re-labelling of some emergency admissions as non-emergencies – could all produce the same result for profoundly different reasons. Similarly, improving quality of life and independence for vulnerable old people (the objective) may result in an increase in the numbers of elderly people who remain in their own home rather than entering residential and nursing home care. But the same result might be achieved by constraining access to residential and nursing home care through limits on local authority budgets for these services, or by increasing the proportion of people who are asked to meet these costs from their own resources through means-testing. In short, these targets are inexact and uncertain measures of the PSA objectives to which they are attached.

Of all the PSA targets, it is target five – ensuring no-one waits longer than 18 weeks from GP referral to treatment – which has commanded the greatest investment of time and energy from the Department of Health and from NHS organisations. Through its established performance management systems, the Department has made the achievement of this latest waiting time target a very high priority for both primary care trusts and NHS trusts – and it has a strong record of achievement for past targets (for twelve, nine and six month waits). In fact almost all of the PSA targets and objectives relate to the health domain or to the NHS – and it is notable that the Department of Health's responsibilities for social care are barely covered except perhaps in target eight (which is concerned with the health and social care of the elderly).

Some targets set in previous Comprehensive Spending Rounds continue to be monitored and measured. For example, in the CSR in 2002, the Department of Health agreed to ensure that virtually all accident and emergency department patients were treated within four hours; that all patients were guaranteed access to a primary care professional within 24 hours and with a GP within 48 hours; and that patients would be given choice in booking hospital appointments. These targets have not been uncontroversial but the first two have been both met and sustained. Progress towards the third is somewhat obscured by the problems of the NHS "choose and book" electronic booking system, and the limited enthusiasm among GPs for offering patients choice at the point of referral.

Looking forward: the 2007 CSR and beyond

After five years of real-term annual increases in resources of around 7-8% pa, it is hard for observers to understand why the NHS is in the midst of a financial crisis. Before turning to the future direction of travel for health policy, and the approach to the CSR in 2007, it is worth taking some time to analyse the present situation[9].

The NHS went into financial crisis in 2006, as it became clear that spending was out of control. An annual overspend of around £790 million was projected, and the chief executive and permanent secretary was effectively sacked. But the crisis was largely the result of decisions made by ministers and civil servants in the Department of Health in recent years. While government (with the surprising support of the Audit Commission) laid the blame largely on NHS organisations and their financial management, the reality is that during a period of resource largesse, a whole series of uncosted and poorly thought through policy commitments were made, with little thought to their financial consequences. The NHS remains in financial intensive care – the overspend has been brought under control through the traditional finessing of NHS accounts, but the underlying position remains highly problematic.

The most significant – and irreversible – errors were made in NHS pay policy. The Department of Health negotiated new contracts with both GPs and NHS consultants which involved paying them substantially more for doing the same or less work. It significantly undercosted the implementation of those contracts, despite warnings from senior NHS managers, and it did not fund implementation properly. It is still implementing a similar comprehensive regrading exercise for all other NHS staff, which has the same potential to drive up pay costs substantially. Given that staff costs represent around two thirds of NHS spending, the long term effects of these pay awards on NHS costs will be very significant.

---

[9] Maynard A, Street A (2007). Health service reform: seven years of feast, seven years of famine – boom to bust in the NHS? British Medical Journal 332:906-908.

But in other, crucial areas of policy, the Department of Health has again failed to understand or cost the consequences of its actions. Many NHS organisations were driven into financial overspend by the Department's own access targets. Meeting the six month waiting target required increases in activity levels (to deal with backlogs and to sustain performance) and changes in services and processes of care, which NHS organisations were expected to absorb. The 18 week target, referred to above, imposes even more demanding activity expectations, at a time of financial constraint. Again, the effects of the 18 week target on NHS activity levels and costs have been at best poorly estimated, are unlikely to be properly funded, and will therefore push many organisations into overspend.

The Department of Health's own marketisation reforms have added to the financial crisis, by creating powerful new financial incentives for individual NHS organisations to drive up their turnover, and by reducing the scope for brokerage and flexibility in local health economies. By adopting a fixed-price tariff for acute care treatments, based on the full (rather than the marginal) costs of care, and routing 100% of funding for acute care provision through this tariff system, the Department of Health ensured that NHS trusts would stimulate rather than manage demand, and would account for activity in ways that maximised their income. Foundation NHS trusts, able to retain any financial surplus from their activities, benefited most from this new system. In the past strategic health authorities were able to arrange to provide short term brokerage or transitional funding between healthcare organisations within a health economy, but the new system made this more difficult.

All of this has taken place at a time of growing policy incoherence and repeated reorganisation within the NHS – again, led by the Department of Health. The Department's programme of reform has been often ill-considered, and its implementation has been rushed, with predictable consequences. Having reorganised the NHS in 2001[10] creating 28 strategic health authorities and about 315 primary care trusts, the Department reorganised it again in 2005[11], and further reorganisation (involving changes to the roles of primary care trusts and the provision of primary care for example) seems likely. The substantial financial costs of reorganisation have never been measured, and the transitional and longer term impacts on service delivery are almost always deleterious[12,13].

A highly critical internal review of the Department's management arrangements last year led to the departure of the permanent secretary and chief executive of the NHS and some other senior staff, and to an internal

---

[10] Department of Health (2001). Shifting the balance of power within the NHS: securing delivery. London: Department of Health, 2001.

[11] Department of Health (2005). Commissioning a patient-led NHS. London: Department of Health.

[12] Smith J, Walshe K, Hunter D (2001). The redisorganisation of the NHS. British Medical Journal, 2001; 323:1262-3.

[13] Walshe K, Smith J, Dixon J, Edwards N, Hunter DJ, Mays N, Normand C, Robinson R (2004). Primary care trusts: premature reorganisation with mergers may be harmful. British Medical Journal, 329:871-2.

restructuring. But the fundamental and problematic issues concerning the role and function of the Department of Health and its relationship with the NHS have not been tackled.

In this context, it will be difficult for the Department of Health to argue in the current Comprehensive Spending Review for continuing substantial increases in NHS spending of the kind it has enjoyed since 2002, and most observers expect a return to rises which marginally exceed general inflation, but which arguably do not reflect either the real impact of inflation on healthcare costs, or the rising demand for healthcare. In a more constrained financial climate, the NHS is going to have to deliver future improvements in services and access through increased productivity, not increased spending.

In conclusion, despite five years of increased spending and some important achievements particularly concerning waiting times and access to treatment, these are not good times for either the Department of Health or the NHS. Their performance – in the eyes of the Treasury and more broadly of politicians and the electorate – has been poor, and the implicit or explicit contract – more money for the NHS, in return for improved health services – has not been met. But the Comprehensive Spending Review provides a welcome opportunity both to learn from some of the problems of the last five years, and to put them right. I would put forward two areas for consideration.

Firstly, if we learn anything from recent experience it is that the Department of Health is not well equipped to manage the NHS, and its woeful track record demonstrates that a fundamental reassessment of the Department's own role and function is long overdue. Despite much recent policy rhetoric about devolution and decentralisation, the Department remains locked in a vicious cycle of ever tighter performance management – its response to each problem or difficulty in the NHS is to intervene, and to institute more intrusive and controlling systems of measurement and monitoring. It is time to consider how best to institutionalise greater autonomy and independence for the NHS at both a national and a local level, while sustaining and improving its proper public accountability. This means a radical redesign of the Department of Health, and a dramatic downsizing in its staff, role and function to match. History suggests that the Department is skilled in appearing to engage in change of this kind, while in reality continuing much as it did before. A new relationship between the Department of Health and the NHS cannot be brought about through aspiration or exhortation, however well meant. It will require a new legislative framework, in which the statutory existence, responsibilities, accountability and autonomy of NHS organisations at a local and national level is clearly established.

Secondly, as was noted earlier, countries that already spend more than us on healthcare (as a proportion of GDP) face similar pressures on healthcare spending. The substantial increase in NHS funding over the last five years, funded through general taxation, was never going to provide a solution to issues such as how we meet the rising healthcare costs of an increasingly elderly population, or who funds the costs of new, effective but expensive treatments for medical problems, or how we respond to rising user or patient expectations of treatment availability and health outcomes. The CSR in 2007 should be used to start a serious national debate about the future financial settlement for the NHS, or more broadly for healthcare services, and how they should be funded. The sustainability of general tax-funding for the NHS should be re-examined, and other approaches to healthcare funding (such as hypothecated taxation like payroll, income or sales taxes, or mandatory systems of social insurance contribution) should be considered. Systems of funding which tied healthcare spending more directly to levels of national productivity and prosperity, and made healthcare costs more explicit at both a collective and an individual level, would make for a more sustainable future for the NHS in which it could continue to command the level of public support it still enjoys.

6. Local Government

Carole Johnson

Introduction

With the creation of the so called 'new settlement' between local and central government and a forthcoming comprehensive spending review based upon a local government funding freeze, it would be easy to predict a CSR containing few surprises. However, despite the widely acknowledged constructive ways in which local and central government now work together, there are many issues which will not be easily resolved. Ongoing efficiency gains, a less burdensome performance system promised from 2009 and the aftermath of the Lyons Review of Local Government Finance are just a few problematic areas. The current strategic context of local government may require something more radical. Whether we will get it is another matter.

As I write, the publication of the Comprehensive Spending Review appears to be pushed back to as late as October, allowing time for Gordon Brown to stamp his mark on it (as Prime Minister rather than Chancellor) and perhaps also to take proper account of Lyon's. This is because, in part, there remain some fundamental problems around local government structures and the mixed messages emerging from central government keen on both localism and centralism.

Local Government, it has to be recognised, has done brilliantly overall during New Labour's decade in office. However, a funding freeze may lead to the withering away of the improvements in quantity and quality which we have seen of late[1].

There are a number of reasons for this. Firstly there has been an increase in outsourcing, up from £10bn in 2000/01 to £18bn in 2004/05[2]. This, combined with the use of ring fenced funds by the centre and funds pooled or aligned to support Local Area Agreements (LAAs) can leave a shrinking percentage over which certain local authorities, and indeed other service providers, have discretion. Added to this there are cost pressures – from services as diverse as construction to care homes. In the latter case directives from central government to keep down wages undermines their other stated objectives of securing better working conditions for women and high quality services. Demographic changes from an ageing population and migration can also strain the purse strings at local level, especially when accurate data on the local population does not exist. All this suggests that nothing short of a miracle will be required if local government are to continue improving in the current financial context.

---

[1] Clark, D. (2007). Get ready for the spending review. Local Government Chronicle.

[2] Local Government Association (2006). Meeting the Challenges Ahead: LGA Autumn Statement 2006. London.

This chapter focuses on Local Government rather than its parent department, the Department for Communities and Local Government (DCLG). The newly named DCLG has a broad remit, a large part of which is local government. It gained responsibility for community policy and equalities from the Home Office in a recent reshuffle. Otherwise DCLG has retained the responsibilities of the former Office of the Deputy Prime Minister. This remit includes: community regeneration policies; regional and city region development, fire and resilience, planning, housing and the specific development of the Thames Gateway and Olympic Legacy. Local government plays a significant role in many of these areas, either providing directly or enabling an array of local services. They do this in addition to their core roles, such as maintaining local democracy, providing education and social services and raising local taxes. In addition, as the role of Local Government as direct service provider has diminished it has taken on the role of 'place shaper'[3]. This new remit brings together its democratic function and service enabling role within the community to actively shape the future of local places as towns and cities which can effectively compete globally in industrial and services production and as educational and cultural venues.

After a number of years when local government was discussed in the context of not just its form and function but also whether or not it would exist at all[4], the New Labour Government and local government have come to a mutual agreement on the terms under which it will exist in the future. This agreement is now being referred to as the new settlement[5].

Over their ten years in power, New Labour has taken a carrot and stick approach, varying the proportion of each according to the importance of the topic. Local government have responded constructively with improved performance across a wide number of areas including the ubiquitous partnership working. Current performance levels are described in the White Paper as unrecognisable compared to those of 10 years ago. There are of course still performance issues. On the floor targets, the decent homes target has slipped and challenges remain on Key stage 3 attainment in basic education (11-14 year olds). Some whole service areas such as children in care have not made the leap required and some local authority areas still lag behind[6][7]. It is unlikely that PSAs in these areas will be candidates for cutting in the new streamlined performance approach being developed.

---

[3] Healey, P. (1999). Institutional Analysis, Communicative Planning, and Shaping Places. Journal of Planning and Research. 19(2): 111-121.

[4] Blair, T. (1997). Leading The Way: A new vision for local government. London, IPPR.

[5] Department for Communities and Local Government (2006). Local Area Agreements Research: Round two negotiations and early progress in Round 1. London, Office for Public Management, University of the West of England & University of Warwick.

[6] Department for Communities and Local Government (2006a). Strong and Prosperous Communities - The Local Government White Paper. London, The Stationery Office.

[7] Department for Communities and Local Government (2006b). Annual Report 2006. London, HMSO.

Alongside this drive for performance improvement has been a broader attempt to engage with Local Government in recognition of their democratically elected status and potential to engage directly with citizens. In the first term of office New Labour introduced a new Local Government Act which invited local authorities to reform their constitutions and take on new roles. Out of this policy has emerged a cabinet style of government through which Local Government have strengthened their democratic role as well as improving service management and acting as 'enablers'. Local Government is once more respected for having a distinctive role to play in governance at local level. Key to their place shaping role is the development of partnerships and local government have largely welcomed the ideas of local strategic partnerships and local area agreements, both of which are ways in which quality service provision can be supported through improved local performance.

Against this backdrop, this chapter discusses the resourcing of local government, and in particular the possible changes which the Comprehensive Spending Review of 2007 may bring. The chapter is organised as follows: the first section discusses the policy challenges facing local government. It is argued that these are representative of the relatively stable situation in which local government finds itself. The second section outlines the spending issues and constraints which face local government. Here it is argued that the broad direction for resourcing is explicitly one of greater efficiency in the use of resources. In the final section, on possible developments in the CSR 2007, the details already outlined in the White Paper are discussed. It is suggested that given the stability, the attention already paid to efficiency and in the design of a new performance framework, there is limited scope for further changes in the CSR. All that remains is for central government to define more closely the national priority outcomes, national indicators and floor targets for this area. There are two issues here: the first is how the CSR will combine newly identified performance indicators and targets - for example, to those relating to local carbon emissions. In less than two years central government hope to reduce the overall number of performance indicators to 200. The problem here relates to the already acknowledged situation where less 'essential' service producers are concerned with how their work will be effectively prioritized (either by the centre or locally), and therefore the degree to which they can expect fair resource allocations in the future to continue to provide these services. The concern is that some services will have to drop from the radar. The second issue concerns how the balance will be achieved between improving and maintaining quality in services in a frozen budget allocation given the context of an extended remit of responsibility for local government and escalating costs.

The policy challenges facing local government

It appears that New Labour has managed to effectively secure a positive relationship and, as a result, many of the old tensions have diminished between local and central government with the relationship defined mostly by its constructive nature.

The new Local Government White Paper (2006) outlines the centre's perspective on the current policy and delivery challenges, in which local government:

- have to develop to take the leadership role in providing or enabling improved service provision;
- need to provide democratic accountability through encouraging greater 'participatory democracy';
- should be taking a new 'more integrated' approach to partnership working;
- need to be given more power to support economic development at the city and city region level; and
- needs a new streamlined and proportionate performance regime which enables them to carry out the above without the previous level of central direction.

To a large extent, these themes build on the content of the Modernising Government White Paper[8] and on the developments previously outlined. The general approach to policy has changed little. The substantive changes are around community cohesion; a commitment to efficiency and the new performance regime through which the double devolution of power – to local government and to citizens will be provided. Issues of the environment while becoming more pressing get a mention but do not dominate.

However, despite the new settlement, debates still rage between local government, usually represented by the Local Government Association, and the centre. Some issues which have emerged of late include:

Council tax rates have increased by 65% in real terms since the late 1990s causing disquiet in many areas. These increases have been necessary to meet the shortfall in contribution from the business rates which has fallen from 26% to 21% of local spending. In particular, some areas have campaigned for the business rate to be relocalised providing them with some scope for raising more revenue this way.

Two further issues are essentially related to funding. Local Government are happy to take their leadership role seriously but argue that the pressures on costs, demands for better services and demographics mean that some reprioritisation is necessary of either demands or funds. The LGA's report Meeting the Challenges Ahead (2006) paints a disturbing picture of the future if conditions do not change. Pressure will come from an ageing population, many

---

[8] Cabinet Office (1999). Modernising Government. London, The Stationery Office Ltd.

of whom today are not getting the services they require, and from population growth through migration which often places more demands on key services. The diversity this creates alone can put a strain on community cohesion. In addition, climate change and pressures on natural resources and also global competition will ratchet up further pressure. All this in a situation in which local government finance has already come under extreme pressures from increased costs in care for the vulnerable (children and elderly); construction; road maintenance; energy and bus contracts.

The LGA argue that there is a gap between central government's stated intentions and the funding they are prepared to provide to deliver these services. While there have been increases, the real terms increases across the majority of services has been 14%. This sounds substantial but taken against the higher demands made on local government through central government policy and regulation, the EU Waste Directive and the increases in costs mentioned above, there is often less room for local priorities than central government acknowledge.

The demands by 26 councils to form further unitary councils is in some ways indicative of the pressures and the desires of local government to respond to local need and to have more choice over how local money is spent. Preston, for example, want their city to be better able to look after the needs of the area by having control over a bigger budget and also how this budget is divided between the various needs of the city. Efficiency savings are also to be made by avoiding the costly two tier system Preston currently inhabits. Unitary status could further bring about more direct accountability of elected councillors for their council's services. At present two thirds of the council tax goes straight to the County but the lines of accountability are not necessarily clear for the local electorate.

The constraints

The Gershon Report[9] has already influenced the general direction of a local government 'meta policy' in relation to finance with further reforms possibly emanating from the Lyon's Review on local government form and finance. However, this is reported to be quite tame and likely to be so late in the spending review cycle that it may not have the impact envisaged. Gershon's influence is reflected in the White Paper in preparation for the CSR.

The resourcing of local government has been relatively stable since the upheaval caused by the introduction of the Poll Tax and its speedy 1992 replacement of Council Tax. Funding, although stable, has not been entirely static for local government. Over the past nine years, some areas have seen increases in funding such as education, social services and to an extent regeneration policy. However, it is unlikely to be increased further under present circumstances, as New Labour's spending spree is over. As Gershon argues, the main opportunity for investing more in frontline public services is to make efficiency savings

---

[9] Gershon, P. (2004). Releasing Resources for the Frontline: Independent Review of Public Sector Efficiency (Gershon Review). London, HM Treasury.

elsewhere in the system. It is likely therefore, that the current direction, set by the Gershon efficiency agenda of better procurement, re-engineering or merging back office functions, increasing productivity and transforming transactional services will frame the future CSR 2007 resource debate.

Local Government have made some important contributions to the estimated £21 billion of savings suggested as possible by Gershon over the current spending review period. The White Paper states that Local Government is likely to meet the £3.0 billion target of efficiency savings, a year ahead of schedule[5]. Despite this success, Gershon has been troubled at local government's lack of attention to procurement, where the biggest savings are to be found, and being over keen on establishing long-term contracts with the private sector whilst 'drip feeding' the local voluntary sector[10]. Neither of which may guarantee quality and efficiency long-term. Gershon continues to argue that efficiency savings can be made.

What will the CSR 2007 bring?

Given the previous discussion it is no surprise that the content of the White Paper does not imply increased resources will be needed for local government. The overwhelming message from central to local government is that local authorities can now be trusted to continue the good work already started in terms of improving performance and acting as leader and place shaper.

But buried in the small print of this message is the caveat that this must be achieved at no or little extra cost. Local government, however, do not necessarily agree that this can be achieved. A key part of freeing up local government to get on with the job is the new performance framework based on the concept of double devolution: devolution to citizens as well as local government. Given that this has already been forged the future CSR will simply add detail to the targets and performance indicators and even here it seems that a methodology has been developed to shape these.

The concept of double devolution is new. The centre, in this vision, will do less and local communities together with their local elected leadership and broader service providers will be left to shape local service delivery, thereby doing more. Three year funding settlements will provide greater stability in which to do this. Downward accountability is the watchword with local service charters and the requirement of local government to produce service standards information for public consumption. This new performance framework, called the 'the comprehensive area assessment', *may* actually help local government to achieve efficiency savings itself as it *could* be less burdensome for both local and central government.

In the new framework, priorities, targets and performance indicators will be in four tiers. At the first level, central government will set broad national priorities.

---

[10] Gershon,P. (2006). Public Sector Efficiency - did the Gershon Review make a difference and what comes next? IDeA Efficiency Matters Conference.

At the second level, there will be 200 indicators on which all local partners will report. This will allegedly reduce the burden from the current estimate of 1,200 indicators collected locally. At the third level LAAs will set 35 targets which will be agreed amongst local partners and with the centre. Again these will contribute to the overarching priorities of the centre but with freedoms and flexibilities in their exact nature. There will, though, be some 18 additional targets in education and childcare effectively making the local targets number 53 instead of 35. The floor targets will still exist as part of the 35 for LAAs. Local areas may, in addition, want to set themselves a fourth level of targets and indicators.

While this process, if successful, may reduce the performance burden in terms of data collection, it does not take into account the costs of negotiating the LAAs. The evaluations of round one and two LAAs suggests that the transaction costs among local providers, government offices for the regions and across central government, outweighs any benefits[11] [5]. The LAA process itself will have to be amended if it is to match up to the claims that government will measure less and give more power to local actors.

A further part of the new performance regime, and an additional way in which savings may be made, are the changes to external assessment and inspection. In future, external assessment and inspection will be coordinated and proportionate to risk. Following in the footsteps of the new NHS Health Check performance framework which uses two aggregated indicators: quality of service and efficiency in the use of resources, the new local government assessment process contains: an annual risk assessment focusing on outcomes and service delivery; a scored use of resources judgement; a scored direction of travel judgement and inspection for those whose risk levels are identified as high.

The White Paper set against the context of the Gershon Review provides a good indication of the direction of local government resourcing and the relationship between resourcing and performance. Local government and its partners will receive financial rewards for good performance and good performance will lead to less inspection freeing up yet more resources locally.

Conclusion

This chapter has argued that there is little scope for surprises and radical policy in the CSR07, thus leaving, at the very least, large sections of local government wondering what they are to do next. It is not at all clear how more improvements in quality and quantity of services can be made, more demands on local government as place shaper can be met and how increased costs and year on year performance improvements can be squared by the slight reduction in the burden of performance management and variable scope for efficiency savings. It is even less clear how this adds up to devolution of any kind.

---

[11] Office of the Deputy Prime Minister (2005). A process evaluation of negotiations of pilot Local Area Agreements. London, HMSO.

So what might the CSR07 contain? In the existing PSAs, local government are subject to a range of objectives, targets and floor targets. The four basic objectives for local government are briefly: tackling social exclusion and deprivation; delivering better services, including improving effectiveness and efficiency; delivering a better balance between housing supply and demand and improving the quality of housing.

CSR 2007 could introduce some new objectives. It is possible that community cohesion could emerge, but given the recent establishment of the Commission on Community Cohesion, any objective is likely to remain rather loosely worded until it reports. Performance indicators and targets for reducing carbon emissions were promised in the White Paper. Likewise, the development of city region economies. The question will be how many objectives or 'broad national priorities' will government want to have overall especially in the context of reducing burdens in the new performance regime by 2009? Surely we will need to start this process now.

Regarding the associated PSA targets under PSA 1 – social exclusion and deprivation - local government work to support the achievement of the floor targets on worklessness, education, crime, health, housing and liveability: essentially areas largely beyond their direct control. They contribute to these indirectly through partnership working and through their direct interactions with citizens in associated areas. A further economic development PSA concerns the regional development agencies and ostensibly has no impact on local government although, in much the same way, local government has played a role here too in terms of helping to deliver regional strategies[12].

In the new performance framework, floor targets will remain and it is difficult to see how these will be changed substantially. While there has been success across most of these targets it is unlikely that any one of these areas will be abandoned as they remain crucial to the New Labour project. Targets may be made more demanding or different elements attached to them. For example, we might see better developed efficiency targets. Overall, what the CSR 2007 process will do is clarify the Treasury's perspective on which objectives, targets (including floor targets) it now needs for local government. But the scope for anything other than an incremental approach which fits firmly with the White Paper proposals seems unrealistic.

In general, incrementalism is as satisfactory an approach as any other, but if central government are really serious about taking forward this twin agenda of better services and efficiency they need to focus more on reducing the burden of performance management, which they argue they want. However, for the first two years of the CSR, the system will be the one currently in use and the new approach does not appear to factor in the burdensome LAA negotiations. The centre may need to think again about just how streamlined the new performance

---

[12] Johnson, C. (2004). "Strategic Superboards: improved network management processes for regeneration?" International Journal of Public Sector Management 18(2): 139-150.

regime will be. An alternative solution may be to accompany this less burdensome performance regime with fewer policy proposals from the centre – truly leaving localities to design their own systems of intervention. However, there seems to be no plans to develop this direction further. If anything the LAAs are characterised by more central direction than many previous policies as the response to the pilots has been to rationalise the content.

Working these issues through in the context outlined above will not be easy. No doubt there are some very heated discussions going on in Whitehall over the shaping of the CSR07. One thing is certain; central government will not manage to balance all these competing demands and priorities, which impact on local government budgets. The process is increasingly likely to be marked by incrementalism and compromise to avoid head on collision or appearing to step down on the need for more and better services. No doubt the CSR will leave much debate around how policy is implemented within the funding priorities set. Local government together with their partners will be the ones trying to solve the contradictions, live with the compromises and make ends meet in practice. The price we might have to pay for ill thought through policy is that outcomes in the future may be less than those we have come to expect from local government.

7. The Home Office

Stephen Brookes

Structure and Function of the Home Office

The Home Office is one of the oldest and largest Whitehall Departments. In the last 18-months the department has had one of the most challenging and difficult times in its 250-year history. The period has culminated with the most radical change since the Home Office was first created in 1782. With almost immediate effect the department will lose its responsibility for the prison service (which it has held since 1823) and the probation service. In its place it will take on a stronger role in tackling the threat of terrorism, alongside its responsibilities of the police service, crime reduction, immigration and asylum, identity and passports[1]. It is what some have called "the biggest hospitals pass in the history of Whitehall"[2] given the difficulties recently experienced in relation to the 'prison crisis'. As part of this process a new Ministry of Justice will be created to provide a stronger focus on the criminal justice system, and on reducing re-offending.

The department is without doubt one of the most complex to lead. The capability review of the Home Office[3] also noted that it has one of the most challenging briefs, including reducing crime and managing offenders, providing visible and accountable policing, managing immigration, and ensuring effective counter-terrorism.

Change, however, is not a new feature for the Home Office, as its structure and functions have changed significantly in recent years. It has moved from what has been described as being a business whose main purpose was to pass legislation, fund services and issue guidance, to become a department that is sharply focused on delivering important outcomes for the public.

Until May 2007, the core Home Office employed 73,700 staff[4] which represents around 14 per cent of the civil service permanent staff. Of these, just over 20,000[5] staff are classed as central core staff, of whom approximately 17,000 work for the Immigration and Nationality Directorate. Approximately 48,000 staff work for the prison service (which will have a significant impact given its move to the Ministry of Justice), 2,822 for the UK Identity and Passport Service and a similar number for the Forensic Science Service.

---

[1] Prime Ministers' announcement to the House of Common 29 March 2007.

[2] Radio 4 'Today' programme 29 March 2007.

[3] PMDU Capability Review of the Home Office, Prime Minister's Delivery Unit, July 2006.

[4] Public Expenditure Statistical Analyses Quarter 4, 2005.

[5] Home Office (2006) Departmental Report 2004-05, Table 6.9: Staff numbers 2004-05.

The most recent changes build on the 'Security Crime and Justice' strand of the Government's policy review and introduce the following main functions to each new department[6]:

Table 7.1 Main functions of new departments

Home Office	Ministry of Justice	Attorney General's Office
- Office for Security and Counter-terrorism - Policing - Crime Reduction and Drugs Strategy - Serious and Organised Crime - RESPECT and Anti-social Behaviour - Border and Immigration Agency - Identity and Passport Service	- Existing functions of the Department for Constitutional Affairs - National Offender Management Service, including the prison and probation services - Criminal Law and Sentencing Policy - Sponsorship of relevant inspectorates and NDPBs, including the Prison Service, Parole Board, Youth Justice Board	- Existing functions remain, including superintendence of the prosecuting authorities and other existing criminal justice responsibilities

The period under review (and no doubt leading to the radical changes) has seen three successive Home Secretaries and witnessed a number of crises including evident systematic failings in dealing with foreign national prisoners. This has been further exacerbated by the number of prisoners reaching record levels, with some prisoners having to serve custodial sentences in police cells in October 2006. Shortly afterwards it was revealed that the Home Office were unable to identify the number of serious offenders who had absconded from custody in open prisons. The debate as to whether the Home Office is 'fit for purpose' has been a consistent theme in the national media.

---

[6] Machinery of Government: Security and Counter-Terrorism, and the Criminal Justice System

Funding and Priorities

The Home Office has a total annual budget of £13 billion which represents almost three per cent of total government expenditure. Of this, 40% is spent on policing, and 11.5% on immigration services.

Successive spending reviews have seen changing emphases. For example, in 1998 the first CSR linked funding to targets, delivery and a greater customer focus. This and further spending reviews was supported by legislation (such as the Crime and Disorder Act 1998 which introduced statutory partnerships), improved structures and processes that supported a performance framework and shifting emphasis to functional responsibility. Public Service Agreement (PSA) targets underlined this change of emphasis.

Performance

The level of recorded crime is the indicator most often used to judge Home Office performance. During the past ten years, the British Crime Survey suggests that crime is down by 35% since 1997 and there are record numbers (over 141,000) of police officers and 11,000 Community Support Officers. Record numbers of people received drug treatment with an increase of 118% since 1998/99. The Home Office has also delivered more than £1.5 billion efficiency savings by March 2006.

The Home Office had seven PSA targets set out in the 2004 spending review:
1. Reduce crime by 15%, and further in high-crime areas, by 2007/08.
2. Reassure the public, reducing the fear of crime and anti-social behaviour, and building confidence in the Criminal Justice System without compromising fairness.
3. Improve the delivery of justice by increasing the number of crimes for which an offender is brought to justice to 1.25 million by 2007/08.
4. Reduce the harm caused by illegal drugs, including substantially increasing the number of drug-misusing offenders entering treatment through the Criminal Justice System.
5. Reduce unfounded asylum claims as part of a wider strategy to tackle abuse of the immigration laws and promote controlled legal migration.
6. Increase voluntary and community engagement, especially amongst those at risk of social exclusion. (moved to DCLG)
7. Reduce race inequalities and build community cohesion. (moved to DCLG)

The capability review suggested that good progress has been made towards delivering its PSA targets since 2004. This includes a reduction in the number of unfounded asylum claims, meeting the target on bringing more offenders to justice and being above target in relation to the number of problem drug users entering treatment programmes. Furthermore, confidence in the Criminal Justice System is increasing. This is encouraging given the creation of the Ministry of Justice.

Policies and Programmes

While some commentators may be of the view that the Home Office has passed over responsibility for managing offenders to the new Ministry of Justice with "a hospital pass", significant areas of reform remain. In addition to the major structural changes, will be the creation of new executive agencies (such as the transfer of the Immigration and Nationality Department (IND) to agency status and the creation of the Serious Organised Crime Agency (SOCA)). Widely reported as applying to the Home Office itself, John Reid's pronouncement that IND "was not fit for purpose" underlines the barriers that need to be addressed in relation to immigration and asylum.

Added to this, is the renewed focus on security and counter terrorism. The Government has been evolving and refining its long-term strategy for countering terrorism. The strategy[7] has been to prevent terrorism by tackling the radicalisation of individuals that leads to violent extremism. Of relevance to the spending review is the fact that investment in this programme has increased. Annual spending on counter-terrorism, intelligence, and resilience will have doubled to £2¼ billion by 2007-08. There have been significant operational successes. However, the threat of terrorism has also increased, and there have been attacks, here in the UK in the London bombings of July 2005, but also abroad, with British citizens caught up alongside others of many nationalities in attacks in Bali, Egypt, Turkey, and elsewhere. Given the increasing role of the Home Office the priority is one that the spending review is likely to endorse.

In summary, the spending review process will be equally as challenging as it was prior to the Home Office reform.

The Future: Departmental Reform

The Home Office reform announced in March by the Prime Minister and the Home Secretary's own plans for transformational change[8] announced earlier will clearly have an impact on the future public service agreements negotiated during the next spending review. The core purpose of the Home Office has been re-defined as 'public protection' (rather than creating a 'safe, just and tolerant society') and is supported by the five new objectives to guide its work.

In line with the Home Secretary's announced changes designed to reshape the Home Office, the key aims are to focus on frontline delivery, develop its people and leaders, match resources to priorities and transform systems and processes.

Detailed proposals have been put forward to implement these reforms. One of the most significant for the purposes of the spending review is the commitment to reduce the total size of the Home Office headquarters by 30% by 2008. This will also see a further reduction of 10% by 2010. The cumulative effect of these changes will be to reduce the size of the headquarters of the Home Office and its

---

[7] Countering International Terrorism: The United Kingdom's Strategy, (Cm 6888, July 2006)

[8] Home Office (2006) ibid, p.11

agencies from 9,200 in 2004 to 6,500 in 2008, and to 5,900 by 2010. Anticipated savings will amount to approximately £115 million per year by 2010. A key question for the spending review must be that of seeking assurances that these savings will be applied to the priority areas and how the wider changes and the transfer of responsibilities to the Ministry of Justice will enable this.

Managing Offenders

The process of managing offenders has undergone its most radical change in recent history through the creation of the National Offender Management Service (NOMS) in 2004, which combines the probation and prison services. This scale of change continues with the transfer of NOMS to the Ministry of Justice.

As the capability review's earlier cited findings point out, performance in relation to existing criminal justice related PSA targets has been encouraging. The number of people who believe that the criminal justice system is effective in bringing people who commit crimes to justice has increased from 39% to 44% and the target of 1,250,000 offenders being brought to justice was exceeded well before its target date of 2008.

These apparent achievements raise some interesting questions for the spending review. Having brought these additional offenders to justice, what impact has this had on the prison system? Can the increasing prison population be attributable to these offender strategies? And are these offenders being successfully re-settled and rehabilitated? These are key questions to be addressed if one is to consider the public value outcomes of the future spending review/s.

The creation of NOMS followed the recommendation of the Carter Report.[9] The overall vision was to create "end-to-end management of sentenced offenders". Some would argue that this is not before time given the current crisis of overcrowding and other related problems pertaining to offenders. There are clear benefits to this change of approach although not all academics and practitioners are convinced that the changes are for the better[10]. The issues underpinning this change have been topical of late. For example:

- Overcrowding of prisons has been a constant feature in the media. At the time of publication the population is now just four places short of 80,000[11]. This may pass the mid-point of the Home Office six year prediction[12] for the period commencing 2005 through to 2011 which suggests a population between the ranges of 76,000 to 87,500 in mid-2011.

---

[9] Carter, P (2003) 'Managing Offenders, Reducing Crime – a New Approach', Home Office Strategy Unit, London, HMSO.

[10] Goode and Brookes (2006) Managing offenders and reducing crime, in Moss, K. and Stephens, M. (eds) 'Crime Reduction and the Law', Routledge: London

[11] HM Prison Service. Prison Population and Accommodation briefing for 13th April 2007.

[12] Da Silva (2005) 'Prison Population Projections 2005 – 2011' RDS Briefing Paper 01/05

- The cost of prisons currently stands at £2.4 billion per year[13]. Plans to build an additional 8,000 prison places[14] could equate to an additional expenditure of £220 million.
- Views differ in relation to the extent to which 'prison works'. The Prison Reform Trust challenges this view and have argued that the number of offenders dealt with by the courts has remained static whilst the prison population has increased.
- Post-custody analysis also challenges this view. In 1992 just over one half of all released prisoners re-offended following release. By 2004 this had increased to 67%. Released prisoners were responsible for one million crimes per year (equivalent to 18% of all recorded crime)[15].
- If two thirds of those released re-offend, a significant impact is felt on the national economy. This was emphasised in a Home Office study undertaken in 2002. Ex-prisoners commit nearly one-fifth of all crime, costing victims and the country £11bn a year[16].

The Ministry of Justice will be responsible for policy on the overall criminal, civil, family and administrative justice system, including sentencing policy, as well as the courts, tribunals and legal aid. It will help to bring together management of the criminal justice system, meaning that once a suspect has been charged, their journey through the courts, and if necessary prison and probation, can be managed seamlessly.

Prison, as the Government has made clear, will continue to be necessary to protect the public from the most serious offenders, although some non-dangerous offenders do not need to be in custody as their offending can better be addressed through non-custodial means. The Government has announced plans to build a further 8,000 prison places by 2012, having already increased capacity by 19,700 since 1997.

Carrying through reforms of the criminal justice system and its critical workforces will be vital to restoring public confidence. The reforms set out in the Offender Management Bill currently before Parliament will ensure that the National Offender Management Service has the powers to commission high-quality services from the best provider, whether in the public, private, or voluntary sector.

Immigration and Nationality

The crisis concerning the failure to deport foreign prisoners has been the latest in a line of failures by an Immigration and Nationality Directorate (IND) which

---

[13] Howard League for Penal Reform (2006). http://www.howardleague.org/ accessed January 2007.

[14] Machinery of Government: Security and Counter-Terrorism, and the Criminal Justice System

[15] ODPM (2002) 'Reducing Reoffending by ex prisoners', Social Exclusion Unit Report, July 2002.

[16] Independent Newspaper (2002) Give ex-prisoners more money, says No 10 poverty unit

struggled to cope with the increased volume of asylum applicants in the late 1990s. The costs of supporting applicants awaiting a decision imposed additional costs of up to £200 million.[17] The Home Office's review of IND, published in July 2006, proposes a number of reforms to improve IND's performance.[18] Immigration law and processes are to be both strengthened and simplified in order to speed up decisions and removals. Leadership and management within IND are to be strengthened and additional investment in new technologies will assist better enforcement and tracking of cases. Furthermore, it is intended that better strategic partnership and collaborative working, which was so absent in relation to the foreign prisoners' crisis, will enhance performance and co-operation with other government agencies and the private sector.

It is intended that these proposals be achieved through better use of existing resources, generating substantial savings in the long-term while productivity efficiencies will fund technological and infrastructural change. But while the reduction of asylum applicants will reduce support costs, the removal of the backlog of an estimated 400,000 failed asylum applicants is likely to require additional investment. Furthermore, there is the broader difficulty of better enforcement of immigration law given a lack of statistics on the number of illegal entrants.

Policing and Community Safety

Policing is one of the most important public services and one of the key areas of responsibility for the Home Office. It is fundamental to the safety and well-being of communities and represents 40% of the Home Office funding allocation. Although significant improvements have been made to the PSA targets and police numbers, many challenges lie ahead. The key challenge is to ensure that the police reform programme continues and seizes the opportunities presented to add real value to safety and well-being. Proposals put forward by the previous Home Secretary were halted on 19 June 2006 when John Reid stated that he would not pursue the enforced mergers of police forces due to concerns around a number of issues that were raised during the amalgamation debate.

The two main reform aims in relation to policing are:
- Addressing what is perceived as a gap in dealing with serious and organized crime and tackling cross border crime.
- Introducing neighbourhood policing to all areas in England and Wales by 2008.

These two main reform aims will need to strike a very delicate balance as one could easily be counter-productive to the other. Responses to the reform proposals from key stakeholders were initially mixed. Government was clearly

---

[17] National Audit Office (2004) Improving the Speed and Quality of Asylum Decisions.

[18] Home Office (2006) Fair, effective, transparent and trusted: Rebuilding confidence in our immigration system.

supportive and viewed the reform as a key part of its aim to "deliver community policing for today's world and face the new challenges of changing criminality" (HMSO 2004:5). The Conservatives were strongly opposed to the notion of regionalisation and call for policing that is "closer to the people – not further away" (Cameron 2006)[19].

In the meantime, the Home Office continues to drive forward the neighbourhood policing model and in November 2006 allocated a further specific grant of £315 million[20] to Police Authorities to fund Police Community Support Officers (PCSO's) and neighbourhood policing for 2007/08. This will help forces to fund 16,000 PCSO's who are being deployed towards the continued rollout of neighbourhood policing. While there is not enough space here to consider in detail the whys and wherefores of this programme it is important to sound a warning note that many police authorities themselves have done – what happens when the pump-priming money runs out and community expectations have been raised? Is there a long-term aim for the development of sustainable policing for the future?

In acknowledging the vital importance of aligning future police funding to the structural and governance reform proposals, it is worth mapping out some suggestions. Police funding comes from two main sources. First, central government (Home Office and DCLG) provides approximately £9 billion through, respectively, the Police Grant and the Revenue Support Grant/National Non-Domestic Rates. Second, Police Authorities – which are corporate bodies - raise revenue to fund the operation of their police forces by levying a precept on local authorities through the council tax. This amounts to approximately £2 billion.

Within the context of reform, strong representations have been made for a review of the funding formula, most notably from chief constables and police authorities in areas where the formula is seen to be unfair (see, for example, Surrey Police Authority 2006)[21]. Nationally, the APA agrees in as much as it calls for the formula to be reviewed to ensure that "police funding is resilient, fair and adequate in all areas"[22]. It is also suggested that the focus includes both the sources and allocation of funding beyond the formula.

---

[19] Cameron., D (2006) Changing our party – changing our Country, speech to the Conservative Party Spring Conference, April 8th., Manchester.

[20] Home Office (2006) Local Policing – Allocations of specific grant for police authorities in England and Wales for 2007/08.

[21] Surrey Police Authority (2005) Surrey Police and Surrey Police Authority urge the Government to end chronic under-funding, Press Release 21 December, accessed April 2006 http://www.surreypa.gov.uk/presspubarchive_story.asp?id=257

[22] APA (2006) 'Listen to Communities on Police Restructuring', January, Association of Police Authorities, London

Future Challenges

Three areas are considered within the concluding section, those of performance, structural change and funding.

Performance

The continued emphasis given to performance management through increasingly centralised performance regimes could represent both an opportunity and a threat. The opportunity is presented by an apparent commitment to implement simpler performance arrangements such as those for policing, crime and drugs and the creation of the National Policing Improvement Agency which was implemented in April 2007. The threat is to embrace vastly increasing 'real-time' data such as that in relation to crime with a view to closely controlling the emphasis of performance regimes for matters that should rightly fall to frontline leaders. Similar arguments can be employed in relation to managing offenders, immigration and nationality. Do the measures take account of public value? The challenge is to ensure consistent standards of performance but to do so in a way that minimises the burdens on frontline services and resists any further attempts at what frontline leaders would describe as 'micro-management'.

Structural Changes

Of pressing importance will be the ongoing implementation of recent reforms and the transition period. Equally important will be the need to introduce mechanisms for cross departmental collaboration. The new structure of the Home Office was illustrated in the earlier section of this chapter. Of particular interest will be the creation of the Border and Immigration Agency – a new executive agency of the Home Office. The main focus should be to examine how the stronger accountability arrangements are established and operate, the extent of operational freedom given to the Chief Executive and the Board and the impact that these have on improved performance. Similar monitoring of the efficacy of the Identity and Passport Service (established as an Executive Agency in April 2006) would be of benefit. Another focus will be on the arrangements for an independent immigration regulator to oversee the agency's performance.

The police reform programme represents further structural challenges. Whilst policing remains a core function for the Home Office there may be a further opportunity to re-examine this once the wider changes settle into place. There may be an argument to look at the Home Office key responsibility as that of protecting the public through cross border approaches (regionally, nationally and internationally) and then look at different ways of managing locally based policing perhaps in closer collaboration with DCLG and local authorities. This would sit well with the local authorities developing role as "first among equals" in the coordination of local public service delivery.[23] The review may ask "should local police commanders have a more direct line of accountability to local authority chief executives (given the substantial financial investment from local precepts and non domestic rates)? This would certainly have an effect of raising the game of local partnership activity and support the move towards the creation and demonstration of increased local public value. It would assist the focus on neighbourhood policing and potentially 'free-up' the Home Office and a re-constituted regional governance role for strategic chief constables and police authorities to focus on terrorism, protection of borders and cross-border and organized crime whilst leaving those who 'know the frontline' to lead local delivery.

The new Home Office will include a Corporate Centre. This will be a smaller and more focused strategic centre, supporting the Board to shape the strategy and drive performance.[24] In implementing these structural changes, it will be interesting to see how the Home Office responds to its commitment to reduce the total size of its strategic and operational headquarters by 30% by 2008. This will be a major challenge and the extent to which it is able to divert the anticipated savings of £115 million per year by 2010 will have a substantial impact on the next comprehensive spending review. Perhaps these savings, if realized, can be re-directed to support more innovative and boundary-crossing approaches to offender management, policing and immigration.

Funding Arrangements

The key challenge – which will certainly apply to the Home Office – is in managing the tension between central and local priorities[25]. The link between changes to the local government system of funding, activities and structures and those of other parts of the public sector such as the police, will all affect council tax bills hence the need, quoted by Lyons in his interim report[26], for a disciplined discussion of potential reforms of a more effective approach to managing pressures. This is a challenge that the Home Office must rise to alongside local authorities. The strong priority given to delegation and devolution to locally based neighbourhood policing teams needs to be clearly linked to the wider modernisation agenda of 'choice' and 'voice'[27], accountability and governance arrangements and the overall performance management framework[28]. There will

---

[23] DCLG (2006) Strong and Prosperous Communities, The Local Government White Paper.

[24] P.10, Machinery of Government: Security and Counter-Terrorism, and the Criminal Justice System

[25] Sir Michael Lyons update to the central Local Partnership meeting at Local Government House on 19 January 2005

[26] Lyons (2006) National prosperity, local choice and civic engagement: A new partnership between central and local government for the 21st century, Lyons Inquiry into Local Government, published May 2006.

[27] Cabinet Office (2006) UK Government's Approach to Public Service Reform,

[28] Cabinet Office (2006) as above.

be implications for the role of police authorities and how precept funding is applied and who is accountable.

The move towards commissioning arrangements will represent a further challenge for the Ministry of Justice. This will be introduced to the National Offender Management Services as a way of managing offenders and driving up the performance of the probation and prison services.

The emphasis given to local area agreements will be as important to the Home Office as it is to other departments. The allocation of programme funding, previously done in a rather ad hoc way[29] has the potential to be devolved closer to the point of delivery. The devolution of resources to the frontline is a stated priority of the Home Office but it will be interesting to observe how this is applied in practice particularly as the Home Office has stated that it actively supports the development of Local Area Agreements to increase local flexibility in reducing crime and improving community safety. The next spending review offers an excellent opportunity to put the responsibility of the Home Office at the centre stage of LAA's along with local government.

Conclusion

As previously outlined, the Home Office has one of the most challenging briefs holding some of the most significant challenges across government. The opportunity is available to think in a different way about leadership and how the leadership of not just the Home Office, but the whole of government, can help in achieving the ambitions outlined in the latest review and the plans for transformational change.

The commitment for transformational change is certainly encouraging. If we draw on the thinking of John Kotter[30], the Home Office may consider the following eight steps for transformational change:

1. Establish a sense of urgency;
2. Create the guiding coalition to drive and sustain change;
3. Develop a vision and a strategy as an investment in the delivery of a better future;
4. Communicate the change vision to develop a common and broad understanding of its goal and direction;
5. Empowering people for broad-based action which stimulates the desire for change;
6. Secure short term wins to keep up motivation;
7. Consolidate change
8. Anchor the change in reality and embed within the culture.

---

[29] National Audit Office (2004) The Home Office: Working with Crime and Disorder Reduction Partnerships.

[30] Kotter, John P.(1999) John P. Kotter on What Leaders Really Do. Boston, MA: Harvard Business School Press and Kotter, J.P. (1996) 'Leading Change', Harvard Business School Press, Boston.

The sense of urgency is now apparent, particularly given the various "not fit for purpose" pronouncements recently made and the major changes already announced. The guiding coalition must include all of the relevant stakeholders – not just Whitehall – but all those who lead frontline delivery and others who have a real stake including local authorities and other public bodies.

It requires not only a commitment to change but also a change to the way in which the Home Office thinks. Such a huge mandate needs radical re-thinking and the spending review provides that very opportunity, building on the changes brought about by the government paper 'Machinery of Government: Security and Counter-Terrorism and the Criminal Justice System'. This approach needs to be translated into the local delivery of Home Office priorities and its links with the government's wider aim of promoting social, economic and environmental well-being[31].

---

[31] Local Government Act 2000, Section 2.

8. Foreign and Commonwealth Office[1]

David Steven

Introduction

Across the democratic world, elections are primarily fought on domestic issues. Policies on jobs, crime and access to social services propel politicians into power. But once in government, an international dimension intrudes, most often suddenly, unexpectedly and dramatically. Tony Blair is one of many leaders whose legacy will be defined by his foreign adventures, not his actions at home. As John F Kennedy put it during his own turbulent presidency: "Domestic policy can only defeat us; foreign policy can kill us."[2]

Foreign policy matters most when the chips are down. Even those who favour a lean public sector accept that national defence is a vital public good. A broad foreign policy is vital for any country, and especially for a porous island economy like the United Kingdom.

All this heightens the importance of the Foreign and Commonwealth Office's fate in the 2007 comprehensive spending review (CSR). Little money is at stake – around half a per cent of total government expenditure – but this has not stopped negotiations with the Treasury turning rancorous. Treasury mandarins believe the FCO's position in Whitehall has never been weaker, with Gordon Brown thought to share his old department's poor opinion of its neighbour. Foreign Office staff feel beleaguered and morale is low. "The entire organisation needs to be challenged and reformed, but the leadership lacks the skills needed and the will to upset the status quo," concluded Collinson Grant, a firm of consultants engaged by the department[3]. All is not gloom, however. A new Permanent Secretary has made a fresh commitment to reform. His staff is among the most talented and resourceful in the civil service and possesses a body of expertise that could not be easily replicated. Years of accumulated investment, for example, mean that British Ambassadors are more likely to be fluent speakers of the local language than their counterparts from other countries. In London, unfamiliar challenges such as climate change have triggered a wave of innovation, while the FCO's delivery of services to the public has become steadily more effective and efficient.

---

[1] This paper is based on research undertaken with Alex Evans, senior policy associate at New York University's Center on International Co-operation, where he leads the Global Risks program. All content is the responsibility of the author, however, who writes in a personal capacity.

[2] Lee Sigelman, A Reassessment of the Two Presidencies Thesis, The Journal of Politics, Vol. 41, No. 4 (Nov., 1979), pp. 1195-1205

[3] Collinson Grant Ltd, Efficiency, effectiveness and the control of costs in the Foreign and Commonwealth Office, 2005

Nevertheless, the department needs to be held to a higher standard than incremental improvement. Like Tony Blair, Gordon Brown is likely to find that his foreign policy has the character of a journey into the unknown. He will need a strong Foreign Office to act as his navigator. He should therefore expect his first Foreign Secretary to lead the department into a period of intellectual renewal, as it fundamentally reinvents its role in the modern world. The alternative is likely to be hard to swallow. Already, there are those prepared to ask how much of the FCO the UK really needs. Perhaps, they speculate, it could be stripped back to its most basic functions, with the 'real' work of making policy shifted permanently to somewhere else in Whitehall.

Spending Reviews and the FCO

It may be less than ten years old, but New Labour's first comprehensive review of Foreign Office spending reads like a document from another era[4]. Hailing 'a new approach to investment in foreign policy', the government is focused on export promotion, investment in the UK, and 'showcasing' modern Britain. Policy objectives are vague. The FCO will ensure fifty more countries are 'committed to co-operating with the UK.' It will also combat the trade in drugs, cross-border crime, abuse of human rights, and environmental degradation. A 'radical' IT upgrade is planned to allow a quicker response to 'global foreign policy issues'.

What is missing is a reflection of the shift that was then underway in Blairite attitudes to the international arena. The Prime Minister had been surprised by the suddenness of the East Asian financial crisis in 1997. The aftermath provided a window for the reform of the global economic system, but there were few ideas about what should change. War in the Balkans acted as a further reproach to the new world order. In 1999, Blair laid out his 'doctrine of the international community' in a speech to the Economic Club of Chicago[5]. Surveying the 'awful crimes' then taking place in Kosovo, the Prime Minister was clearly shocked by the pace at which chaos had impinged on Europe. He hailed the 'just war' that had been declared in response. "We are," he said, "all internationalists now, whether we like it or not. We cannot refuse to participate in global markets if we want to prosper. We cannot ignore new political ideas in other countries if we want to innovate. We cannot turn our backs on conflicts and the violation of human rights within other countries if we want still to be secure." The 1990s had seen ad hoc and reactive responses to global problems, he argued. The future would require a more strategic approach. Narrow national interests must no longer be allowed to predominate. Instead, a 'sustained and serious' approach was needed to delivering global public goods.

---

[4] HM Treasury, Modern Public Services for Britain: Investing in Reform, The Stationery Office, 1998

[5] Tony Blair, Doctrine of the International Community, at the Economic Club, Chicago, 24 April 1999

The attacks of 9/11 strengthened Blair's confidence in his vision and it is unsurprising that a (stripped down) version made its way into the 2002 spending review[6]. The UK would build on its "proud tradition as an outward-looking nation' and 'play a leading role in promoting peace and prosperity around the world, and in combating global poverty, conflict, and terrorism." For the FCO, this meant responding to a 'major shift in foreign affairs'. Economic cheerleading had moved down the agenda. Instead, the department would focus its energies on two themes: European enlargement and worldwide engagement. Two years later, the FCO's first formal strategy – and its first major policy statement under New Labour – reinforced the new approach. It set out eight 'strategic international policy priorities' for the UK (these are now referred to as international strategic priorities or ISPs)[7]. For each priority, the FCO committed itself to a list of objectives. In order to contribute to a 'safer world', for example, the department committed itself to leading "a systematic strategy across Government for engaging with the Islamic world and promoting peaceful political and social reform in Arab countries." The FCO updated this strategy in 2006, this time engaging in greater consultation with other government departments[8]. Most of the ISPs emerged unscathed. Shortly thereafter, a new ISP on climate security was added to the list at the insistence of Margaret Beckett, who had just arrived as the UK's first female Foreign Secretary.

The spending review architecture has meshed rather poorly with the new strategies. In 2002, twelve public sector agreement (PSA) targets were set. By 2004, this had been reduced to nine, which were then mapped against the ISPs in an ad hoc fashion. Three ISPs did not have any targets at all under the 2004 spending review. The resulting patchwork has proved deeply unsatisfactory, especially in 2005/2006 when the FCO found itself reporting against both the 2002 and 2004 targets[9]. The traffic light system used to demonstrate impact has proved particularly contentious. In 2005/2006, for example, Iraq was marked as 'on track' to becoming a stable democracy by March 2008. A year later, the assessment had changed dramatically, with the target marked as 'not on course – major slippage'[10]. FCO systems for assessing progress are generally qualitative and informal, with the FCO's lack of skills in this area standing in stark contrast to best practice in the international development field. The perceived lack of credibility of the FCO's performance management regime has undoubtedly damaged its negotiating position in the 2007 spending review.

In practice, the FCO has used its PSA targets purely for external accountability purposes, with internal performance management more closely focused on the ISPs. This raises important questions. Is the FCO's strategy driving performance

---

[6] HM Treasury, *Opportunity and Security for All: Investing in an enterprising, fairer Britain*, 2002

[7] Foreign and Commonwealth Office, *UK International Priorities: a Strategy for the FCO*, 2003

[8] Foreign and Commonwealth Office, *Active Diplomacy for a Changing World: the UK's international priorities*, 2006

[9] Foreign and Commonwealth Office, *FCO Departmental Report 2005/2006*, 2006

[10] Foreign and Commonwealth Office, *FCO Departmental Report 2006/2007*, 2007

as intended? Or is the department chiefly reactive in its approach, with resources allocated according to historical precedent and expressions of short-term need?

FCO – Fit for the Future?

The FCO's recent departmental Capability Review provides an unequivocal answer to these questions. Completed by a senior team from the private and public sectors, it concludes that:

> The Department has weak business planning, resource allocation and prioritisation processes. The International Priorities do not directly drive the allocation of resources across the organisation. There is limited clarity on the relative importance of FCO's contributions to the various International Priorities. As a result, many Posts are pursuing most of the International Priorities, resulting in resources being spread very thinly across these priorities. At the same time, resources are slow to get to some Posts located in countries that are a priority for UK foreign policy[11].

While the Capability Review found areas of high performance in the FCO, in general its tone is critical. Staff are praised for their passion and commitment, but the department as a whole is criticised for failing to articulate a clear mission. The result is a lack of 'clarity, pace and coherence in the direction of the Department's strategic change.' The department needs urgently to set a clearer direction, to prioritise its resources more effectively, and to become better at exploiting the undoubted talents of its staff. Its lack of a systematic approach for measuring impact is also a further cause for concern.

These criticisms have been echoed by a number of other studies. In 2000, Robin Cook tasked a team of young officials to think about the FCO's future. The Foresight Report, which they produced, found that the department was good at tactics, short-term practical problems, 'understanding foreigners' and gaining access to decision makers[12]. However, it was judged to be weak at long-term strategy and planning, focusing on concrete outcomes, reallocating resources to meet new priorities, learning from mistakes, and implementing change. The FCO's organisational structure and business processes have also come in for repeated criticism. Only 28% of staff believes the department is well managed, while Collinson Grant has found that processes "are not thought through logically but have been built on past methods, with cumbersome modifications to meet perceived changes to requirements."[13] [14] Moreover, the department's experience with IT is chequered at best. One 'lessons learned' report, commissioned after a high-risk IT project hit the buffers, found that inadequate planning, a shortage of relevant skills, and the failure of the Board to engage

---

[11] Civil Service 2007, Capability Review of the Foreign and Commonwealth Office, 2007

[12] Foreign & Commonwealth Office, Foresight Report, 2000

[13] ORC International, Foreign and Commonwealth Office Employee Engagement Survey 2006: narrative report, 2006

[14] Collinson Grant Ltd, Efficiency, effectiveness and the control of costs in the Foreign and Commonwealth Office, 2005

effectively had all caused major difficulties for the project. The FCO's investment in public diplomacy has also been regularly criticised. Lord Carter's 2005 report put a brave face on what was being achieved, but his private message was much stronger[15]. The FCO could only provide rough estimates of how much it spent on public diplomacy. It did not have an effective strategy for what it was trying to achieve. Nor did it have firm evidence to show results.

Legitimate questions have also been raised about whether the FCO has the right staff with the right expertise, deployed in the right places. The department makes a £6m investment in languages, but has not developed equivalent expertise in global issues. The Foreign Affairs Committee, meanwhile, has accused the department of an 'amateurish approach' to filling senior posts. The new Finance Director, for example, is the first to have relevant professional qualifications. Human resources policies are weak, with only 0.8% of staff receiving an unsatisfactory grade in their appraisals, despite widespread acceptance that, especially at senior levels, a rump of poor performers is blocking the organisation's development[16]. The Capability Review criticised the department for failing to manage its staff strategically, as well as for limited external competition for senior posts. The weakness of the FCO's knowledge management is another area of legitimate concern. Knowledge was correctly identified in the Foresight Report as the FCO's most important commodity. However, it found that the FCO failed to make the most of its expertise, with an 'intellectual machismo' stopping staff from turning to their predecessors for advice and assistance. The Capability Review shows that too little has changed in the past seven years. In particular, an obsession with secrecy has stopped knowledge being shared effectively across the FCO network.

The bigger picture

In part, the causes of the Foreign Office's weakness lie outside the department. While Tony Blair has not been actively hostile towards the Foreign Office during his ten years in power, he has done little to assist the department's development. Faced with a series of escalating and complex global challenges, his impulse has usually been to centralise foreign policy decision-making within Number 10. This reflects the ever-increasing role played by heads of state in modern policy making. It can also work, especially to create momentum behind pressing, short-term policy issues such as the 2005 deployment to Helmand province in Afghanistan or the 2003 London conference on Palestinian reform.

Centralisation, however, has led to a widening gulf between the Prime Minister's staff and the wider foreign policy apparatus. It has also sapped the strength of the FCO. As one former Cabinet Office staffer ruefully put it: "Information and analysis is faithfully reported up a vast pyramid. Then four people at the top read the Economist and make a decision." The dangers of this

---

[15] Lord Carter of Coles, Public Diplomacy Review, 2005

[16] Collinson Grant Ltd, Efficiency, effectiveness and the control of costs in the Foreign and Commonwealth Office, 2005

approach were most obvious in the run-up to the invasion of Iraq, where a narrow group of advisers controlled policy development. Less noted has been the difficulty Blair experienced in persuading government departments to develop ambitious and far-sighted policies on key global risks like climate change. The run up to the UK's presidency of the G8 and EU in 2005 provides an example, with Nigel Sheinwald, the Prime Minister's Foreign Policy and Defence Adviser, charged with chivvying Whitehall departments into developing a long-term climate strategy for the UK. The results were frustrating for all those involved, and the UK arrived at the G8 Gleneagles summit without a clear vision of what a comprehensive and global solution to climate change would look like. It was not until Summer 2006 that an outline strategy was finally drafted by DEFRA, DTI, DFID and the FCO.

Gordon Brown's approach to foreign policy will take time to develop. As Chancellor, he largely left foreign policy to the Prime Minister. However, he proved an enthusiastic supporter of increased British investment in international development and promoted a number of new multilateral mechanisms, including the International Financing Facility and the Education for All Fast-track Initiative. In Downing Street, he is likely to be less evangelical in style than Tony Blair, but the emphasis on interdependence seems certain to remain. And so it should. The UK will continue to face a palette of unpredictable risks. Throughout the world, the threat from non-state actors to cause chaos will only increase, while every failed or failing state will export disorder to its neighbours and beyond. It is no wonder that Brown has proved a strong advocate for a co-ordinated response to security issues, calling for 'all methods of diplomacy, all means of intelligence, all tools of law, policing and our security and military forces' to be brought together to protect British citizens from security threats. Under Brown, the focus on security is likely to lead to something of a 'back to basics' approach to international relations. The Prime Minister is, however, highly unlikely either to want or to be able to ignore the wider global risks that the UK faces. Ongoing attempts to tackle the underlying structural problems that lead to radicalisation will continue, but the slow-burning drivers of instability – state failure, global economic imbalances, infectious diseases, climate change and energy security – will also jostle for his attention. The UK's capacity to respond to international and domestic shocks may have improved in recent years. Its ability to prevent them, however, has lagged far behind.

The problem should not be seen solely as a British one. Indeed, we have been pushed into a position of leadership on many issues because the world's multilateral systems are in such woeful disarray. Early reports on the new UN Secretary General, Ban Ki-Moon, are discouraging, while commentators wonder whether the UN system is in terminal decline. Paul Wolfowitz has run the World Bank into the ground, NATO is a shadow of its former self, and the European Union is yet to find a foreign policy voice commensurate with its size. Other major powers have, if anything, more fragmented government responses to international issues. At the same time, we are in the midst of what might be termed a global interregnum, as the leadership of many countries and international institutions changes hands. This will only culminate in 2008 when George Bush leaves power, to the fervent prayers (and realistic hope) that the global superpower never again elects such an incompetent leader.

For Brown, all this change provides an opportunity. Angela Merkel has already shown how quickly a leader can gain influence in a period of such fluidity. A new US president, whether Republican or Democrat, is almost certain to want to re-engage internationally as he, or perhaps for the first time she, attempts to clear up the damage that the Bush administration has done. Brown may prove pragmatic in his foreign policy, but he is unlikely to put all ambition aside. Like Blair, he is likely to want to show bold leadership overseas as he promotes long-term solutions for deep-seated problems. Effective frameworks cannot be created without painstaking effort, however. Neither will they be adopted without concerted efforts to influence opinion overseas and build broad coalitions for change. Brown will therefore be deeply reliant on Britain's foreign policy apparatus to if he is to make lasting achievements. Without reform, however, that apparatus is more likely than not to fail him.

Redesigning the foreign policy apparatus

If he is to succeed internationally, Brown must demand much greater agility and flexibility from his foreign policy system. This means clarifying the role of the centre. As head of state, he will remain the UK's most important foreign policy asset. However, he must resist the temptation to attempt to micro-manage foreign policy from Number 10 or the Cabinet Office. The centre's role is to act as a catalyst, setting clear missions, providing intellectual challenge, and using shared strategies to drive departmental performance.

Tackling fragmentation is the key challenge, but this work will differ markedly from the 'joined-up government' agenda of Labour's first term. Domestic policy is above all about delivery – how effectively government can deploy the proportion of the national wealth over which it has control. Internationally, money matters less. Instead, influence is the prime currency. This is becoming increasingly clear to all departments that work globally. Security threats, for example, are generally asymmetric and cannot be defeated by force alone. Donors, meanwhile, cannot simply 'buy' development. Attempting to do so simply strips capacity from the national institutions they most want to reinforce. As a result, changes are rippling through the system. The new Office for Security and Counter-Terrorism will have a research, information and communications unit at its heart, charged with supporting the 'struggle for ideas and values'. The military is busy re-learning the lessons of counter-insurgency, as Sir John Kiszely, head of the Defence Academy, has pointed out[17]. For Kiszely, "military leaders, and not just senior ones, need a high level of understanding of factors such as the political dimension of counterinsurgency, the constituent elements of good governance and prosperity, the role of ideology and religion,

---

[17] Lieutenant General Sir John Kiszely, Learning About Counterinsurgency, Military Review, March-April 2007

the nature of societies and culture, and of minds and people." DFID is also broadening its approach, with its Capability Review underlining that "the world of development is changing and becoming more complex, with poverty reduction becoming increasingly interconnected with the global economy, global environment and security."[18] In response, the department is attempting to grapple with the challenge of what power is, where it is held, and how external forces can influence a state to deliver more effectively to its people[19].

The Brown administration needs to draw on these developments as it attempts to integrate the foreign policy system; build an interface between the UK's security, international development, and foreign policy programmes; and deliver a 'whole government' response to the our most pressing international problems. This will require much more than a simple process of organisational engineering. At present, the UK is flying blind internationally because it lacks a clear 'theory of influence'. The international arena is characterised by a growing number of clashing ideas and values on the one hand, and loose networks of government and non-government actors on the other. Many of the old rules of diplomacy no longer apply. A programme of intellectual renewal is therefore needed. Departments must draw insights from the study of complex and adaptive system, learn how to analyse social networks, and adopt new communication models that take account of radical changes to the media landscape. From this, we could expect a 'common language' to emerge, which would allow a shared understanding of problems to develop and facilitate greater interoperability across departments. Themes to be explored include the power of narrative to mould international opinion; the growing role of campaigns staffed by teams that cut across existing bureaucracies; and the need for greater ambition, with resources concentrated on initiatives that have the potential to achieve decisive, and often disruptive, change. The Stern Review on the Economics of Climate Change, run from Brown's Treasury, provides a model for the new approach[20]. The government could have commissioned an internal analysis of the issues. Instead, it used the review to set an agenda internationally and to integrate an economic perspective into the climate change narrative. The launch was a global media event, with impact on other governments, electorates and big business. Subsequently, the campaign has continued with Nicholas Stern travelling extensively, to amplify key messages, while other countries are encouraged to sponsor 'mini-Sterns' that look at impacts on national or regional economies.

As I have argued in a recent report on the future of the UK's foreign policy apparatus, Brown's first cabinet will need to make hard decisions about where

---

[18] Civil Service, Capability Review of the Department for International Development, 2007

[19] Department for International Development, Governance, Development and Democratic Politics: DFID's work in building more effective states, Department for International Development, 2007

[20] Nicholas Stern, The Economics of Climate Change: the Stern Review, HM Treasury, 2006

the UK should focus its energies[21]. I have recommended the development of a global issues strategy, which sets out long term plans for how the government intends to protect its citizens against the most significant slow-burn risks. I also believe that a central 'challenge function' should be created to provide the cabinet with analysis of global risks and ideas for how to respond to them in a more dynamic and innovative fashion. This work would set the stage for renewal at the Foreign Office. Domestic departments will clearly continue to lead on their own areas of policy. This leaves only one role for the department: to forge an effective synthesis across issues, while planning and co-ordinating the deployment of all available tools to achieve change internationally. This does not mean starting from scratch. Far from it. Many reforms are already underway and there is a growing appetite to take on new challenges. However, there is resistance to change and a sense that, despite ten years of steady development, a decisive breakthrough has yet to be made. A considerable investment of ministerial time will be required to give the FCO a renewed sense of direction and achieve a lasting shift in mindset – from 'lead department for foreign policy' to a 'platform for global issues management'.

FCO renewal

I cannot lay out a complete plan for reform of the Foreign Office in this chapter. Instead, consider a different question. If one looks beyond the next general election to a fundamental review of government expenditure in the future, what are the signs that would show the department had really changed? Here are eight areas where I would expect to see a substantial shift in the department's performance.

1. Intellectual leadership. The FCO has great intellectual reserves, but this is not always evident. The contrast with other government departments is marked. A major study of failing states was led from the Cabinet Office. The Treasury sponsored the Stern Review. DFID is at the forefront of the international development debate. The FCO should follow these examples, adopting an increasingly 'open source' model for developing and disseminating policy. In the future, we would expect the department to master a two-step process: first, create an intellectual resource, preferably packaged in a powerful narrative; second, use it to reframe an issue and shape innovative policy responses. To succeed, the department will need to attain international authority in crucial areas like global public goods and the resilience of complex, transnational systems.

2. Issue synthesis. The FCO cannot fulfil its role as a 'platform' for foreign policy if it reinforces silos between policy areas. Domestic departments lack the ability to tie global risks together, a serious disadvantage when

---

[21] David Steven and Alex Evans, Fixing the UK's Foreign Policy, Global Dashboard, 2007

progress in one area may require a 'grand bargain' that cuts across departmental responsibilities. The FCO's Permanent Secretary has already announced the creation of a new Policy Planning team, which will report directly to him. It is essential that this team quickly becomes a dynamic force within the FCO and that it focuses its efforts on the area where the department can add most value – policy synthesis. Again, narrative is important. A revitalised department will use it to shape debate within government as well as internationally.

3. Campaign leadership. The FCO has been a willing participant in recent international campaigns. The next step will be for it to initiate and lead new ones. It is surprising, for example, that the UK has not done more to create momentum behind the stalled Doha trade talks. Avian flu could be another area where action is suddenly needed to galvanise a large number of government and non-government actors to participate in a comprehensive response. This will require the department to develop new skills and create more effective structures for its network to act as one on priority issues. Successful development and execution of even a single flagship campaign will provide clear evidence that the organisation is adapting to its new role.

4. Issue ambassadors. The FCO has traditionally been configured around bilateral relationships. However, Margaret Beckett's decision to appoint a Special Representative for Climate Change has shown the potential for 'issue ambassadors' to cut across geographical boundaries and create progress on key policy priorities. The result has been new authority for the FCO on climate change and a strong reference point for all FCO staff working on the issue. The FCO should build on this experience. A key issue for the future will be the number of 'thought leaders' it has, with credibility across government and internationally.

5. The new public diplomacy. As discussed above, the Carter Review was strongly critical of the FCO's investment in public diplomacy. Since then, a new public diplomacy board has been established, with an FCO minister in the chair. The board has scrapped public diplomacy's old mission – massaging the UK's 'brand' – and is promoting a new approach, which aims to use broad social engagement to achieve UK policy goals. This is an important development, but there is still a long way to go. Public diplomacy remains a low status function within the FCO. A dramatic reversal of attitudes is needed to push public engagement to the heart of the organisational mission. In the future, the organisation will need a new breed of diplomat, comfortable with a rapidly changing media landscape and able to deploy networks of non-governmental contacts to achieve concrete results. Real change will occur when public diplomacy experience is seen as an asset to any Foreign Office career.

6. A more agile network. In 2006, the Foreign Affairs Committee criticised the FCO for failing to take 'a fundamental look at the reason why it has the Posts it has, and why those Posts are where they are.' To date, the FCO has proved most willing to be innovative in its delivery of services. UK Visas has reconfigured its operations on a regional basis, while FCO Consular Services has pioneered the use of rapid response teams. Both innovations could usefully be applied to the FCO's policy work, with regionalisation reducing fragmentation across the network, and rapid response teams helping to streamline posts and eliminate redundant capacity. Influence is about pace and momentum, but, at present, embassies take months if not years to realign themselves to new priorities. In the future, the network will need to be demonstrably more flexible, responsive and efficient. Evidence of a radical reallocation of resources will be needed, with the FCO beginning the process of rebuilding key posts from the ground up.

7. Better systems. The FCO has recently appointed a new Director General to lead its change programme. This is not an area where it has a good track record. We suggest four yardsticks for the future. First, Future Firecrest, its next generation IT platform, must deliver the benefits predicted by its business case. Second, the department must become more effective at modelling and tracking its target audiences. Third, its performance management system needs to be more robust and systematic. And finally, the Foreign Office should become a recognised centre of excellence for the new generation of online technologies (blogs, bulletin boards and so on) that are reshaping the way people socialise across national borders.

8. A transformed culture. Cultural change is the key to progress in all other areas. To meet its challenges, the Foreign Office needs to become a far more outward-facing organisation. A cross-departmental cadre of international civil servants must be developed, with members sharing an understanding of the synergies between global issues and a commitment to achieving results rather than defending departmental turf. This means opening up recruitment for all front-line policy posts and ensuring secondments are a key part of the career of all civil servants working on international issues. At the same time, the FCO needs to develop a more concerted programme to equip its generalists with policy expertise, helping them learn about issues in the same way they learn languages. Finally, the department should recognise that talking about new approaches will not deliver real change. It should develop the ability to bring together departments to 'war game' comprehensive responses to global challenges.

Conclusion

The Foreign Office will not achieve wholesale change overnight. However, the Permanent Secretary has recognised the urgency of reform and has set a two-year deadline for achieving results. It is vital that Brown's first Foreign Secretary makes the department's transformation one of his or her top priorities.

Together, they need to challenge the department to become much more assertive, ambitious and determined in its approach. At present, diplomats have the same 'investment mindset' as bank managers. They hold a large portfolio of assets from which they expect incremental returns. Their appetite for risk is low and there is an expectation that failure will be punished. This approach is not well-suited to the contemporary international arena, where bold attempts are often needed to reframe issues and build coalitions. Diplomats therefore need to start behaving more like venture capitalists. They need to slim down their portfolios, pumping more resources into fewer activities. These activities will be more risky – some will be dramatically successful, others will make little impact. It is on the dramatic successes, and not on being a 'safe pair of hands', that careers should be founded. An incrementalist approach is no longer justifiable. How much, for example, has the UK spent on attempting to save the Doha trade talks compared to its ongoing support for individual British businesses overseas? The failure of Doha will have implications for the whole of the UK economy, for our development objectives, and for confidence in the multilateral system's ability to broker complex agreements. Success in the latter can only help a small number of businesses, some of whom would find other ways of accessing export markets.

In essence, diplomacy must be about achieving influence disproportionate to the resources employed. That is why we need a foreign affairs department that can identify and exploit opportunities for achieving lasting change. It is time for a new model at the Foreign Office.

9. Department for International Development

Willy McCourt

Government and public commitment to aid

The Labour government's support for poor countries, mostly in Africa and Asia, has been remarkable in a number of ways. If political commitment is about putting your money where your mouth is, then there is a sense in which this government has been more committed to the welfare of poor countries than to education, health, law and order or any single issue in its own backyard. Once its 1997 election promise to stick to its Conservative predecessor's spending plans ran out, it opened the floodgates: real terms increases of 6.2, 8.1 and 9.2 per cent respectively following the Spending Reviews of 2000, 2002 and 2004. The Department for International Development (DFID)'s budget will increase to more than £5.3 billion a year in 2007-08 compared to £3.8 billion in 2004-05, the highest percentage increase of any government department.

But what is equally remarkable is that this has been a popular increase. The equality agenda of Labour-led local authorities in the 1980s ran ahead of public opinion and contributed to the downfall of many of them, but this even more utopian social experiment enjoys considerable public support. It was dramatically evident in the Make Poverty History campaign in 2005, when thousands marched round Edinburgh Castle in the run-up to the G8 Summit at Gleneagles and the 'Live 8' pop concerts were watched by millions more on TV. With the major parties in all four countries of the United Kingdom united on the importance of development aid, and with Gordon Brown if anything even more personally committed to development than Tony Blair, the political climate will tolerate high spending and may even expect it to increase even more.

How we got here

This is one area of the public sector where the government has plenty of room to manoeuvre. Still, even a Comprehensive Spending Review is not a policy 'year zero': aid policy after it will be in the light of what went before. So how did we get to where we are now?

In international development, the 1980s and early 1990s were the period of the 'Washington consensus'[1], when the decisive development actors, notably the Washington-based International Monetary Fund (IMF) and the World Bank, came to believe that development's overriding goal should be economic growth, from which all other good things would follow. Also, since nationalised industries were seen to have underperformed, delivering growth was to be the job of the private sector. The job of government was merely to act as 'watchman', maintaining law and order by all means, particularly property rights, possibly also providing some 'safety net' social services, but otherwise keeping out of the wealth creators' way.

If government in the rich countries was 'the problem, not the solution', as Ronald Reagan had famously declared in his first Inaugural Address, then Third World governments with their perceived corruption, 'rent-seeking' and general inefficiency were a very big problem indeed. This was a view that left little room for traditional development assistance, which had focused on government-to-government aid. It duly declined, with more of what was left bypassing governments to go straight to the burgeoning NGO sector.

That view was already changing when Labour came to power, for four reasons:

- **Politics and the electoral cycle.** Centrist or leftish governments were taking over or already in office in France, Germany and the US around the same time.
- **The experience of structural adjustment** sponsored by the World Bank and IMF, and seen to have failed to produce significant growth in most developing countries (or, equally importantly, in most of central and eastern Europe after the fall of the Berlin Wall).
- **Ideas**, and in particular the emergence of a human development paradigm sponsored by the United Nations. It put measures of well-being, especially education and health, alongside income measures. Economic growth might not be enough on its own. There could be 'bad growth' which increased the gap between rich and poor. When the new paradigm was taken up by NGOs refusing to be confined to the low-cost development service provider role which conservative governments had earmarked for them, it influenced the Jubilee Debt Campaign at national level, and internationally became the basis just after Labour came to power for the UN Millennium Declaration and the Millennium Development Goals (MDGs).
- **The strategic management model**, a seductive soft technology borrowed from the private sector. Its apparatus of time-bound numerical outcome indicators was used to give utopian aspirations a tough veneer.

---

[1] Williamson, J. (1993) 'Democracy and the "Washington consensus"', *World Development* 21: 1329-36.

Thus in line with Labour's traditional socialist beliefs, poverty eradication was the single goal of the new government's first White Paper in 1997[2]. Economic growth remained central, just as it was in the Washington consensus, but it now had to be 'pro-poor'. However, as the Millennium Development Goals (MDGs) built up a head of steam, the goal broadened to encompass education, health and gender equality as well as income poverty. To compensate for this 'mission creep', the goal also sharpened in strategic management terms: advancing the MDGs became the be-all and end-all of government policy, expressed in DFID's admirably succinct (less than two pages) Public Service Agreement (PSA) with the Treasury for the period 2005-8.

Box 9.1   **DFID Public Service Agreement 2005–8**

AIM: Eliminate poverty in poorer countries, in particular through achievement by 2015 of the Millennium Development Goals:

TARGET 1: Progress towards the MDGs in 16 key countries in Africa, demonstrated by:
1) A reduction of 4 percentage points in the proportion of people living in poverty across the entire region, against the 1999 baseline
2) An increase in primary school enrolment by 18 percentage points and an increase in the ratio of girls to boys enrolled in primary school by 5 percentage points, both against their year 2000 baseline
3) a reduction in under-5 mortality rates for girls and boys by 8 per 1000 live births, against the year 2000 baseline; and an increase in proportion of births assisted by skilled birth attendants by 11 percentage points, against the year 2000 baseline
4) A reduction in the proportion of 15-24 year old pregnant women with HIV
5) Enhanced partnership at the country and regional level, especially through the G8, to increase the effectiveness of aid and ensure that international policies support African development
TARGET 2: Progress towards the MDGs in 16 key countries in Asia
TARGET 3: Improved effectiveness of the multilateral system
TARGET 4: Ensure that the EU secures significant reductions in EU and world trade barriers by 2008 ([joint target with Department of Trade and Industry [DTI])
TARGET 5: By 2007/08, improved effectiveness of UK and international support for conflict prevention (joint target with the Foreign Office [FCO] and Ministry of Defence [MOD])
TARGET 6: 90 per cent of DFID's bilateral programme going to low-income countries; and achieve a sustained increase in the index of DFID's bilateral projects evaluated as successful.

---

[2]DFID (1997) Eliminating world poverty: A challenge for the twenty-first century, http://www.dfid.gov.uk/pubs/files/whitepaper1997.pdf, accessed January 19 2007.

DEVELOPMENT SPENDING AFTER THE CSR: WHAT SHOULD CONTINUE, AND WHAT SHOULD CHANGE

Emerging priorities

The trouble with the strategic management model is that strategies are never set in stone: managers have to adjust to Harold Macmillan's dictum, 'events, dear boy, events'. So we should not be surprised that only half-way through the current PSA, two new priorities have already popped up. The first is governance. It was highlighted by the report of Tony Blair's Africa Commission[3], and it was duly the subject of DFID's latest White Paper[4]. It ratified the PSA obligations, but it also added objectives for state capability, responsiveness and accountability, and vowed to make British aid conditional on developing countries' commitment to fighting corruption.

We can expect governance, along with security (a barely acknowledged but effective post-Iraq priority), to be part of the CSR picture. Also, with Tony Blair having already declared his intention to resign at the time of writing, we can expect the CSR to reflect the priorities of his successor, prime minister Brown. Mr Brown showed his hand in a speech in 2005, which announced that Britain will write off its 10 per cent share of Africa's debts to the World Bank, press for fair trade terms for developing countries, help African countries upgrade their infrastructure – physical facilities like roads, but also institutions - underwrite free primary education for every child and support health care. He has continued to emphasise education in speeches and interviews.

So that is what Labour has done, or is pledging to do: more work to advance the MDGs, focusing on priorities in education and health supported by a stronger physical and institutional infrastructure   But is it on the right track? There are perhaps three issues that the CSR should address:

- The MDGs: big push, or lots of tiny pushes?
- To whom should aid spending be accountable?
- Climate change and trade

---

[3]Africa Commission (2005) Our common interest: Report of the Africa Commission, http://www.commissionforafrica.org/english/report/introduction.html, accessed January 17 2007.

[4] DFID (2006) Making governance work for the poor: A White Paper on international development, http://www.dfid.gov.uk/pubs/files/whitepaper2006/wp2006foreword-preface-section1.pdf, accessed January 17 2007.

Achieving the MDGs

No one disputes the desirability of goals like ending child poverty by 2015. But how realistic are they? The American economist and former World Bank official William Easterly[5] has trenchantly argued that:

> The utopian (MDG) agenda has led to collective responsibility for multiple goals for each (aid) agency, one of the worst incentive systems invented since mankind started walking upright.

Aid agencies, he believes, would do better to concentrate on obvious goods like vaccines and food supplements, and seek out other piecemeal solutions at country level.

Certainly some readers scanning the grandiose ambitions of the PSA might be tempted to mutter, 'If wishes were horses, then beggars would ride.' But those who favour the 'big push', like the American economist Jeffrey Sachs[6] and others grouped around the UN, argue that ambitious goals galvanise efforts. They also point to the runaway economic growth in Asia, particularly China and India, that is lifting millions out of poverty there. With Asia taken care of, they say, we can focus on sub-Saharan Africa and the few remaining outlier countries which the UN estimates are not on track to achieve the MDGs[7].

Nor do ambitious goals have to be at the expense of local, piecemeal solutions. In fact, Sachs is sometimes caricatured as having an obsession with such homely initiatives as using impregnated bednets to combat malaria. So there is room for prioritising and even opportunism in the choice of initiatives that Britain's limited aid resources should be spent on. Gordon Brown's declarations on education, health and infrastructure, and country-level initiatives like support in Malawi for free anti-retroviral treatment for HIV/AIDS and salary top-ups for health workers, show that the government recognises this. Of course the wrong priorities could still be chosen. With the very first MDG target - halving the number of people living on less than a dollar a day – it is growth that has put Asia on track. But growth, the number one priority in the Washington consensus era, seems to have been pushed to DFID's margins, relegated in the main to support for what other agencies are doing[5]. This shift in priorities is reflected in the dramatic switch in aid expenditure, including DFID's, on the economic versus the social sector from a ratio of 4: 1 in 1978 to a ratio of 1: 4 in 2004[8].

All in all, the MDGs should stay at the centre of British aid policy. The jury is still out on whether they can be achieved in Africa by 2015, and we may end up

---

[5] Easterly, W. (2006) The white man's burden: Why the West's efforts to aid the rest have done so much ill and so little good, New York: Penguin.

[6] Sachs, J. (2005) The end of poverty: Economic possibilities for our time, New York: Penguin.

[7] United Nations (2005) The Millennium Development Goals Report 2005, http://www.unfpa.org/icpd/docs/mdgrept2005.pdf, accessed January 17 2007.

[8] Killick, T. and M. Foster (2007) 'The macroeconomics of doubling aid to Africa and the centrality of the supply side', Development Policy Review, 25, 2: 167-92.

having to retreat from them with our fingers burnt - but not now. Switching from the MDG-led approach would also be stop-go policymaking at its worst, and would damage British credibility with First and Third World governments. In aid policy it is mostly the boring virtues of perseverance and patience that we need at the moment, not attention-grabbing new initiatives.

Accountable to whom?

The point of public service agreements is to make government departments accountable to the Treasury and to citizens. But making the MDGs the centrepiece of DFID's PSA makes DFID accountable for something it has no jurisdiction over, and for which it is developing country governments that are meant to be responsible. When DFID makes itself accountable for poverty in developing countries, developing countries cease to be accountable themselves. DFID is ready to share responsibility for two of its six PSA targets with the DTI, FCO and MoD but not, apparently, with developing country governments.

And yet DFID's governance White Paper[7] is all about making developing country governments more accountable to their own citizens. Moreover, as a signatory to the 2005 Paris Declaration on Aid Effectiveness, DFID is also committed to respecting developing country leadership and ownership, and basing its aid on its partners' own national development strategies.

In response to this concern, DFID could point out that its partners have all committed themselves to the MDGs, and that it is now giving more of its aid through general 'budget support', allowing governments more freedom, rather than earmarked projects. So they have, and so it has. But Britain committed itself likewise in 1970 to spending 0.7 per cent of GDP on aid, which did not stop aid spending from dwindling in relative terms while the Conservatives were in power after 1979. In the same way, developing country governments, increasingly democratic as we should remember, have their own real priorities which may not be the ones they pay lip-service to. Moreover, budget support arguably just adjusts donors' grip on the aid purse strings. It is still conditional on donors' approval, particularly the IMF's, of the overall shape of government policy. Donors like DFID can still influence government policy in order to do the things they want to do. But that is not what developing country ownership was supposed to be about.

There is a real contradiction, in fact, between doing the democratic thing and the developmental thing in many countries; or, to put it another way, between being accountable to British citizens, with all our fickle preferences, and to developing country citizens via their governments. Keeping everyone happy by finessing the contradiction will be at the expense of producing development programmes that collapse as soon as the donor withdraws, as they have so often done in the past.

The solution is to recognise that aid is a special case of accountability. DFID cannot ignore its accountability to UK citizens. The thousands if not millions who were mobilised by the Make Poverty History campaign would be betrayed if the government walked away from the MDGs, whatever individual African governments might think of them. But accountability to British people has to be reconciled with the principle of developing country leadership, so that accountability is shared with people in developing countries – and their governments in particular: DFID should not be in the business of hand-picking congenial partners among NGOs, trade unions and civil society.

In practice, this means two things:

1. **Being more rigorous in pursuing DFID's self-imposed accountability for the MDGs.** Despite DFID's tough-seeming performance indicator regime, the House of Commons Select Committee on International Development[9] noted that 'Where targets are not on course, there is often no specific information in the Departmental Report 2006 of the remedial action that DFID is taking').

2. **Combining the MDG commitment in DFID's next PSA with a new commitment to respecting the priorities of its country partners.** More practically still, it means allowing greater discretion to DFID's country-level staff to support initiatives that are worthwhile on countries' own terms (and will put an even greater premium on those staff being steeped in the reality of those countries). At a global level that will give DFID a slightly incoherent grab-bag of activities. But this messiness will be the sign that DFID is really prepared (perhaps for the first time?) to take country ownership to its logical conclusion. That may well do as much for good governance in poor countries as anything else that DFID can put its hand to.

Climate change and trade

There are two areas where consolidating or refining the existing agenda isn't enough: climate change and trade. They are also areas where the problem of ownership doesn't arise because it is mostly our own mess, not poor countries', that we will be cleaning up. With the environment, that is because 'the most vulnerable – the poorest countries and populations – will suffer earliest and most, even though they have contributed least to the causes of climate change', as the Government's Stern Report noted[10]. We did not understand the threat of climate change to the environment so well when the MDGs were drawn up. Even

---

[9] House of Commons Select Committee on International Development (2006) Department for International Development Departmental Report 2006: First Report of Session 2006–07, http://www.publications.parliament.uk/pa/cm200607/cmselect/cmintdev/71/71.pdf, accessed January 17 2007.

[10] Stern, N. (2006) The economics of climate change: The Stern report, http://www.hm-treasury.gov.uk/independent_reviews/stern_review_economics_climate_change/sternreview_summary.cfm, accessed January 19 2007.

the UN's MDG progress report of 2005[8] worked its way through forest and species loss before dispatching global warming in a single paragraph. That lack of awareness explains climate change's relatively low profile in DFID's work.

Trade is the other area where business as usual won't do, and where again it is mostly up to us to act. DFID already has a joint target with DTI for improving trade terms in the current PSA (Box 9.1). But with the World Trade Organisation's 'Doha Round' suspended acrimoniously in July last year and only laboriously revived at the 2007 Davos Conference while this chapter was being written, more may need to be done. In the absence of a new agreement, protective quotas are disappearing (for example, for Bangladesh's garments industry) and adverse terms of trade for developing countries persist. There may also be a case for an increase in 'aid for trade', partly to offset the switch of aid spending from the economic to the social sector which we commented on earlier: a member of DFID's International Trade Department has already argued that case[11].

Primary responsibility for action on climate change and fair trade should stay with the Department for Environment, Food and Rural Affairs (DEFRA) and the DTI respectively. But alleviating the impact of climate change on poor countries needs to become a central DFID role, for which DFID's Global and Local Environment Team as currently constituted may not be adequate. And subject to the success or otherwise of attempts to revive the Doha Round (we should know the outcome by Easter), DFID's International Trade Department needs an expanded role to promote the developing country trading interest, both in Whitehall and internationally.

THE WAY AHEAD: KEEP THE MDGs, PUT PARTNERS IN THE DRIVING SEAT, DO MORE ON CLIMATE CHANGE AND TRADE

This departmental section has not been able to cover everything. I have not been able to talk about DFID's continuing work in influencing international bodies like the EU and the World Bank (Gordon Brown was in India calling for the World Bank's reform as I wrote this chapter). I have assumed that Britain's historically high spending on aid will and should continue, as an expression of our moral responsibility towards our fellow human beings, and also our enlightened self-interest, even though I have not been able to look at the evaluation evidence for British aid effectiveness. Likewise, I have space to do no more than hope that Britain will come to terms with its real or imagined enemies in Muslim countries,

---

[11] Prowse, S. (2005) Aid for trade: Enhancing trade capacity in poor countries – a proposal, http://www.ycsg.yale.edu/focus/gta/aid_for_trade.pdf, accessed March 7 2007.

putting an end to the contamination of aid by national security. But I hope I have managed to cover what I see as two fundamental priorities for DFID's new PSA. They are:

- Maintaining the emphasis on the MDGs and monitoring DFID's contribution to them more closely, while balancing that emphasis with respect for poor countries' freedom to determine their own priorities
- Giving DFID an expanded role in dealing with climate change and fair trade

10. Department of Trade and Industry (aka Department of Technology and Innovation[1])

Francis Chittenden & Ray Oakey

Background

The Comprehensive Spending Review 2004 forecast a growth in the DTI budget from £4.9bn in 2004/5 to £6.2bn in 2007/8. To place this in the context of other government departments the DTI budget is approximately similar to that of the (then) Office of the Deputy Prime Minister, and smaller than the Northern Ireland Office, but slightly larger than the Department for International Development. In 2004/5 the DTI budget represented 1.9% of all departmental expenditure and, although as a proportion it rose over this period, in 2007/8 it was expected to remain at less than 2% (2004 Spending Review p182[2]). The DTI is not, therefore, a major spending department. Further, recently its budgets have been under significant pressure as a consequence of the support for the Rover Group in its last few weeks of life and the subsequent closure of that business.

The DTI's public service agreement comprises six key objectives to be achieved, sometimes in conjunction with other departments. In summary these objectives are (Public Service Agreements 2004, Ch 12[3]): raising the rate of sustainable productivity growth; promoting world class science and innovation; ensuring fair, competitive markets and empowering consumers; enabling successful enterprise and business; working to deliver equality and to maximise potential in the workplace; provision of safe, secure, cost-effective and environmentally friendly nuclear clean-up.

In addition, related targets remain based upon earlier spending rounds. The DTI's 2006 Autumn Report[4] draws all of these themes together and argues that progress towards each of these combined objectives is on target, except for:

1. The UK domestic goal of reducing carbon dioxide emissions (as opposed to all greenhouse gases) by 20% below 1990 base levels by 2010. More action will be needed in order to meet this target. Latest projections suggest that, taking into account the impact of the EU Emissions Trading Scheme (ETS) and other measures in the Climate Change Programme, the UK will have reduced CO_2 emissions by around 16% by 2010, as opposed to the 20% target. Higher than anticipated levels of economic growth and

---

[1] DTI 5 Year Programme, Nov 2004, p11.

[2] Available at http://www.hm-treasury.gov.uk/media/381/63/sr2004_annexa.pdf, accessed 9th October 2006

[3] Available at - http://www.hm-treasury.gov.uk/media//94F79/sr04_psa_ch12.pdf, accessed 9th October 2006

[4] Available at - http://www.dti.gov.uk/files/file28500.pdf, accessed 9th October 2006

the recent rise in global energy prices, have altered the relative prices of coal and gas in favour of coal-fired generation, and led to increases in CO_2 emissions in recent years. The Government has used the new Climate Change Programme Review and the recent Energy Review to assess both the impact of existing policies and the potential contribution of new policy options (DTI 2006 Autumn Report pages 24/25[5]).

2. The number of households in fuel poverty in 2004 remained the same as 2003, at 1.2 million households in England, with 1.0 million of those being vulnerable households. However, analysis of the effects of fuel prices and incomes, excluding energy efficiency improvements, suggests that the total number of vulnerable households in fuel poverty is likely to rise, by around 1 million vulnerable households in England between 2004 and 2006 with proportional increases in the Devolved Administrations. (DTI 2006 Autumn Report pages 28/29).

3. Ensuring that the EU secures significant reductions in EU and world trade barriers by 2008 leading to improved opportunities for developing countries and a more competitive Europe. This objective, for which responsibility is held jointly with the Department for International Development (DFID) is hampered by the slow progress towards the Doha Development Agreement being negotiated in the World Trade Organisation.

4. In 2005, 11.6% of adults in England were considering going into business, the same as in 2001. The PSA target level was set at 12.3%. However, it could be argued that these targets are inappropriate since the majority of UK small firms are self-employed people who employ no-one else, and a significant proportion of these continue to work for their previous employer but in different ways[6]. The choice of self-employment is presently encouraged by tax breaks for the 'own account worker' and the increasingly onerous employment responsibilities being placed on employers. A re-focussing of this target based on the formation of genuinely entrepreneurial businesses would be more appropriate.

In addition to the four targets where progress is slower than expected there are two themes for which progress cannot yet be measured. These are the PSAs introduced in 2005 relating to ethnic diversity and cooperative employment relations in the workplace for which new baseline targets were set in June 2006[7]; and the commitment to reduce the civil nuclear liability by 10% by 2010, to establish a market for nuclear cleanup by delivering annual 2% efficiency gains from 2006-07; and ensuring successful competitions have been completed for the

---

[5] Available at http://www.dti.gov.uk/files/file36067.pdf last accessed 11th January 2006.

[6] Chittenden, F. and Sloan, B. Quantifying Inequity in the Taxation of Individuals and Small Firms, British Tax Review, B.T.R. 2007, 1, 58-72.

[7] PSA Target 10 – Maximising Potential in the Workplace, Revised Technical Note (June 2006), www.dti.gov.uk/files/file14301.pdf , last accessed 10th January 2007

management of at least 50% of UK nuclear sites by end 2008. The Nuclear Decommissioning Authority (NDA) came in to existence on 1 April 2005 and there are no PSA deliverables until the end of 2006-07.

It is likely that the Comprehensive Spending Review 2007 will renew commitment to most of these and especially relating to the environment and energy. However, three elements of the DTI strategy are likely to be subject to closer review: the provision of services to small and medium-sized firms; the DTIs performance on regulation; and the much vaunted strategy on science technology and innovation. Each will be discussed in turn.

Much of the DTIs provision of services to small businesses have now been devolved to the Regional Development Agencies[8], leaving the SBS as a small (50 staff) internal DTI unit with access to another 50 civil servants within the DTI 'policy pool'. The SBS will retain specialist expertise in key areas, including: business support policy, small business finance, specific enterprise policy issues including women and ethnic minorities and research, statistics, analysis and performance evaluation[9]. The main themes in their work at present relate to the provision of advice about small firms to government departments[10]; trying to persuade other Ministries to 'think small first'; and rationalising small business support, in line with the Budget 2006 commitment to reduce the number of small business schemes from 3,000 to just 100. In practice this latter target is challenging, and probably impossible to achieve given that small business support is administered through the regional development agencies, seven government departments - including the Treasury - and various assorted 'non-departmental public bodies', and local authorities[11].

The Comprehensive Spending Review should provide a useful starting point for the process of rationalisation, since there are questions about the cost-effectiveness of the brokerage model currently being espoused by Business Links[12]. Treasury estimates of the cost of SME support policies, excluding agricultural and tax benefits, suggest this was £2.5bn per year in 2002. This is £600 per business per year, or £2,100 per established business of at least one employee. Arguably, the best way of reducing the number of schemes would be to scale back the funds available. From a policy perspective this could be justified on the grounds that business support is now accessed by the majority of small firms through the market[13].

---

[8] NAO 2006, Supporting Small Business, HC 962 Session 2005-2006, 24 May

[9] Announcement by Margaret Hodge, Small Business Minister, 26th October 2006, available   at http://www.gnn.gov.uk/environment/mediaDetail.asp?MediaDetailsID=180901&NewsAreaID=2&ClientID=201&LocaleID=2, last accessed 27th December 2006 .

[10] In this respect the NAO report acknowledged that the SBS had made considerable progress and that it required greater institutional support within government in order to consolidate this, NAO 2006, p6.

[11] Financial Times 9th October 2006

[12] Government SME policy since the 1990s: what have we learnt? Robert Bennett 2006

[13] Bennett, op cit.

In addition, whilst initiatives such as the National Council for Graduate Entrepreneurship appear to be having a positive impact on the number of younger people considering entrepreneurial careers, the DTI and Government should redefine small firms to exclude the self-employed with no employees. In certain volatile industries, such as construction and media production, efficiency gains probably accrue from own-account skilled individuals working together in informal teams that can form and reform in response market opportunities. However, the existing tax regime encourages employees to become own-account self-employed workers, often through single person companies. In addition, increasingly onerous employment laws lead to businesses preferring to use sub-contract workers. As a consequence, business decisions are distorted. There is no economic logic in the CSR encouraging the DTI or any other government department to encourage these forms of quasi-employment that, perversely, lead to declining tax revenues[14].

Turning now to a consideration of the performance of the DTI on regulation. The department is in the vanguard of producers of new regulation[15]. However, a criticism that could be levied is that in the process of introducing new regulations, whilst the DTI are experienced at estimating the costs of new regulation they seek to value the benefits on too few occasions, thus providing ammunition for liberals who suspect that the regulatory process is driven by the wishes of politicians[16] in Westminster and Brussels rather than being founded on an objective strategy for creating public value.

The DTI's simplification plan[17] includes measures that will result in around £1 billion of net undiscounted deregulatory savings over the period 2005-2010 (circa £700m discounted). However, these 'savings' are modest compared with the discounted cost of regulation on, for example, business, charities and the voluntary sector that amounted to £15.5bn in 2004/5 alone[18]. The DTI has also promised a 25% reduction in administrative burdens, against the baseline estimate of £5.3bn. The baseline figure has been calculated from data collected by PwC, but reduced from £13bn to just £5.3bn by the estimating 'Business as Usual' costs (BaU) i.e. costs that it is argued businesses would incur anyway, even in the absence of regulation – for example it is claimed that companies would prepare annual accounts whether required by the Companies Act or not. The voracity of such BaU cost estimates is questionable[19], and it is apparent that the

---

[14] Chittenden F and Sloan B, Budget Report 2006, prepared for the DTI Small Business Service, 31st March 2006

[15] Ambler T, Chittenden F and Hwang C, Regulation: another form of taxation?, British Chambers of Commerce, 2005.

[16] Stigler, George J. (1971), The Theory of Economic Regulation, Bell Journal of Economics and Management Science 2, 3-21

[17] Better Regulation; simplification plan, December 2006, available at http://www.dti.gov.uk/files/file35872.pdf, accessed 11th January 2007.

[18] Ambler T, Chittenden F and Ahuja K, Regulators; Box Tickers or Burden Busters?, British Chambers of Commerce, 2006

[19] Ambler T and Chittenden F (2007) Deregulation or De ja vu? UK Deregulation Initiatives 1997/2006, British Chambers of Commerce, forthcoming.

Administrative Burdens savings that result as a consequence of introducing this 'concept' will be lower than originally expected when the Administrative Burdens initiative was announced.

The promotion of new technology and innovation

Although a key policy objective of many recent DTI funding initiatives has been support for new technology and innovation, the scope for exerting a meaningful impact where large firms are concerned has been limited. A sharp decline in the number of United Kingdom large 'flagship' high technology firms over the past twenty years (e.g. Ferranti; GEC; ICL), and the growing importance of foreign owned multi-national corporations has led to a dearth of 'home grown' large firms with which to develop a policy agenda. In addition, any policy initiatives would have little impact on the often damaging global investment decisions of foreign owned and headquartered firms that have replaced 'home grown' corporations (e.g. the recent decision of Peugeot to close production in the English West Midlands). Moreover, the 'free market' imperative of the present government not to intervene to protect prestige national business assets (e.g. the Stock Exchange; British Aerospace's sale of their share in the Airbus project) has further reduced the scope of the DTI to encourage innovation and growth in key indigenous large firms since, following foreign acquisition, control over such decisions has been progressively relocated to other foreign jurisdictions. Because of this decline of United Kingdom large firms, and a lack of influence over foreign corporations, much recent emphasis has inevitably fallen on the potential contribution to innovation of the small firm sector in general, and new small high technology firms in particular. Policies to encourage academic entrepreneurship, for example, through the DTI supported Science Enterprise Centres (SECs), have sought to develop the undeniable technical potential of gifted academics through the establishment of 'spin off' new high technology small firms. However, here too, the scope for the rapid growth of such firms from small beginnings to 'world leader' large enterprises as evidenced by United States firms such as Apple or Google is, in practice, very small due to the frequent absorption of any promising new technically advanced firms by existing large multinational competitors (e.g. Google's recent acquisition of You Tube).[20]

The encouragement of invention and innovation in high technology firms by the DTI has inevitably addressed problems associated with the acquisition of investment capital, particularly because high technology product development requires substantial amounts of 'front end' capital investment before a return can be achieved. A consistent objective of the DTI has been to use incentives to improve the penetration of financial assistance to high technology small firms by providing additional support beyond the unsatisfactory level that has occurred 'naturally' without government intervention. While 'additionally' is an accepted means of measuring the impact of incentives, it is a particularly relevant issue to

---

[20] Oakey, R. P., (2003) Technical entrepreneurship in high technology small firms: some observations on the implications for management, Technovation, Vol. 23. pp. 679 – 688.

the funding of high technology small firms, since they have persistently experienced funding problems over many years[21][22]. From the birth of the venture capital industry in the early 1980s, there has been a steady decline in the proportion of 'early stage' firms funded by the industry[23], and a move to fund management 'buy outs', 'buy ins' and expansions, since they involve lower risks due to their previous proven 'track records'. Indeed, it has been confirmed by the Bank of England[24] that an enduring problem exists with the funding of 'early stage' high technology small firms in the United Kingdom.

While grant aid through the DTI sponsored Smart award scheme and its recent modifications have been welcome, importantly, this type of finance has never guaranteed the much-needed *long-term* financial security of recipient high technology small firm (Oakey 2003b). More importantly, DTI attempts to coax the private sector banks and venture capital firms, to increase their level of risk and move respectively to give loans or take equity in high technology small firms that were previously judged unfundable (thus creating additionality), have been less than impressive. A past criticism of the DTI's Loans Guarantee Scheme has been that banks have often tended to use this incentive to provide additional 'insurance' on loans that they would have advanced *in the absence of the scheme*, thus questioning whether this incentive meets the additionality test[25].

Similarly, the recently introduced Venture Capital Trusts (VCTs), while in part devised to address the problem of shortcomings in early stage funding by underpinning private investment with government financial support on the basis of a pound of support for every two invested, risk falling short of closing gaps in the market for the funding of new high technology ventures for two major, yet familiar, reasons. First, there is a strong risk that problems found with the loans guarantee scheme will be repeated again in circumstances where government money is used by VCTs to fund investments that would have been undertaken by the private sector without such support. Second, another long standing criticism of the venture capital industry might also not be addressed by VCTs in that the size of the 'deals' to emerge from this new scheme are likely to be far *too large* for most early stage high technology small firms. Also, it could be argued that schemes of the VCT type, designed to correct such gaps in funding, will probably fail because they lack a radical edge, and are too mindful of the sensitivity of private sector capital market actors who are unprepared to increase their level of risk by funding high technology small firms although they,

---

[21] Oakey R. P., (1984) High technology small firms: innovation and regional development in Britain and the United States, Frances Pinter, London.

[22] Oakey, R. P., (2003) Funding innovation and growth in UK new technology-based firms: some observations on contributions from the public and private sectors, Venture Capital, Vol. 5, No. 2, pp. 161-179.

[23] Murray, G. and Lott, J. (1995), Have venture capital firms a bias against investment in high technology companies?, Research Policy, 24, 1, pp 283-299.

[24] Bank of England (2001), The financing of technology-based small firms, February, London.

[25] House of Lords Select Committee on Science and Technology (1997), The innovation exploitation barrier, HL Paper 62.

perversely, vehemently complain if the DTI seeks to fill the gap they leave with incentives based on tax payer's money. Certainly, experts concerned with the funding of new high technology small firms remain sceptical as to whether any existing public or private funding mechanisms have yet been created that solve the continuing problem of a low level of 'early stage' high technology small firm funding support[26].

Furthermore, it might be argued that, in the current political climate there is a broad political consensus against a strong interventionist role for the DTI. Thus, the future for any meaningful industrial development arm of government looks bleak. This negative political attitude stems from a belief that a 'free market' approach to the development of the economy is preferable to interventionist industrial development polices based on government industrial planning and financial support to industry in instances either where market failure occurs, or where the strategic development of new industrial sectors is deemed essential, and cannot be left to the 'free market' alone (e.g. biotechnology). Although the United Kingdom economy is currently relatively strong, the decline in our manufacturing industrial base over the last twenty years has been unremitting. While, to some extent, this change can be explained by the growth of international competition in medium technology sectors (e.g. motor vehicles; electronics), as noted above, there is a danger that capital market imperfections may inhibit (or destroy) the future development of our high technology industrial potential. There is also a danger that the devolving of industrial development to the Regional Development Agencies (RDAs) of the United Kingdom will result in anarchistic confusion and wasteful inter-regional competition. Such an approach is no substitute for a coherent policy led at the national level by an active Ministry for Industry. Without the capacity to strategically develop new industrial growth and nurture such initiatives through strong publically funded incentives, the DTI will be reduced to duplicating the functions of an Industrial Association. Unfortunately, in the current political climate such a role might be deemed appropriate.

Conclusions

Thus arguments about the future of the DTI abound and the need for government to exercise strong financial discipline in the Comprehensive Spending Review means that some re-organisation is likely. Whilst industry appears to support the existence of a ministry to represent its views at the Cabinet table[27], spending reductions in support to industry would be much more attractive to government and the electorate than cutbacks in, for example, Education or Health. In certain areas the DTI's remit overlaps with other Departments, especially in respect of Energy and the Environment where DEFRA also has important responsibilities and employment which overlaps with both

---

[26] Herriot W. (2005), Improving early-stage financing in the East of England, Report by St John's Innovation Centre, Cambridge.

[27] British Chambers of Commerce, 18th September 2006

Education and Skills and Work and Pensions and the remaining responsibilities for consumer affairs could be transferred to the Office of Fair Trading. Thus reallocating some the DTI's current remit to other Departments might offer the prospect of improved clarity in areas that are likely to continue to attract political and policy interest at home and abroad. There are other less ambitious opportunities for re-focussing the DTI around a narrower range of responsibilities such as science, technology and productivity.

The appointment of Alistair Darling at the head of the DTI could also be seen as a signal of impending change, since he is tipped[28] to be the next Chancellor of the Exchequer. Who could be better placed to agree the re-allocation of responsibilities and pairing back of the functions currently conducted by the DTI than a senior Minister with detailed knowledge of that Department?

However, whatever the political pressures the commercial realities remain. The UK is a major economy that is fully exposed to changes in the patterns of world trade, and especially the rise of competition from China and India. In order to remain internationally competitive it will be necessary to fully exploit our competitive advantages based upon a very strong science and intellectual property base, a skilled workforce and excellent infrastructure and global linkages. In order to take full advantage of these strengths we need higher levels of innovation, investment and productivity to underpin continued economic growth and business needs to believe that its views are adequately represented inside government through a robust DTI. However, *refocusing* the DTI on these critical tasks could be a viable strategy, and this is currently being debated in Whitehall[29].

---

[28] Jean Eaglesham and Nicholas Timmins, Review casts spotlight on DTI's future, Financial Times, 13th December 2006.

[29] Toby Helm, Brown plans to abolish DTI, Daily Telegraph, 12th December 2006.

11. Department for Environment, Food and Rural Affairs

Joe Ravetz

Introduction

A £200 million (7%) deficit in this year's budget for Defra has forced the Environment Agency to make deep cuts to its programme... Because of the unexpected cost of preparing for avian flu, overspending by the rural payments scheme, and cross-departmental changes to government accounting procedures.[1]

This is a snapshot of an organization charged with tasks that may be beyond its means. The Department of Environment, Food and Rural Affairs was 'thrown together' in 2001 from a national crisis in the foot and mouth disease episode. What became apparent was that the direct loss to agriculture was far outweighed by the knock-on effects on tourism, leisure and rural services in general. A picture emerged of the British rural economy and landscape, and indeed the environment at large, as vulnerable and inter-dependent, driven by psychological and cultural pressures, and increasingly used as the receptacle and backdrop for urban lifestyles.

Underlying this is Defra's core mission of sustainable development (SD) – an agenda which spreads right across the UK government and beyond. SD is subject to myriad interpretations, but one fundamental principle is that of reducing the impact of economic activity, in order to live on the UK's share of the resources of 'One Planet'. As such, this cuts right across the pro-growth assumptions of almost every other department of government, creating a fundamental policy dilemma.

It may be this 'dilemma' of SD which is at the root of the problems of Defra as an organization – the result is the pervasive ambiguity on questions such as 'value', 'services' and 'front-line delivery'. If this dilemma can be grasped, in return there may be opportunities and imperatives for the mainstreaming of SD practices right across government, in which case Defra may shift its role from the margins to the political high ground.

This chapter looks firstly at the agenda for Defra, in the context of its priorities and performance. It also discusses the wider SD agenda, as this remains paramount to realizing the potential of the Defra mission.

---

[1] ENDS Report 383, Dec 2006, p12

A department of many parts

Defra since its creation has been a kind of 'camel', an experiment in departmental design. Its largest Grant in Aid operation, the Environment Agency, is also a kind of 'kludge', notorious in the environmental professions as the forced marriage of the former National Rivers Authority, HM Inspectorate of Pollution, and many Waste Regulation Authorities.

Defra's permanent secretary, Sir Brian Bender, argued in 2004 that "we're doing pretty well considering the circumstances surrounding the creation of the Department.... an unplanned merger, at a time of national crisis" arising from the foot and mouth outbreak (FMD)[2]. The FMD episode forms the ghost in the departmental memory, which was determined to avoid similar 'elephant traps' in the future.

However, another kind of elephant trap came up in 2006, when a large deficit in the Defra annual budget forced the Environment Agency in turn to make drastic cuts to its programmes for water, waste, research and other areas. The budget for 2006-7 was cut by nearly £200 million because of the unexpected cost of preparing for avian flu, together with overspending by the rural payments scheme. The Environment Agency was forced to cut its enforcement measures in precisely the areas which needed it most: for instance it was reported by IMPEL, the EU network of environmental regulatory bodies, that the UK has the biggest illegal waste export problem in Europe. The House of Commons found that the bulk of these financial shortcomings came from "budgeting commitments based on careless assumptions about the attitude of HM Treasury—especially in respect of the use of unspent budget covered by its End-Year-Flexibility arrangements—in a tight fiscal period"[3].

Generally, and apart from technical errors in financial management, how much does this indicate overlap or confusion of policy with operations and delivery? This is apparently what the management has been trying to avoid since the Spending Review 2004.

Mission to accomplish?

Having said that, it is fair to say that Defra is still seeking its role in the political community, beyond its reputation as the 'NGO of Whitehall' – is it a policy development or policy maintenance body, purchaser of operations or grant manager, leader or follower in Europe, or some ideal combination of all of these? Is it basically a 'land manager' with farmers as its agents, or is it a campaigner for

---

[2] Public Accounts Committee (PAC) 2005: Ninth Report, Foot and Mouth Disease: applying the lessons (HC 563)

[3] House of Commons Environment, Food and Rural Affairs Committee: Defra's Departmental Report 2006 and Defra's budget: Second Report of Session 2006–07: HC 132: London, House of Commons.

the whole of government? How does it define its value in terms of 'public benefit / public money'?

Environmental policy making and policy targets are increasingly inter-dependent on other departments, such as transport, communities, trade and industry, and international development. In many cases environmental policy is driven by the EU, and the transposing of Directives to UK law and industrial practices is often controversial and unpredictable. Operational licensing and regulation is devolved to the Environment Agency and other Grant in Aid (GIA) bodies, which regularly change their configuration, with their own financial pressures, and constantly review their relation to the parent body. Even grant administration itself can be far from simple, as shown by the problems with the Rural Payments scheme.

Over-arching this is the Defra lead on the UK Sustainable Development Strategy, certainly a challenge for any department to deliver.[4] The letters to and from the Environment Secretary and Tony Blair in 2006 reveal the direction of thinking:

The challenges we now face in the environmental arena are of a different order of magnitude... we are living beyond our environmental means. The best illustration of this is the fact that if everyone in the world consumed as ... we do in the UK we would need three planets to support us. So, put simply, I see Defra's mission as enabling a move toward what the WWF has called One Planet Living. (Open letter from D.Miliband to the Prime Minister, July 2006)

Such commitment is laudable and far sighted. However it follows that the suggested reduction in consumption could possibly bring on a direct clash with the growth-oriented paradigm of virtually every other department of government.

Efficiency saved?

In the Spending Review 2004, the Chancellor announced that he was looking for savings of £610 million from Defra by 2007/08. Half of the total was expected to come from efficiency gains in local authority waste services. At present Defra is on course to meet its target £299 million in efficiency savings in local authority waste services by 2007/08, a 5% saving over the period.

The target is part of a broader goal to achieve £610 million in efficiency savings by 2007/08 that was included in the 2004 SR[5]. Defra met its interim target to achieve £52 million in waste management savings in 2004/05, and aims at further savings up to £82 million in the coming years. These are judged against a 'business as usual' scenario which assumes annual municipal waste growth of 2-3%, and excludes the effect of non-cash efficiency measures such as the advice services offered to authorities by the department's Waste Implementation Programme and Waste and Resources Action Programme.

---

[4] HMG (Her Majesty's Government), (2005), Securing the Future: the UK Sustainable Development Strategy, CM6467, London: TSO

[5] ENDS Report 355, October 2004, p 6

By 2008 the core Department will be some 60% smaller than when Defra was created in 2001, from 8,000 staff to around 3,200. Alongside transfers outside the Defra core, there will be a 21% reduction – 2,400 - in the number of posts in Defra and its Executive Agencies. This transformation of policy, delivery and corporate support is anticipated to result in a "leaner, more efficient Department, providing value for money and achieving results for the public"[6].

Strategic priorities & PSA targets

This is slimming on an impressive scale – and if only the UK's climate emissions could reduce at the same rate! But we need to keep in mind what kind of efficiency is being achieved here, and how far this is effective or efficacious for the purpose. We could start with the 'strategic priorities' of the Department, and the PSA targets attached to them, and look at the underlying challenges that these represent[7].

a) Sustainable development – promoted across Government, in the UK and internationally, as measured by – the achievement of positive trends in the Government's headline indicators of sustainable development… etc[7].

The 'SD' concept is of course all embracing, and despite the rhetoric on integrating social, economic and environmental issues, it is significant that one of the smaller and weaker departments has the job of promoting SD right across government and internationally, and responding to several of the 'long term challenges' identified by the Treasury for the Comprehensive Spending Review[8].

In terms of PSA targets there are positive trends in the SD 'headline indicators', and 'progress' towards international commitments. However, both the industry and the NGOs point out the potential flaws and gaps in the measurement of such concepts. For instance the objective to "reduce trade-distorting agricultural support, recognising the importance of this for our own and developing countries' economies"[9] is surely a hostage to the fortunes and internal politics of the WTO, GATT, CAP reform and so on.

b) Meeting the challenge of climate change. This agenda overlaps on the province of the DTI, who are responsible for energy supply and the construction industry: DCLG representing the built environment and the largest source of climate emissions: and DfT who represent transport as the fastest growing source of emissions. Less obviously, the activities of DFID are instrumental in the agenda for carbon offsets and 'Joint Implementation' of carbon saving projects, but such policy integration is still rare. Thus with its new-found enthusiasm for climate change policy, Defra is the first to be held to account for the failings of

---

[6] DEFRA and the Forestry Commission (2006): Departmental Report 2006: CM6827: London, TSO

[7] DEFRA (2004) Delivering the Essentials of Life: Defra's Five Year Strategy, London TSO

[8] HM Treasury (2006) Long-term opportunities and challenges for the UK: analysis for the 2007 Comprehensive Spending Review: London, HM Treasury

[9] DEFRA 2004 Spending Review

others, and could be trapped in the 'advice and exhortation' zone, of responsibility without mandate[10].

This same PSA target is also shared with the DfT, to "reduce greenhouse gas emissions to 12.5 per cent below 1990 levels in line with our Kyoto commitment…"[6]. This is reported as 'on course', although the industry view is that this modest achievement is clearly the result of shifting from coal to gas since 1990, driven by North Sea economics, clean air legislation, and the politically-driven destruction of the UK coal industry[11].

c) Sustainable consumption and production (SCP):

Breaking the link between economic growth and environmental degradation and resource use through promoting and enabling more sustainable patterns of consumption and production[7].

This is perhaps the most dispersed of all the themes, covering DTI, DfID, DfT and others, and there are major questions in how to define SCP or make policy against the tide of economic growth. The core activity under this heading is waste management, a sector well-known for being fragmented, short sighted, and subject to political interference. And as every environmentalist knows, waste problems are rarely solved at the end-of-pipe, rather they are much better addressed upstream, across many sectors of production, distribution and consumption.

The PSA target most directly covered here is "To enable at least 25 per cent of household waste to be recycled or composted by 2005-06, with further improvement by 2008"[6]. This quite modest target is reported as on course. However the implications of the EU Directives on waste landfill and recycling are more challenging and still quite uncertain.

d) Protecting the countryside and natural resource protection

Creating a robust policy framework and evidence base in order to promote the sustainable use and enhancement of the country's natural heritage and ecosystems[7].

Such 'sustainable use' is of course open for debate, but there are some recognized success stories, such as the Countryside Right of Way (CROW) programme, and the gradual return of biodiversity to farmland. Here there is a sense that Defra is at least moving with the tide, in a field where targeting and monitoring is (relatively) straightforward.

This involves specific PSA targets such as those for air quality, again shared with the DfT, where there is continuing concern on the lack of management of the nations' vehicle fleet. The parallel targets on the rural environment, show improvement mainly due to the CAP reform and EU agricultural policy framework.

---

[10] DEFRA 2007a & 2007b

[11] Milne, S (2004) The Enemy Within: Thatcher's Secret War Against the Miners: London, Verso Books

e) Sustainable Rural Communities

Encouraging sustainable regeneration in disadvantaged rural areas, promoting social inclusion and reducing deprivation: ensuring higher quality, more accessible public services to rural communities[7].

This agenda again is a hostage to fortune, being mainly the result of housing and planning policy at the DCLG, transport policy at DfT, competition policy at the DTI and so on. The closure of up to 8,000 post offices, indirectly the responsibility of the DTI, shows the scale of the challenge in rural communities. And how to define a 'sustainable rural community', in an age of mass transport and tourism, digital communications, second homes, and centralization of almost all services such as schools, health, leisure and so on? The rhetoric is often a long way from the reality, and the shake up of the delivery agencies has possibly destabilized many slower-paced policy initiatives at ground level. The Haskins Review asked the question – 'what (or who) is the countryside for? – and it seems that this question is still open[12].

f) Sustainable Farming & Food, including animal health & welfare

…helping to create a sustainable food and farming supply chain serving the market and the environment; putting in place systems to reduce risks of animal diseases, and being ready to control them when they occur[7].

This is the mainstay of the department and the inheritance from the former Ministry of Agriculture, Fisheries and Food (MAFF). However, in practice the mechanics of CAP reform, Single Farm Payments and Environmental Stewardship schemes have often proved contentious - technical issues such as computer mapping, delivery issues such as half yearly payments, and industry issues such as the price of milk, seem to generate unending problems for farmers. The animal health agenda, for example, seems to be one of the most volatile and risky briefs in government: the PSA targets for animal health are aiming to be achieved 'through sharing the management of risk with industry', and many are reported with 'some slippage'. However the current CAP reform 'modulation' of up to 20% of farm support into stewardship schemes, although complex, is a sign of the potential for Defra to be a pro-active steward of land and environmental assets.

Generally, and outside of Whitehall reporting, a real world view of these performance benchmarks invites mixed approval with criticism from the environmental professions and policy community. For instance Defra's publicity for the Emissions Trading Scheme continues in the face of obvious failings, as does the insistence that air quality is improving, when pollution levels in the summer of 2003 were the worst for a decade. Troublesome areas such as hazardous waste exports, redundant fridges and sulphurous combustion plants are quietly shifted away from the report front pages. The UK climate emissions trends can be interpreted as both good and bad news, depending on the frame of reference.

---

[12] Haskins C (2003) Rural Delivery Review: A report on the delivery of government policies in rural England: London, DEFRA

Cross-cutting theme – behaviour change

Each of the above themes raises cross cutting issues. Two of these are highlighted here: behaviour change issues, and the science/evidence base. Both show how the SD challenge is endemic to the way Defra performs and is perceived.

Behaviour change is at the core of the Defra mission at many levels – individuals, households, businesses, farmers, communities and sectors. To its credit, the Defra policy centre sees that environmental and SD policy cannot be achieved by command, control or economic incentives alone. The Downing St Strategy Unit ran a background programme, looking at the scope and means of behaviour change, and pointing out the role of incentive systems, gaming strategies, collective cultures and so on[13]. This then aims to inform policy developments such as the Sustainable Consumption and Production programme, and the related Sustainable Procurement agenda[14]. The problem with targeting behaviour change is that the agent of deliberative change here is the least powerful or well resourced, and this characterizes the Defra mission in relation to larger departments such as DfT or DCLG.

Perhaps the first and foremost behaviour change target is many of these government departments, who are regularly called on to put their house in order in the face of clear failings[15]. This illustrates the scale of the challenge facing Defra, as the champion of what is often seen by other departments as unnecessary and uneconomic.

Cross-cutting theme – evidence base

Meanwhile, the 10 year strategy 'Science Forward Look' shows how a strong science base is essential for effective policy, and requires close co-operation with academia, independent institutes, R&D units, businesses and other departments[16]. One application is 'Horizon Scanning', a variation developed for Defra of the established methods of 'Foresight' based at the DTI. This is used to identify rapidly emerging risk areas as well as strategic priorities. Experience shows that effective horizon scanning is as much an art as a science, depending very much on organizational communications, and the Unit has been through several phases of re-orientation.

One topical feature of the emerging science strategy is where a policy platform can be linked with an information platform, for example the evidence base being assembled for the Sustainable Consumption and Production unit. This is sponsoring a series of studies on 'decoupling' and modeling of resource flows

---

[13] PMSU (Prime Minister's Strategy Unit) 2005: Personal Responsibility and Changing Behaviour: the state of knowledge and its implications for public policy: London, TSO

[14] Jackson, T. and Michaelis, L. (2003), Policies for Sustainable Consumption, London: Sustainable Development Commission: available on www.sd-commission.gov.uk

[15] Sustainable Development Commission (2006) Redefining Progress: report on consultation London, SDC

[16] DEFRA 2005b, Science Forward Look 2004 – 2013: London, TSO

and footprints, which are in a sense being led by a methodology programme, which then seeks applications and users at various levels[17].

Underlying the science strategy is the emerging SD agenda, and particularly the themes of inter-dependence and multi-level/lateral governance. This has implications for the way in which scientific knowledge is produced and disseminated; it also showed how the challenges of SD are driving a new kind of scientific paradigm which is holistic, inter-disciplinary, reflexive and transparent, in contrast to previous more reductive and technology-focused methods[18]. This then has implications for the institutional structure and the funding base of £300 million per year (in 2006) for all forms of Defra science/research/monitoring, which funds a large family of internal programmes, grant-in-aid bodies, central laboratories, devolved services and other agencies. Again there are difficult questions on public benefit in 'knowledge management' in a complex set of organizations.

Implications for the CSR

Given all this, it would be simplistic to argue that Defra needs to increase its much reduced expenditure through the CSR. It would be more constructive to propose better targeted investment, with a finer evidence base, more leverage on other Departments, more intelligent combination of policy and delivery and with better lock-in to private sector utilities and service providers – all this with more visible and measurable 'public benefit'.

This outline of a problematic department should not be taken as negative criticism; rather it shows an interesting picture of challenges and responses. As far as the CSR goes, three themes emerge with implications for future fiscal policy.

Improved efficiency and apparent savings: the 'efficiency' equation depends very much on how the results are defined, measured and benchmarked. If we factor in the value of clean streets, clean air and so on, in both economic and wider terms, then it is clear that much apparent 'cost' is in fact 'investment'. This wider 'investment case' should in principle be measured and factored into the CSR, by whichever method is most relevant. Although such measurements are typically difficult to define and agree on, there is a case for showing a transparent process and the scope of the debate, with a series of best guess proxies. The recent panel on 'Redefining Prosperity' is one example where some very fuzzy but important measures were debated at length[9].

Policy, operations and delivery: the organizational split aims at transparency, performance monitoring and a framework for management incentives. However, it is questionable whether this is appropriate for the kind of joined-up, multi-

---

[17] Barrett, Ravetz & Bond, 2006: DEFRA 2005a

[18] Flanagan et al (2004): Exploring Future Science Needs for Defra: Part of the Science Forward Look 2004-2013: PREST / TNO, available March 2007 on http://www.defra.gov.uk/science/documents/forwardlook/FinalSynthesisReportDefraFut ureScienceNeeds.pdf

sectoral, value-laden issues which Defra has to deal with. Such cross-cutting institutional issues as behaviour change, participation, citizenship and corporate responsibility are crucial for local environmental action, and important to bring into the frame of added value, efficiency savings and management targets.

As far as corporate structures go, the current Defra Delivery Strategy is based on the accepted management strategy of an organizational separation between the two types of function – policy and delivery – underpinned by consistent and well-understood principles. There is also a commitment to partnership working beyond Defra's boundaries, for example through the Sustainable Energy Policy Network, or the Waste Implementation Programme. The Policy Centre Review Programme is also looking at the skills and expertise needed to deliver effective policy, and this aims to further refine the distinction between 'policy development' and 'policy maintenance'[19].

Environmental stewardship and One Planet fiscal policy

The third theme is the challenge of pro-active stewardship and strategic investment, to enable market transformation towards a One Planet Economy, as highlighted by David Miliband.

The One Planet Economy agenda aims at a pattern of production and consumption where resource efficiency is raised by a factor of four. The basic idea is very simple – to manage assets and liabilities, risks and opportunities in a strategic way, considering short and long terms, and the interests of suppliers, customers and employees[20].

This is often framed in terms of the carbon footprint, but the real agenda is deeper and wider. The issue is not only carbon, but other climate change effects, which count for half as much again. Then, we need to consider not only climate change but other kinds of resource use – water, forests and productive resources of all kinds. And for developed nations, the problem is not so much what we produce, as what we consume from around the world. The One Planet Economy agenda aims to turn such problems into 'opportunities' for economic growth and social progress.

All of this adds up to a full industrial evolution – a sector by sector transformation strategy – including low impact technologies, integrated supply chains and sustainable consumption. Such a strategy will involve new kinds of tax and public investment: and new kinds of arrangements between public, private and community sectors. The fiscal agenda follows from the current state of the art with 'Market Based Instruments' (MBIs)[21]. The current set of MBIs are

---

[19] DEFRA 2006

[20] Ravetz J (2007): Taking the first steps – Pathways to a One Planet Economy: Surrey, WWF-UK: available March 2007 www.ecologicalbudget.org.uk

[21] EEA (European Environment Agency) (2006): Using the market for cost-effective environmental policy: Market-based instruments in Europe: Technical Report 1/2006, Copenhagen, EEA: available on www.eea.eu.int

generally effective for 'environmental mitigation', but the One Planet Economy agenda looks beyond this:

From environmental mitigation to environmental transformation. It is becoming clear that the challenge of raising resource efficiency by a factor of four requires a step-change across the whole economy, with a combination of technological change, institutional change and behavioural change.

A **supply chain approach**: individual measures can be combined on an upstream – downstream basis, which makes it more clear and transparent how and where producers interact with consumers.

An **integrated asset management** approach: progress on the ground becomes possible when collective responsibility is taken, for instance for the building stock of a city, or the travel demand of a region.

Stewardship and stake-owning approach: both from government as the 'steward of last resort', but also from other stakeholder communities, as in the 'Business Improvement District' principle.

This suggests a new agenda for fiscal policy, where the conventional set of MBIs are combined with stewardship, procurement, supply chain management, integrated asset management, and market transformation, in a 'new institutional economics'[22]. Some possible directions can be charted out on the 'upstream / downstream' supply chain framework:

'end fate deposit' – applies to all materials / products / ancillaries such as packaging, at the point of sale, in lieu of a known recovery / recycling / re-use pathway.

'eco-credit transfer' – this applies a levy / duty on higher impact activities / technologies, which provides a token / 'air-mile' type credit or rebate, for lower impact activities / technologies.

'lifetime levy' – a 'downstream' application of producer responsibility on the 'polluter pre-pays precautionary' principle. E.g. car purchase tax which reflects their lifetime emissions, set at levels which provide real incentives.

'R&D investment' – on the principle that users & beneficiaries of services or technologies should re-invest in the upstream direction, for the improvement of those services or technologies.

Each of these is at the research and consultation stage: but clearly there are many possibilities, which put stewardship and fiscal responsibility in the hands of the public sector. It could be guessed that the current proportion of UK environment-related taxation, at 8.3% of total revenues in 2007, could double within 20 years[23]. The topical issue is how much of this may in new fiscal arrangements rather than conventional taxation – new types of corporate or consumer responsibility, environmental market trading systems, and systems of re-investment and innovation. One example is the Tax Increment Financing

---

[22] Jacobs M (1997): Environmental valuation, deliberative democracy and public decision-making institutions: In: Foster J (Ed) Valuing Nature: economics, ethics and environment: London, Routledge

[23] Leicester, A (2006) The UK Tax System and the Environment: London, Institute of Fiscal Studies

scheme, as used in the US and Australia, where local decision makers borrow against anticipated tax revenues following public infrastructure – as a way of enabling innovation and re-investment[24].

As these innovation and re-investment partnerships tend to cross departmental boundaries, for instance between DCLG, DTI, DFT and DFES, there is a clear role for an intermediary to take up the facilitation and coordination across government. For any environmental or land-based issue that role should fall to Defra, which would need to enlarge its remit accordingly.

The CSR 2007 is likely to take a more conventional approach to marginal tax and spend adjustments, in transport, waste management and so on – and there is still much room for improvement[25]. It may be for future CSRs to fully explore the implications for Defra and the government as a whole. There are new paradigms emerging which combine policy, operations, facilititation, investment and partnerships. Following these through could then help to resolve some current dilemnas in the policy-operations split of Defra, and the question 'what is Defra for' would shift towards the centre ground of the political landscape.

Conclusions

Generally, we can see with Defra a young department with ambitions for great challenges, cross-cutting not only the UK government, but with a potentially leading role on a world stage. It has seen a vigorous process of shake-out and re-orientation in the last five years, and has also some impressive mistakes to learn from. With the rapid climb of environmental and SD issues up the agenda, there is now a growing policy space where Defra has great potential to play a very active role.

To follow this through may involve a rapid increase in fiscal flows, Much of this may well be formed in novel fiscal arrangements based on the 'stewardship' concept, and outside of conventional tax and spend operations. By implication, Defra may have a crucial role to play as facilitator and enabler of the 'market transformations' which such flows should enable. All in all, there should be interesting times ahead.

---

[24] Webber C & Athey G (2007): *The Route to Growth: Transport, density and productivity.* London, Institute of Public Policy Research

[25] Hislop H (2006) Beyond Stern: the environmental challenge for the comprehensive spending review: London, Green Alliance

12. Department for Work and Pensions

Jay Wiggan

The challenge of delivery

In the 2006 Budget the Chancellor announced that along with HM Treasury, HM Revenue and Customs and the Cabinet Office, the Department for Work and Pensions (DWP) would see a real terms reduction of 5% per year over the 2007-08 -2010-11 period of the next CSR in their Departmental Expenditure Limits[1] [2]. The ambitious value for money reforms envisaged over the CSR period creates a challenging delivery environment for the department. The 2006 Capability Review of the Department for Work and Pensions, for example, identified a continuing need to improve management of people and resources. Coordination of overall departmental priorities and resource allocation across the department remains limited. In the context of ambitious efficiency reforms this may impact on the ability of the department to effectively reallocate resources across the department's agencies to priority areas[3]. Anticipated efficiency gains have to be realised in tandem with improvements in service delivery underpinning key Government objectives. These include the raising of the overall employment rate; the raising of the employment rate for various 'hard to reach' groups as part of the welfare to work strategy and continued improvements in the levels of child and pensioner poverty. Progress has been made in these areas but its sustainability is in doubt. In a climate of increasingly scarce resources and unwillingness on the part of the Government to step outside of the economic and political constraints it has imposed upon itself, questions remain as to whether the ambitious welfare reform and anti-poverty programme will prove achievable.

Performance against the 2004 Spending Review Public Service Agreement (PSA) targets

The 2004 Spending Review (SR 2004) set out a total of 10 targets for the Department for Work and Pensions covering the years 2004-07. The targets

---

[1] HM Treasury (2006) A strong and strengthening economy: investing in Britain's future, Economic and Fiscal Strategy Report and Financial Statement and Budget Report, The Stationery Office, London. http://www.hm-treasury.gov.uk/budget/budget_06/budget_report/bud_bud06_repindex.cfm

[2] Emmerson, C. & Frayne, C. (2006) 'Analysis – Something's got to give', Public Finance, April 3rd, http://www.publicfinance.co.uk/features_details.cfm?News_id=27054

[3] Cabinet Office (2006a) Capability Review of the Department for Work and Pensions, http://www.civilservice.gov.uk/reform/capability_reviews/publications/pdf/Capability_Review_DWP.pdf

themselves are often made up of more than one part. Consequently a target can be partially met if one part of the target is achieved whilst other parts make no or limited progress. Analysis contained within the DWP 2006 Autumn Performance Report[4] shows that the 24 parts which make up the 10 SR 2004 PSA targets were rated as follows: five reported as 'not yet assessed'; eight on course to meet their targets; seven are reporting slippage where progress is slower than expected; three targets have been achieved and two targets have been met ahead of schedule. In the course of this review I consider some of the challenges that present themselves in the key areas of employment, children, pensioners and fraud and error that DWP policy and the PSA targets address. Some possible reforms to PSA targets are also outlined.

Employment opportunity for all (SR 2004 PSA targets 4, 5 & 8)

The Government's strategy to increase the numbers of lone parents and disabled people moving into paid employment while modernising welfare to deliver a responsive and personalised service to customers[5] relies heavily on Jobcentre Plus and the success of efficiency and delivery reforms currently being implemented. The sheer size of Jobcentre Plus means it is vital to many of the efficiency gains the department are attempting to realise. The drive for efficiency gains combined with the Spending Review 2004 PSA targets has prompted an ambitious programme of reform and overlapping organisational change. Jobcentre Plus is to account for 50% of the departmental commitment to reduce their number of civil service posts by a total of 30,000[6]. The pace of change has been intense. Ambitious reforms such as the headcount reduction target of 15,000 FTE (full time equivalent) staff between February 2004 and March 2008 has gone hand in hand with the roll-out of Contact Centres as part of a restructuring of customer interaction with the organisation. This has raised some concerns with the House of Commons Work & Pensions Select Committee questioning whether Jobcentre Plus and the DWP have been trying to do too much, too quickly[7].

The pace of reform within Jobcentre Plus has brought about some problems for performance and delivery of services for customers. Of particular concern to the Work & Pensions Committee was the performance of Jobcentre Plus Contact Centres in 2005. The recorded performance of some Contact Centres against the

---

[4] Department for Work and Pensions (2006f) Autumn Performance Report: Progress against Public Service Agreement Targets,
http://www.dwp.gov.uk/publications/dwp/2006/autumnreport/

[5] Jobcentre Plus (2003) Jobcentre Plus Vision 2003-07,
http://www.jobcentreplus.gov.uk/JCP/static/Dev_007275.pdf

[6] HM Treasury (2004) Stability, Security and Opportunity for All: Investing in Britain's Long Term Future: New Public Spending Plans 2005-2008, Spending Review 2004,
http://www.hm-treasury.gov.uk

[7] Work and Pensions Committee (2006a) The Efficiency Savings Programme in Jobcentre Plus Second Report of Session 2005-06 Volume 1, HC834-I, House of Commons, The Stationery Office Ltd, London.
http://www.publications.parliament.uk/pa/cm200506/cmselect/cmworpen/834/834i.pdf

Jobcentre Plus Customer Service Target (the Customer Service Target is one of six targets guiding JCP activity. The others include a Business and Delivery Target; Job Outcome Target, Employer Outcome Target; Monetary Value of Fraud and Error Target and the Average Actual Clearance Time Target www.jobcentreplus.gov.uk) in the second quarter of 2005-06 ran far below the acceptable standard of performance, at an average of 34%, although there was some recovery towards the end of the year[7]. The Contact Centres are an integral part of the reforms designed to improve the customer experience. DWP envisage them freeing up staff resources and enabling the customer to avoid the need for travelling to their local office initially. The poor performance provided by the Contact Centres may have been a temporary blip as the Government have suggested[8]. It does, however, raise questions about the ease with which substantial efficiency reforms can be delivered alongside ongoing modernisation and organisational change without detracting from the quality of provision. The vulnerability of some of the Jobcentre Plus customer base makes this an important concern.

How the tension between rapid implementation of efficiency reforms, organisational change and broader welfare reform policy resolves itself will be fundamental to the DWP meeting its PSA employment targets. The Government's reform of welfare has centred on labour market activation policies such as the various New Deal schemes for young people, lone parents, disabled people and partners of the unemployed and 'making work pay' strategy of tax and benefit reform[9] [10] [11] [12] [13] [14]. The 2006 Green Paper on Welfare Reform proposes a further expansion of activation policies and significant changes to the operation of Incapacity Benefit (IB). From 2008 IB and Income Support paid on grounds of disability will be replaced by an Employment Support Allowance (ESA). For most recipients this change will require them to attend work focused interviews, establish an employment action plan and possibly some work related activity, or

---

[8] Work and Pensions Committee (2006b) The Efficiency Savings Programme in Jobcentre Plus: Government Response to the Committtee's Second Report of Session 2005-06, HC1187, The Stationery Office Ltd, London. http://www.publications.parliament.uk/pa/cm200506/cmselect/cmworpen/1187/1187.pdf

[9] HM Treasury (1998) Work Incentives: A Report by Martin Taylor, The Modernisation of Britain's Tax and Benefit System, No. 2. http://www.hm-treasury.gov.uk

[10] HM Treasury (2002a) The Child and Working Tax Credits, The Modernisation of Britain's Tax and Benefit System, No. 10, http://www.hm-treasury.gov.uk

[11] HM Treasury (2002b) Opportunity and Security for All, Spending Review 2002 White Paper, http://www.hm-treasury.gov.uk

[12] HM Treasury (2005) Tax Credits: reforming financial support for families, The Modernisation of Britain's Tax and Benefit System, No. 11, http://www.hm-treasury.gov.uk

[13] Department for Work and Pensions (2003) United Kingdom Employment Action Plan, http://www.dwp.gov.uk/publications/dwp/2003/uk_action_plan/ukeap.pdf

[14] Walker, R. and Wiseman, M (2003) "Making welfare work: UK activation policies under New Labour", International Social Security Review, Vol. 56, 1.

see the level of benefit they receive reduced[15]. The broadly encouraging results from the Pathway to Work/Incapacity Benefit Reform pilot schemes show greater support can improve engagement with the labour market[16] [17].The House of Commons Work and Pension Committee, while acknowledging the potential of the schemes, has cautioned that Incapacity Benefit Personal Advisors (IBPA) are not all as highly trained in tax and benefits and issues around disability awareness and mental health. With the Pathways to Work Process and ESA being rolled out nationwide for 2008, high quality training and monitoring of the caseload of IBPAs will be important for ensuring they are able to offer customers a full range of services[18].

The DWP five year plan aims to move towards an employment rate of 80% of the working age population partly in order to improve the position of disadvantaged groups and support an ageing society. The department recognises that following the fall in unemployment since 1997 realisation of an 80% employment rate increasingly requires the department to assist those who have a greater distance to travel in achieving job readiness[19]. The Freud Review[20] commissioned by the Government to explore the potential future directions for welfare to work also concluded that more intensive intervention and support is necessary to assist the economically inactive into employment. The task which faces Government if it is to achieve an 80% employment rate is considerable. It will require around one fifth of the current economically inactive population to move into paid work[19]. The expansion of activation policies and support to more fully address the needs of 'harder to reach' individuals is to be welcomed, but it does indicate that Jobcentre Plus Personal Advisors may face a larger caseload and one that is increasingly complex. Maintaining a manageable caseload for Personal Advisors will continue to be critical to ensuring welfare reforms are

---

[15] Department for Work and Pensions (2006a) A new deal for welfare: Empowering people to work, CM 6730.
http://www.dwp.gov.uk/welfarereform/docs/A_new_deal_for_welfare-Empowering_people_to_work-Full_Document.pdf

[16] Corden, A. & Nice, K. (2006a) Pathways to Work from Incapacity Benefit: A Study of experience and use of Return to Work Credit, Research Report No. 353, Department for Work and Pensions, Corporate Document Services.
http://www.dwp.gov.uk/asd/asd5/rports2005-2006/rrep353.pdf

[17] Corden, A. & Nice, K. (2006b) Incapacity Benefit Reforms Pilot: Findings from the second cohort in a longitudinal panel of clients, Research Report No. 345, Department for Work and Pensions, Corporate Document Services,
http://www.dwp.gov.uk/asd/asd5/rports2005-2006/rrep345.pdf

[18] Work and Pensions Committee (2006c) Incapacity Benefits and Pathways to Work Third Report of Session 2005-06, Volume 1, HC616-I, The Stationery Office Ltd, London.
http://www.publications.parliament.uk/pa/cm200506/cmselect/cmworpen/616/616i.pdf

[19] Department for Work and Pensions (2005) Five Year Strategy– Opportunity and security throughout life,
http://www.dwp.gov.uk/publications/dwp/2005/5_yr_strat/pdf/report.pdf

[20] Freud, D. (2007) Reducing dependency, increasing opportunity: options for the future of welfare to work, Department for Work and Pensions, Corporate Document Services, Leeds.

delivered effectively and that the DWP is able to meet PSA target 4. Already there is some concern that the caseloads of Personal Advisors are growing and that promised reforms to lighten their administrative load through the recruitment of Administrative Support Officers has been slow to occur[7]. Freud (2007) suggests that to improve efficiency and effectiveness the Government should look to contracting out support and intervention services to the private and third sectors for long term economically inactive customers. Jobcentre Plus would likely remain as lead agency under such a new contracting system during a customer's first year of a claim, with the customer moving to contracted support at 12 months (although it's envisaged that this might be altered for specific client groups). Over the medium and longer term this might also allow Jobcentre Plus to focus increasingly on delivering a service geared towards its more job ready customers.

The challenge facing Government is to ensure that efficiency reforms, changes in labour market activation services, social security reforms and employment rate aspirations all push in the same direction. The danger exists that increasing caseloads for Personal Advisors alongside greater emphasis on 'personalisation' of delivery and/or repetition of the kind of problems experienced with the introduction of the Contact Centres will reduce the effectiveness of interventions. Nor should an emphasis on activation distract the Government from providing the security from poverty necessary for those who cannot take-up paid employment. If the progressive raising of the employment rate towards 80% is a medium term goal then the Government should consider making this an explicit target (not simply an aspiration) on which it is to judged in 2010-11 by embedding it in the DWP PSA in CSR 2007.

Children and pensioners (SR 2004 PSA targets 1, 2, 3, 6 & 7)

The following section focuses on child and pensioner poverty and the targets associated with these goals (specifically PSA 1 and 6). The government have set itself ambitious goals to reduce child and pensioner poverty[1][21] and John Hutton, the Secretary of State for Work and Pensions, outlines why child poverty is such a priority:

> We cannot have a strong society and a strong economy unless we address the problem of child poverty. That is why it is a shared objective of both the DWP and the Treasury. And it is why I am making tackling child poverty the Department's number one priority[22].

Targets related to the achievement of these goals are likely to continue to feature as highly salient in the 2007 CSR and evidence from previous spending review

---

[21] Chancellor of the Exchequer (2002) Speech by Gordon Brown to the Labour Party Conference Monday 30th September 2002, The Guardian, http://politics.guardian.co.uk/labour2002/story/0,,801869,00.html

[22] Secretary of State for Work and Pensions (2006a) 'Ending Child Poverty and Transforming Life Chances', speech by the Secretary of State for Work and Pensions to the Fabian Society, May 10th, http://www.dwp.gov.uk/aboutus/2006/10-05-06.asp

rounds provides us with an indication of Government progress and challenges ahead.

The SR 2004 child poverty PSA calls for a halving of the number of children living in relative low-income households between 1998-99 and 2010-11. Relative low income is defined as households with incomes of less than 60% of the contemporary median income. The Government have also proposed as part of the next CSR an additional target to halve by 2010-11 the numbers of children suffering a combination of material deprivation and relative low income[6]. Such a target may be more amenable to conveying what poverty means in terms of living standards and opportunities. The proposed use of a 70% below median income measure combined with the material deprivation index suggests it may capture dimensions of poverty that are currently missed. Some households with an income above 60% median may, for example, have a low disposable income due to unavoidably high housing and/or childcare costs[23].

In line with Government objectives, progress has occurred in reducing the number of children living in poverty. The (2004/05) figures from the Household Below Average Income (HBAI) Series showed that from a 1998/99 baseline there has been a reduction on both a Before Housing Cost (BFC) and After Housing Cost (AFC) basis in the number children living in poverty of 700,000[24]. Unfortunately for the Government this positive development has stalled with the latest figures for 2005/06 showing a rise of 100,000 (BHC) to 200,000 (AHC) in the number of children living in poverty[25]. The failure to sustain previous performance means the Government look increasingly likely to fail in their objective to halve child poverty by 2010[10]. The slippage shows that substantial reductions in child poverty will require increased expenditure on social security and tax credits. The Institute for Fiscal Studies (IFS) Green Budget has indicated that such an increase may need to be higher overall than in the period from 1997 – 2004. During this period sustained falls in the number of people registered unemployed increased parental and household incomes assisting the Government in lifting children out of poverty[26]. Ensuring that progress continues to be made in tackling child poverty will require a reduction in the number of

---

[23] Department for Work and Pensions (2004) Public Service Agreement and Technical Notes 2005-2008,
http://www.dwp.gov.uk/publications/dwp/2004/psa/tech_note_2005_2008.pdf
[24] Department for Work and Pensions (2006c) Households Below Average Income Series 1994/95-2004/05, http://www.dwp.gov.uk/asd/hbai/hbai2005/chapters.asp
[25] Department for Work and Pensions (2007) Households Below Average Income Series, 1994/95-2005/06,
http://www.dwp.gov.uk/asd/hbai/hbai2006/pdf_files/chapters/chapter_4_hbai07.pdf
[26] Institute for Fiscal Studies (2006) IFS Green Budget, London,
http://www.ifs.org.uk/budgets/gb2006/gb2006.pdf#search=%22IFS%20green%20budget%22

workless families with children alongside greater expenditure on social security and tax credits[27].

A significant and ongoing commitment to improve the skill levels of the substantial number of adults in the UK who have poor basic skill levels is therefore necessary. Developing improvements in skill levels among the poorly qualified brings gains in employability and goes a long way to providing a more stable base for people to move into sustainable employment. The various New Deal programmes and the recent Leitch review of skills in the UK[28] suggest that Government recognises the need to address poor skills levels amongst the (potential) labour force.

On pensioner poverty substantial progress has occurred, although the take-up of entitlements continues to be less than optimal [26] [29]. Government aspirations to improve pensioner incomes is likely to occur against a background of growing resource constraints and demographic pressures as the baby boomer generation begin to reach state pension age[25] [30]. Despite the progress on pensioner poverty made so far, challenges remain. The Government's SR 2002 PSA target to be paying, by 2006, Pension Credit to at least 3 million households was not met[31] and there is slippage on the current SR 2004 target to be paying, '3.2 million households Pension Credit by 2008 while ensuring at least 2.2 million of the most disadvantaged households are claiming the Guarantee Credit element of the Pension Credit by 2008'4. Maximisation of Pension Credit take-up is necessary, but it is only one part of a wider approach concerning take-up of entitlements needed to tackle pensioner poverty. Yet low income amongst pensioners is only covered by the DWP's PSA Pension Credit take-up target. The National Audit Office reviewing progress made on pensioner poverty have suggested that the challenge of tackling pensioner poverty and encouraging take-up of entitlements should be reflected in a more comprehensive DWP PSA target or targets[28]. The Government has not, for example instituted a specific PSA target for reducing pensioner poverty as it has done with child poverty. The DWP CSR 2007 PSA targets might also usefully expand the Pension Credit target to include targets on Council Tax Benefit and Housing Benefit take-up amongst pensioners, possibly as joint targets with the Department for Communities and Local Government.

---

[27] Brewer, M. Goodman, A. Shaw, J. & Sibieta, L. (2006) Poverty and Inequality in Britain: 2006, Commentary 101, Institute for Fiscal Studies, http://www.ifs.org.uk/comms/comm101.pdf

[28] Leitch, S. (2006) Prosperity for all in the global economy: world class skills, Final Report, http://www.hm-treasury.gov.uk/media/523/43/leitch_finalreport051206.pdf

[29] National Audit Office (2006) Progress in tackling pensioner poverty: Encouraging take-up of entitlements, Report by the Comptroller and Auditor General, HC1178-I, The Stationery Office Ltd, London.

[30] Government Actuary Department (2005) National Statistics News Release 20th October 2005, http://www.gad.gov.uk/News/Documents/2004-based_national_population_projections.pdf

[31] Department for Work and Pensions (2006b) Departmental Report, http://www.dwp.gov.uk/publications/dwp/2006/dr06/

Tackling fraud & error and improving service quality (SR 2004 PSA targets 9 &10)

The social security system is necessarily complex, redistributing resources horizontally and vertically to people in different circumstances and with different needs. It includes a variety of different objectives including income replacement; financial incentives to make work pay; support for disabled people; assistance with bringing up children; rules to ensure proper use of public moneys and equity in administration and high level long term goals such as eradicating child poverty or creating a fairer society[32]. Changes in society and the ever shifting political arena create new needs as new regulations and changes in benefits, advice and guidance are introduced. Yet the very intricacy of the benefits system carries with it the risk that staff struggling to keep up to date with developments will make a high level of errors undermining the quality of service provided. It also creates barriers to customer access resulting in a less efficient use of resources while making it more likely that a context is created within which it is easier to perpetrate fraud[33].

The department is engaged in addressing problems of complexity and has had some success in mitigating its negative effects. Yet it does recognise that complexity is an inherent function of the current system and at least in part exists for good reasons[34]. Since 1997-98 there has been a reduction in losses from fraud and error in Income Support and Jobseeker Allowance Fraud by 38%, yet overall in 2004-05 the level of fraud and error is estimated to have stood at £2.6 billion[33].

Nonetheless, 2002 PSA targets for a 50% reduction in losses through fraud and error in Income Support and Jobseeker's Allowance by 2006 are on course. The Housing Benefit fraud and error target has, however, made slower progress towards the target of a 25% reduction in fraud and error[35]. The comparable targets for the 2004 PSA are a reduction by 15% in overpayments of IS and JSA through fraud and error by 2010 measured against a new baseline. For Housing Benefit the reduction sought is 25% by 2008 against the 2002-03 baseline. Again the 2006 Autumn Performance report draws attention to slippage on the housing benefit target, whilst the progress made towards the IS and JSA elements of the PSA has not yet been assessed[4]. The estimation of fraud and error overpayments in JSA and IS contained in the regular DWP assessment also contains a measurement of overpayment of Pension Credit as part of Service Delivery

---

[32] Millar, J. (2003) 'Social security: means and ends', pp 1-9, Millar, J. (ed.) Understanding Social Security, The Policy Press, Bristol.

[33] Committee of Public Accounts (2006) Tackling the complexity of the benefits system, Thirty-Sixth Report of Session 2005-06, HC 765, The Stationery Office Ltd, London. http://www.publications.parliament.uk/pa/cm200506/cmselect/cmpubacc/765/765.pdf

[34] National Audit Office (2005) Department for Work and Pensions: Dealing with the complexity of the benefits system, Report by the Comptroller and Auditor General, HC 592, The Stationery Office Ltd, London.

[35] Department for Work and Pensions (2006d) Fraud and Error in Housing Benefit April 2002 to September 2005, http://www.dwp.gov.uk/asd/asd2/fraud_hb/HBR_Report_Jul06.pdf

Agreement to reduce this by 20% by March 2006[36]. It is unclear why Pension Credit is not currently included in the overall high level PSA target on overpayment due to fraud and error. Particularly when it is estimated that the highest proportion of official error cases (21.6%) are found amongst the pensioner customer group[34].

Potential PSA target reforms for CSR 2007

The Government might consider in future bundling the Pension Credit fraud and error SDA into the overall PSA fraud and error target alongside JSA, IS and Housing Benefit. We know that customer experience of mistakes made by staff and difficulties encountered in past interactions with the benefits system impact on take-up of benefits in the future. Reducing those mistakes is a necessary objective and Pension Credit is worthy of equal status in the pursuit of minimising fraud and error. The 2007 PSA should reflect this.

The DWP PSA targets for 2004-2007 do not include a target for improving the skill levels of disadvantaged groups and the low paid. Yet the DWP is increasingly directing its attention to assisting harder to reach groups to move into employment. Indeed Jobcentre Plus was created to break through the structural divisions separating the delivery of employment and social security policy embedded in the old Employment Service and Benefit Agency, in order to improve services to the economically inactive.

For the individual the consequences of poor skill levels may be a 'churning' between low paid insecure work and receipt of benefits. For society the persistence of poor basic literacy and numeracy skills is likely to hamper economic growth and the realisation of greater social mobility[37][11]. It would seem prudent for the Government to return to its 'joined-up' government strategy and encourage greater coordination on the skills agenda by considering whether skills should be made an explicit joint target between DWP and DfES.

The current SR 2004 child poverty PSA target contains incongruities between the language which Ministers use to describe their goal, notably the eradication of child poverty, and the description of how this will be judged. The DWP Efficiency Technical notes accompanying SR 2004 indicates that the goal of eliminating child poverty will be judged to have succeeded if the UK's position has improved to where it is amongst the best in Europe. As the House of Commons Work and Pensions Committee have noted this could have a very different meaning to that of eradication. The current UK child poverty rate is currently around 20%[23] while the poverty rates elsewhere in Europe reported by the Work and Pensions Committee included Denmark at 5%, Finland at 6% and

---

[36] Department for Work and Pensions (2006e) Fraud and Error in Income Support, Jobseeker's Allowance and Pension Credit from April 2004 to March 2005, http://www.dwp.gov.uk/asd/asd2/IS_JSA_PC_fraud_full_report_Apr04_Mar05.doc

[37] Centre for Economic and Social Inclusion (2005) A Scheme for full employment: An inclusion policy paper, Policy Paper 3, London, www.cesi.org.uk

Sweden at 10%[38]. Are the UK government aiming for a child poverty rate of between 5-10% by 2020 and do they regard achievement of this as the successful eradication of child poverty? The 2007 Comprehensive Spending Review provides the opportunity to clarify how achievement of the long term objective of eliminating child poverty will be measured. Figures for both the level of material deprivation and relative low income that will be regarded as a true indicator that eradication has been achieved should be given.

A more ambitious step in the 2007 CSR would be to tie the employment and anti-poverty agenda of the DWP more firmly together. The objective being to create a new PSA that aligns policy in these areas with the delivery of increased social mobility. The addition of a 'social mobility' PSA target might face practical difficulties but it would help drive the child poverty target and the employment first agenda and cast greater light on the impact of inequality. The equality of opportunity agenda the Government is ostensibly committed to might for example require delivery of greater equality of outcome if it is to be realised. Ensuring policy is geared towards greater social mobility is central to giving early years anti poverty interventions a life chances perspective. It would also improve the attention given to achieving greater opportunities for progression in employment for the low paid and low skilled. The latter is important if tackling child poverty over the long term is to be addressed[39]. Thus far achieving greater social mobility and embedding this as an overarching objective of public service reform, has not been satisfactorily established[40] [41]. The next round of Public Service Agreement targets should reflect on this and remedy it.

Conclusion

Since 1997 the Government have introduced a series of ambitious reforms concerning employment policy and the tax and benefits system. They have also given themselves perhaps the most demanding and radical social policy objective of any Government in the past 50-years: to eradicate child poverty in a generation. That some progress has been made on reducing the levels of child

---

[38] Work and Pensions Committee (2004) Child Poverty in the UK, Second Report of Session 2003-04 Volume 1, HC85-1, House of Commons, The Stationery Office Ltd, London.
http://www.publications.parliament.uk/pa/cm200304/cmselect/cmworpen/85/85.pdf

[39] Secretary of State for Work and Pensions (2006b) 'What will it take to end Child Poverty', speech by the Secretary of State for Work and Pensions John Hutton to the Joseph Rowntree Foundation, July 6th, http://www.dwp.gov.uk/aboutus/2006/06-07-06.asp

[40] Cabinet Office (2006b) 'Social Mobility - We need to do more' speech to Institute of Public Policy Research April 4th,
http://www.cabinetoffice.gov.uk/about_the_cabinet_office/speeches/murphy/pdf/ippr_social_mobility.pdf

[41] Murphy, J. (2006) Keynote speech on Social Justice and public service reform to the Institute for Public Policy Research April 4th,
http://www.ippr.org.uk/feeds/files/ippr_ea_04-04-2006_murphy.mp3

poverty is to be welcomed, but it also demonstrates the scale of the task facing the Government. Achieving the child poverty objective will require further significant investment in tax credits and benefits and continued progress in moving workless households into employment. Sustaining sufficient support services to help the less 'job ready' to move into paid work is likely to become an increasing challenge for the DWP within existing resource constraints. It is here that the contradictions Labour faces are most clear. When Labour took power in 1997 it identified as key issues for resolution the persistence of large numbers of workless households and children in poverty. Continued economic growth and the inventiveness of the Chancellor of the Exchequer Gordon Brown and HM Treasury have provided the resources and policies to begin to tackle these problems. Yet given the possibility of a future economic downturn, along with Ministers' belief that globalisation, international competitiveness and potential tax payer revolt constrains policy options, New Labour's room for manoeuvre is heavily circumscribed. The question therefore remains as to whether the political and economic limits the Government believes itself to be operating within have left it with enough tools to accomplish the job it has set out to do.

13. An effective centre for government – the future of the Cabinet Office and HM Treasury

Colin Talbot

Introduction

This chapter looks at the roles of the Cabinet Office and HM Treasury as the two central ministries in UK national government. Together with the office of the Prime Minister in Number 10 Downing St, they make up what is effectively the centre of government – although whether it is an effective centre is another question.

Let us begin by acknowledging the very peculiar context for how the centre of power is created. Unlike virtually all modern, advanced, democracies the structures of the machinery of government in the UK are not laid down constitutionally or legislatively[1]. They exist by a strange combination of custom and practice, convention, and the peculiar operation of Crown Prerogative powers by the Prime Minister of the day.

Nearly all ministries – including Cabinet Office and Treasury – exist solely at the discretion of the Prime Minister who can abolish, create, amalgamate and separate at will without recourse to Parliament or even the Cabinet. (The only major exception to this is what is now HM Revenue and Customs, formerly Inland Revenue and HM Customs and Excise, which is based on statute for deep historical reasons about the conflict between Crown and Parliament).

This is important to bear in mind because although Cabinet Office and HM Treasury appear almost immutable, in reality they have changed greatly over the years and may yet change even more fundamentally (and quickly) under a new Prime Minister.

The second peculiarity of the UK system has been the confidentiality that has always bedevilled those who want to study the relationships between these crucial central institutions. Occasionally researchers have been allowed to raise the veil of secrecy[2] [3] but we have had to rely mainly on autobiographies of ministers, mandarins and advisors[4] for insights.

The third peculiarity is the role of HM Treasury (and its impact on Cabinet Office). Our Treasury has always been a fairly rare combination of economic and

---

[1] Harden, I. (1992). The Contracting State, Open University Press.

[2] Heclo, H. and A. Wildavsky (1981). The Private Government of Public Money (2/e), Macmillan.

[3] Thain, C. and M. Wright (1996). The Treasury and Whitehall - The Planning and Control of Public Expenditure, 1976-1993. Oxford, Clarendon Press.

[4] Lipsey, D. (2000). The Secret Treasury. London, Viking.

finance ministry and one with even rarer degree of autonomy from the Prime Minister than is the case in virtually any other Westminster-style government. HM Treasury has always wielded fearsome power across Whitehall but recent years have seen this power both morph and increase. Whilst it has lost some economic power (e.g. through independence of the Bank of England) it has gained enormously in power of over the rest of Whitehall's spending, policies and performance, which we will examine later in this chapter.

As a result the various offices of the Prime Minister (which have included Cabinet Office in various guises as well as a series of ah hoc centres attached directly to Number 10) have been always been weaker than many would suppose. Under New Labour the tension between Number 10/Cabinet Office and HM Treasury has never been greater for both personal and – which gets far less attention – structural reasons.

Before returning to the issue of the relationship between the two centres of power in Whitehall, let us look at each in turn.

Cabinet Office

The Cabinet Office that has gone through numerous changes of status, name and structure over the past quarter-century (and numerous Ministers). But it has always aspired to play a central role in government. Indeed the chapter on the Cabinet Office in the last (2004) Spending Review was headed "an Effective Centre for Government".

As already noted, the fundamental problem for the Cabinet Office is, and always has been, that there are not one, but two, 'centres' in UK government – the Cabinet Office and the Treasury.

This compounded by the Westminster system of Cabinet government, which means that Permanent Secretaries in departments owe a dual accountability to the Head of the Civil Service and to 'their' Minister (see comments to this effect by Sir Gus O'Donnell in the Cabinet Office Capability Review). These twin elements – a very strong Treasury and strong departmentalism – have always undermined this ambition.

This is illustrated very well by a look back at the four Spending Reviews from 1998 onwards. In the 1998 Comprehensive Spending Review[5] Cabinet Office was relegated to section on "The Chancellor's Departments and the Cabinet Office/Office of Public Services" and given a mere two paragraphs (out of 17).

In Spending Review 2000 Cabinet office made some progress – it was still bracketed with the Chancellor's Department's but had managed three paragraphs[6].

---

[5] Chancellor of the Exchequer (1998). Modern Public Services for Britain: Investing in Reform - Comprehensive Spending Review: New Public Spending Plans 1999-2002. London, Parliament.

[6] Chancellor of the Exchequer (2000). Prudent for a Purpose: Building Opportunity and Security for All - 2000 Spending Review: New Public Spending Plans 2001-2004. London, The Stationery Office.

By Spending Review 2002 (and under a new Cabinet Secretary) Cabinet Office finally achieved its own independent chapter, albeit a short one[7]. And finally in 2004 a slightly more substantial chapter of its own, and the "Effective Centre for Government" claim[8].

There have been many efforts over the years to strengthen the role of Cabinet Office – such as the Central Policy Review Staff[9] – over the years, but none has dislodged the Treasury or managed to 'corporatise' the departments. More recently, the New Labour Government of 1997 embarked on an ambitious series of moves to beef up the Cabinet Office.

First, a whole series of units were created which were aimed at creating 'joined-up' policy-making- on drugs, homelessness, etc.

Secondly, some specifically 'whole of government' policy units were established – initially the Performance and Innovation Unit and the Forward Strategy Unit, later merged into the Strategy Unit.

Thirdly, the overhaul of the Civil Service College sought to create yet another vehicle for creative and joined up central thinking about policy. Renamed the 'Centre for Policy and Management Studies' (CMPS) and with the former head of the economic and social research council (ESRC) as its head, this was clearly designed to help create an effective centre for government which – as the title suggested – extended to being both a policy and a management centre with a research component to both.

Fourthly, to answer criticisms of the so-called 'generalist' civil servant being merely a 'gifted amateur', the 'Professional Skills for Government' programme was launched.

And finally, and most recently, as series of 'capability reviews' were launched looking at each department in turn – this was billed as 'CPA for government'. Comprehensive Performance Assessment (CPA) is the process applied to local government by the Audit Commission that has widely been seen as an effective change tool. Capability Reviews are fundamentally different – they are much more internal and they only look at capability, not actual performance whereas CPA does both.

A Failing Organisation?

The Capability Reviews – conducted by teams of Whitehall insiders with a sprinkling of external input – have proved remarkably more honest and critical than anyone expected. They have certainly come as something of a shock to the

---

[7] Chancellor of the Exchequer (2002). Opportunity and security for all: Investing in an enterprising, fairer Britain (2002 Spending Review)(Cm 5570), HM Treasury.

[8] Chancellor of the Exchequer (2004). Stability, security and opportunity for all: Investing for Britain's long-term future (2004 Spending Review)(Cm 6237), HM Treasury.

[9] Blackstone, T. and W. Plowden (1990). Inside the Think Tank - Advising the Cabinet 1971-83, Mandarin.

seven departments – including the Cabinet Office itself – that have been completed (at the time of writing).

The Capability Reviews looked at three key areas: strategy, leadership and delivery. Across a range of ten areas (4 for leadership and 3 each for strategy and delivery) departments were 'scored' as:

1. Strong: good capability for future delivery in place. Clear focus on the actions and improvement required to deliver transformation over the medium term.
2. Well placed: well placed to address any gaps in capability for future delivery. Is making improvements in capability and is expected to improve further in the medium-term.
3. Development area: the department should be capable of addressing some significant weaknesses in capability for future delivery by taking remedial action. More action is required to close those gaps and deliver improvement in the medium term.
4. Urgent development area: significant weaknesses in capability for future delivery that require urgent action. Not well placed to address weaknesses and needs significant additional action and support to secure effective delivery. Not well placed to deliver improvement over the medium term.
5. Serious concerns: serious concerns about current capability. Intervention is required to address current weaknesses and secure improvement in the medium term (category reserved for most serious gaps and should only be used infrequently).

The average 'score' across the seven departments reviewed so far is almost exactly a 3 – i.e. a 'development area' with 'significant weaknesses'. For leadership the score is 2.96 (i.e. a development area) and for delivery it is 3.23. Only on strategy is the picture a bit better – an average score of 2.47 (which on a 'rounding basis' just about squeezes into the well placed' category. On 'build capacity' (one of the sub-categories) the seven departments score only 3.71 – putting them well into the 'urgent development area' range.

The reason for dwelling on these scores (and of course we should treat these scores with some caution given the way they are arrived at. But that only means they could be either higher or lower than the reality) is simple – if the one of the Cabinet Offices core tasks – as set out in its own Public Service Agreement – is to "build the capacity of the Civil Service to deliver the Government's priorities" then it is clearly failing. Nor is it even an effective exemplar – its' own Capability review score is exactly average – with delivery and strategy slightly worse and only leadership marginally better. And to add to the humiliation, the Review team note that if they could have disaggregated the leadership score between leadership of the Civil Service as a whole and leadership of the Cabinet Office itself, they would have moved it up to 'strong' (1) for the former but down to 'development area' (3) for its internal leadership. Put more uncharitably a clear case of 'do as I say, not do as I do'?

So we are left with a Cabinet Office which appears to have failed – based on an assessment process of its own devising – to deliver on one of its key tasks, delivering a capable Civil Service. This is a very serious situation – especially given that over the past two decades or more vast amounts of money have been spent on reform and we have constantly been told that we have a 'Rolls Royce' Civil Service. When the Cabinet Office itself cannot score a 1 – i.e. 'strong' - in any single sub-category and for seventy scores across seven departments only two instances of a 'strong' score appear, something is clearly 'broke'.

Capability Reviews might have been seen as strengthening the role of Cabinet Office vis-à-vis the rest of Whitehall, instead they have – so far at least – merely illuminated its impotence in achieving real change within the 'Whitehall Village'. It is still possible that Capability Reviews – coupled with an imminent change of Prime Minister – may prove historically to have been one of the key factors in the start of a real transformation in Whitehall. This issue is examined further at the end of this chapter.

HM Treasury

In contrast to Cabinet Office, HM Treasury (HMT) seems to have gone from strength to strength since New Labour came to power in 1998. Although one of the new government's first acts was to strip the Treasury of direct control of monetary policy by giving freedom to the Bank of England (BoE) and the 'Monetary Policy Committee' (MPC) this has been more than compensated for by Treasury power gains in other areas. And, indeed, although BoE and MPC independence is undoubtedly genuine in many respects, it is not quite as total as is often assumed (the Chancellor stills sets the MPC's targets and selects its members).

HMT has of course always had considerable power within Whitehall – especially over domestic spending ministries. Under the old PES (public expenditure survey) system which lasted for almost 4 decades HMT was able to use the annual budgetary round to challenge not just spending but also and by implication policy priorities. We do have good accounts of just how powerful HMT was in this arena. And of course, even between Budgets any new policy initiatives that needed money had to be subjected to Treasury scrutiny before being allowed to proceed. All of which means HMT has always had a strong policy role, but it has undoubtedly become stronger of late.

The first major change was the scrapping of the old PES system and its replacement with the current 'Comprehensive Spending Reviews' and 'Public Service Agreements' system. By lengthening the planning horizon and including explicit targets for achievements by spending departments the new system codified and made much more explicit HMT's policy role across the whole of Whitehall. Indeed it brought some traditionally more 'autonomous' policy areas – such as defence and foreign affairs – more into the Treasury's orbit. How effective the whole CSR system – and PSAs in particular – have been remains somewhat of an open question, but at the very least they have legitimised Treasury's policy role.

The second change is a consequence of the first. Just as the whole CSR/PSA system has centralised more power into Treasury, so the whole approach of 'targets' across the whole of UK public service has centralised more power into Whitehall over the 90% of public servants who are not civil servants[10] . This is what might be called a double-centralisation (as opposed to the double devolution currently in vogue) – centralisation upwards into Whitehall and centralisation within Whitehall into Treasury.

The third major change has been the partial merging of the tax and benefit systems. This has brought a whole area of what had been separate social policy squarely within HMT's remit. Not only have policy decisions shifted into HMT, but the merging of the systems means that large administrative resources have moved with it – for example the transfer of the national insurance contributions agency into the (then) Inland Revenue.

A fourth area of shifting power has been within the family of departments under the Treasury. The old Customs and Excise (C&E) and Inland Revenue (IR) were – as already been noted – very unusual in being based on legislation not Crown Prerogative powers. This gave them a degree of independence from direct ministerial interference aimed at preventing corrupt practices emerging. Further – C&E and IR also had considerable policy autonomy to interpret legislation as they saw fit. The merger of C&E and IR into the new mega HM Revenue and Customs – which at its inception employed 100,000 civil servants, one in five of all civil servants – also saw a major shift of power to HMT. Many of the policy powers which had been held by the old 'non-Ministerial' departments were transferred, in the legislation which established HMRC, to the very Ministerial Treasury. It is as yet unclear what impact this has had.

The Balance of Power and the Future

The growth in Treasury power and the rather more mixed fortunes of the Cabinet Office have resulted by 2007 in a situation that – if there is a strong and effective centre in government it is the former rather than the latter. Or as one Treasury mandarin out it, rather disdainfully, to an academic colleague not so long ago – "they've got what, twenty of so decent brains over in Cabinet Office – we've got 200 here in Treasury." When the former Permanent Secretary at HMT and former head of the Civil Service, Lord (formely Sir Andrew) Turnbull spoke to the Financial Times in March 2007 it caused something of a storm. His comments on how Gordon Brown had wielded Treasury power in a 'Stalinist' manner were headline news. Whilst commentators focussed on Mr Brown's

---

[10] Public Administration Select Committee (2003). On Target? Government by Measurement (HC 62-I). London, House of Commons.

personality, the really important point was how Lord Turnbull pointed to the growth in Treasury power.

Another former mandarin – Sir Stephen Wall – said in the FT the same week that:

> I cannot recall a time – and I was civil servant for 35 years, including during the Thatcher period, which was a pretty brutal period – when there has been such a lack of communication between Treasury and the rest of Whitehall, and that is not good for government.[11]

But, as they say, pride often comes before a fall and the present situation may in future years be seen as the pinnacle of Treasury power before the decline began. The obvious architect of such a fall could be Prime Minister Brown. Having spent a decade carefully nurturing HMT's powers, Mr Brown is unlikely to leave then for a successor who could then use them to thwart his ambitions as Prime Minister.

Of course, Mr Brown will be constrained politically by fear of further accusations of 'control freakery' that have dogged him as Chancellor. Despite this however it is unlikely that the current configuration of power between Cabinet Office and Treasury will last under a Brown premiership. And this is not just an issue of personality.

There is a growing chorus – some of which has been noted above – of complaint that Whitehall as a whole is not "fit for purpose". The Capability Reviews are having a traumatic effect both within Whitehall and outside. The Home Office's calamities and a series of other mini-crises have reinforced the view of a system in a sub-optimal state. The position therefore seems ripe for some more fundamental reform.

Two long-standing ministries – the Home Office and the Department of Trade and Industry (DTI) – have their futures very much in question. Given the DTI overlaps with many of the economic competences of the Treasury, its break-up and redistribution of these powers to HMT could be used to help camouflage and sweeten the transfer of powers over spending and targets from HMT to Downing St/Cabinet Office.

This is of course all speculation and PM Brown may opt for minimal structural change and implement a much more collegial, open, style of government tipping the pendulum back towards cabinet government (it has happened before). This is possible, but it seems rather unlikely. Much more possible seems to be that we have seen the apogee of Treasury power. Whether this leads to 'an effective centre for government' emerging is a somewhat more open question. Some would argue that it is rather more fundamental systemic and constitutional, rather than structural, change which is needed to make Whitehall work more effectively[12]. At a recent seminar that included critical former mandarins and various Whitehall-watchers, there seemed to a consensus that only a rebalancing

---

[11] Financial Times, 21 March 2007

[12] Lodge, G. and B. Rogers (2006). Whitehall's Black Box. London, Institute for Public Policy Research.

of powers between Whitehall and town-hall and Whitehall and parliament would lead to fundamental change. These type of rather more fundamental changes have so far not been high on New Labour's agenda and there is so far no sign that a Brown premiership would be any different. The ducking of the Whitehall-town-hall issue in the response to the long-awaited Lyons review of local government finance suggests this will continue to be the case.

Section III: Cross-cutting issues

14. Towards the next phase of employment policy

Jill Rubery

Employment policy is central to new Labour's economic policy. Yet responsibility for employment policy is effectively spread across three departments of government: the DTI is charged with raising the rate of sustainable productivity growth and working to deliver equality and maximise potential in the workplace; the DWP with promoting work as the best form of welfare and improving employment rates; and the DFES with improving skills and participation in education for both young people and adults. These fragmented areas of policy are brought together on an annual basis though the requirement for member states of the European Union to develop and implement an employment strategy (now incorporated into a more general National Reform Programme covering economic policy, macro and micro as well as a separate chapter on employment policy). An even more important integrating force is that of the Treasury; employment and work issues are central to the Treasury's twin objectives of raising productivity and promoting social inclusion through employment. Furthermore the UK's so-called flexible labour market is the cornerstone of new Labour's claim that the UK now represents a model for the rest of Europe to emulate. It is therefore highly appropriate to take employment policy as an area of consideration for the current comprehensive spending review. Although the recommendations will be divided among a range of ministries, it is the coherence of the package as a whole that needs to be reviewed. Three main areas of government employment policy will be reviewed: its welfare to work policy, its labour market regulation policy and its policy for skilling the workforce and raising productivity.

Welfare to work

Activation - the moving of people from passive receipt of welfare benefits to engagement in work and employment - is "an internationally fashionable policy label"[1] that has been embraced by both new Labour and the–European Union. The motivation behind activation is the reduction of both social security costs and short and long term risks of poverty. Three main strands to the policy have

---

[1] Barbier, J-C. (2006) 'Has the European model a distinctive activation touch ?' in M.Jespen and A. Serrano Pascual eds. *Unwrapping the European Social Model* Bristol: The Policy Press

been developed. First there are policies targeted at those in receipt of benefits; here new Labour has continued and intensified the policy started under the Conservatives of withdrawing or threatening to withdraw or cut benefits from those who fail to seek work actively. However, they have combined these punitive policies with the New Deal that provides opportunities for at least partial activation through training and work placement. This contrasts with the Conservative approach that opposed any notion of the state being the "employer of last resort"[1]. The second policy strand is the development of a raft of more generous in work or employment-conditional benefits designed to provide financial support for those taking low paid jobs and who do not have access to support from other working family members. Third, there have been efforts to develop other forms of support to facilitate employment, notably the development of a national childcare strategy and the SureStart programme for those in more disadvantaged areas.

Much has been made of the apparent successes of the policy programme. Particularly notable according to the government has been: the success of the New Deal both in placing participants in work and in reducing the number of people eligible for the programmes; the rise in the employment rate for lone parents - up 11% since 1997; the reduction in the number of families facing punitive claw back rates on benefits as they increase working hours at 70% of increased earnings or above from ¾ million in 1998 to under ¼ million today; and the reduction in rates of poverty particularly for children by 700,000, or 17 per cent between 1998/99 and 2004/05[2]. These claims provide a rather positive spin on a more complex situation; for example, the role of the New Deal in reducing unemployment, compared to the effect of favourable economic trends, is difficult to disentangle; and doubt may be cast on the impact of the policy in motivating benefit claimants into work by the modest overall reduction in workless households from a peak in 1996 of 19.1% to 15.8% in 2006[3], with lone mothers the major area of improvement in employment rates among disadvantaged groups. Similarly, the reduction in claw back rates in excess of 70% has been accompanied by a large increase in the number of families facing effective tax rates of more than 60%, from ¾ million to 1¾ million[4]; and while child poverty rates were reduced by 17% 1998/9 and 2004/5 (or 23% if measured before housing costs are deducted), the target actually set for this period was for the rate to fall by 25% and the 50% reduction sought by 2010 is unlikely to be achieved[5]. Moreover Palmer et al. (2006) show that the reduction is primarily due

---

[2] Palmer, G, MacInnes, T and Kenway,P. (2006) Monitoring poverty and social exclusion 2006 Joseph Rowntree Foundation and the New Policy Institute
http://www.poverty.org.uk/reports/mpse%202006.pdf
[3] ONS 26 (2006) First Release: Work and worklessness among households July
http://www.statistics.gov.uk/pdfdir/wwhh0706.pdf
[4] HM Treasury (2006) Report on the Budget, London: HM Treasury. (http://www.hm-treasury.gov.uk/budget/budget_06/budget_report/bud_bud06_repindex.cfm)
[5] Harker, L. (2006) Delivering on Child Poverty: what would it take?A report for the Department for Work and Pensions
http://www.dwp.gov.uk/publications/dwp/2006/harker/

to overall reductions in risk of poverty both for those in work and those out of work and not as a result of the movement into employment.

Interpretations of the policy changes clearly depend in part on whether they are viewed from a glass half full or a glass half empty perspective. There are also deep rooted disagreements as to whether the policy is coherent, workable and indeed desirable. Five key issues can be identified that require consideration under the CSR. These include the complexity of the benefit system, the limitations of the focus on single breadwinners in households, the persistent problems of job quality, the impact of the increase in migrant workers from an enlarged Europe and the ethical issues raised by policies to increase sanctions on those who fail to gain access to employment.

The first issue is the complexity and cost - both economic and political - of the tax credit system. In contrast to the US system of earned income tax credits, the UK tax credit system is prospective not retrospective; tax credits are paid on the basis of current and anticipated earnings and not, as in the case of a negative income tax, on the previous year's actual earnings. This allows the UK system to provide stronger incentives to enter work but carries with it the much greater likelihood of both under and over payment. These problems, coupled with IT-based problems - have dogged the implementation of the tax credit system and the temporary solution has been effectively to allow for high levels of overpayment without the requirement for pay back as, almost by definition, households in need of tax credits are not in a position to save in anticipation of the benefits being overpaid. This problem led to a tenfold increase in the increased earnings disregarded in 2006-7 before benefits for the year would be reduced - from £2,500 to £25,000[4]. Such a high disregard may prove unsustainable but the problems of how to make adjustments without creating financial instability for claimant families has not yet been solved. The negative publicity associated with the overpayment issue has also potentially reduced the acceptability of tax credits to those families most in need of assistance when in employment. The jury is still out on whether the tax credit systems can survive these problems or whether alternative and less complex systems of support for the working poor need to be considered, including higher minimum wages, a more individualised entitlement to tax credits etc.

The continued and indeed even increased need for support for the working poor is related to the second problem and that is whether the policy has primarily shifted the problem of poverty from the inactive to the working poor. The 2006 Joseph Rowntree report on poverty indicates that the government has underestimated the problems of poverty for the working poor, related to the poor quality of jobs available to disadvantaged adults. The working poor may be supported by the tax credit system but they are also trapped by the new benefits. Tax credits create major disincentives to extend working hours, improve earnings and for partners to enter employment. Evidence suggests that two earners are necessary to move households out of poverty[6] [7]. These disincentives also

---

[6] Women's Budget Group 2005 Women's and children's poverty: making the links

contradict the policy objective of promoting women's employment; in practice the help is primarily directed at those who are main breadwinners, that is lone parents and women in couple households not claiming benefits are not even included in the activation programmes . Women face a higher risk of falling into poverty in part due to lack of continuous connection to the labour market. Indeed, policies that promote discontinuity may result in many women falling into poverty over the lifecourse. At the time of marital break-up, being in employment is a strong predictor as to whether women become active or inactive lone parents[6][7][8]. A recent report to the DWP has stressed that further progress in reducing child poverty requires a new approach targeted at all low income parents irrespective of their current status as benefit claimants.

Helping single earners to progress in work, or supporting non-working partners of single earners (potential second earners) to move into work, will play a crucial part in the next stage of tackling child poverty[5].

The need to address problems of the working poor suggests not only a change in eligibility to participate in support schemes but also a need to address the problems of low pay and insecurity in the jobs available to many of those on new deal programmes or in receipt of tax credits. As Harker again argues "parents 'cycling' between having a job and being out of work, is neither efficient nor effective in tackling child poverty"[5].

The government's policy is based on a belief that any form of work can act as a bridge into better paid and more secure work but experience under this policy approach suggests that many who move from welfare into employment still face a high risk both of remaining in low paid jobs and of returning to welfare dependency. New policies to provide for training at work and for non-employed adults to be able to acquire basic skills and vocational qualifications may assist but the major problem lies in the high number of low paid and insecure jobs that are isolated from ladders into more rewarding or more highly paid jobs. The government through its own promotion of outsourcing of work, particularly in the public sector, is in fact making it more difficult for people to use a low paid job as a bridge into a career as they are often employed in specialised firms including temporary work agencies that have only a limited range of types of jobs available. Experience in narrowly defined job categories tends not to help the development of a career. There are some examples of new approaches towards skill and career development, such as the skills escalator programme in the NHS which provides opportunities for advancement for both direct recruits and

---

http://www.wbg.org.uk/documents/WBGWomensandchildrenspoverty.pdf
[7] Lister, R.(2005) The Links Between Women's and Children's Poverty in Women's Budget Group (2005) Women's and children's poverty: making the links
http://www.wbg.org.uk/documents/WBGWomensandchildrenspoverty.pdf
[8] HM Treasury (2004) Child Poverty Review, London: HM Treasury

contracted workers[9], but many more such schemes are needed if the welfare to work programme to provide real opportunities to those entering employment.

The fourth problem is the impact of high flows of workers from the new EU member states into the UK's labour market. For the Secretary of State for work and pensions, the arrival and employment of these migrants only serves to prove that those who remain unemployed in the UK are work shy as jobs are clearly plentiful[10]. This interpretation discounts any possibility that UK employers are prejudiced against the long term unemployed in the UK and are exercising an active preference for migrants over UK applicants. We need to know more about how employers view those on benefits and with interrupted work histories before placing the responsibility for gaining employment solely on the benefit claimant. Gray (2002) shows that the unemployed often feel they are forced to take jobs with temporary work agencies as according to agencies employers are less concerned and knowledgeable about the work history of temporary agency workers than is the case for direct hires[11]. The entry of migrants is apparently to be used to support stricter sanctions against the unemployed who fail to find work, even though higher migration clearly means more competition for available jobs.

This bring us to the fifth issue and that is the continued intensification of pressure on benefit claimants to seek work or face sanctions with respect to their benefits. Announcements in the budget that job seekers' allowance claimants are to face more intensive work-focused interviews and that all lone parents, even those with a child under 14, would be required to attend work-focused interviews from April 2007 have been followed up in January 2007 with proposals to make receipt of benefits conditional on active work seeking for mothers with children over 12 even before the policy of extending work-focused interviews has been implemented. Currently benefits are not conditional on work seeking until children reach the age of 16 and there are strong hints that the threshold age could well fall below 12 in the future. The ethical issue is whether all the pressure should be placed on the individual claimants in a labour market where employers remain free to discriminate against the unemployed, the incapacitated and those with high domestic burdens. It might be appropriate at this juncture in the welfare to work policy to switch attention from the individual claimants to the practices of employers and to consider providing incentives to employers who hire people who have a history of incapacity or long term

---

[9] The agenda for change in the NHS 'includes a commitment for contractors to introduce systems for job evaluation and staff development, and to work with the NHS on workforce issues such a cleaners progressing to train as health care assistants'
http://www.dh.gov.uk/PolicyAndGuidance/HumanResourcesAndTraining/ModernisingPay/AgendaForChange/AgendaForChangeArticle/fs/en?CONTENT_ID=4120663&chk=fZzK07.

[10] Observer 17.12.06 Minister warns 'can work, won't work' Britons over benefits. Gaby Hinsliff

[11] Gray, A. (2002) Jobseekers and Gatekeepers: the Role of the Private Employment Agency in the Placement of the Unemployed Work Employment Society 2002; 16; 655

unemployed, or who offer flexible packages to lone parents. The policy has become unbalanced with all responsibility on the claimants and little effort made to change the context in which claimants seek employment.

Labour market regulation policy

Labour market regulation has been extended since 1997 on four main impetuses; first there was a raft of commitments made at the initial election including the minimum wage and some trade union recognition rights; second there was the backlog of EU legislation to be implemented once the opt out from the social chapter was given up (also promised prior to election in 1997); third there has been some further expansion of EU legislation, notably relating to information and consultation and to a wider range of areas of discrimination; and fourth there have been some initiatives in the area of support for carers and work-life balance. While the sum total of this legislation amounts to a significant body of new regulation, the UK remains one of the more deregulated labour markets in Europe. Much of the EU legislation has not led to changes in other member states as their existing regulations were already at least as strong as those contained in the EU directives.

There is relatively little prospect of further regulation, except perhaps in the area of work-life balance where rights to request flexible working are to be extended to carers of adults in April and extension to all parents is under consideration. In this context the focus for the CSR should be to concentrate on implementation and modernisation of existing legislation. Four priorities in this respect can be identified.

1. First, more attention needs to be paid to enforcement of legislation through inspection, audit and through awareness raising. This approach is particularly required in the light of high migration and the greater potential for abuse where migrants may be even more unaware of their employment rights than UK citizens. Already more resources have been provided for enforcing the minimum wage but the adequacy of this extra resource needs to be assessed.

2. The real and relative value of the minimum wage needs to be maintained and potentially improved. Such a policy reduces the costs of the tax credit policy as well as improving equity for those not receiving tax credits and promoting productivity in the large low paid labour market. Arguments against further improvement in the minimum wage are likely to continue to be made on the basis that wage structures are becoming too compressed at the bottom end of the labour market[12]. Here again we come back to the actions of employers. While the minimum wage, to be effective and non inflationary, needed to change wage differentials,

---

[12] Cronin, E. and Thewlis, M. (2004) Qualitative Research On Firms' Adjustments To The Minimum Wage. IRS research Low Pay Commission
http://www2.lowpay.gov.uk/lowpay/research/pdf/t0IDZGQ0.pdf

employers in low pay sectors have in fact perhaps been too ready not to make appropriate upward revisions to their skill and pay grading structure to preserve rewards for experience and responsibility. The tax credit system has also removed some responsibility from employers to provide wage advancement in the low paying segments as the increase in earnings may be clawed back in reduced benefits. Policies to promote the principle of equal pay for work of equal value for all employees regardless of gender- as advocated by the CIPD[13] - could be considered as a means of encouraging employers to pay due regard to differences in skill and responsibility in this segment of the labour market.

3. Consideration needs to be given to modernising regulations to meet the needs of employee protection in contexts of more complex inter-organisational contracting where the definition of who is the employer and where the responsibilities for employment protection, training and fair remuneration lie are unclear[14]. Promotion of good employment practices through public procurement policies needs to be further explored and developed, making use, for example, of the new general duty on public organisations to promote equal opportunities that comes into force in April 2007 with the new equality act.

4. Recent initiatives to support working parents need to be monitored for their impact on the gender division of labour. While positive impacts can be expected from the rights to request flexible working - by allowing women to retain their current jobs if they wish to work more flexible and possibly shorter hours after having children – (the proportion of working mothers who change employer on returning to work following maternity leave has fallen from 41% in 2002 to 20% in 2005, which is significant for women because resumption of employment is important in terms of maintaining occupational status, earnings and pension entitlements[15]) - there are also risks that this might reduce the number of women returning to work full-time and in fact reinforcing women's roles as the prime carer and the flexible and part-time worker. As the rights are also available to men there may of course be some opposite and positive outcomes but the overall impact needs careful monitoring and assessment[16]. Proposals to

---

[13] Welfare, S. (2006) 'Equal Pay at the Crossroads', IRS Employment Review and Benefits, 843: 36.

[14] Earnshaw, J., Rubery, J. and Cooke, F-L, 2002 Who is the Employer?, Institute of Employment Rights, London.

[15] Smeaton, D. and Marsh, A. (2006) Maternity and Paternity Rights and Benefits: Survey of Parents 2005, DTI Employment Relations Survey No. 50, March.
(http://www.dti.gov.uk/files/file27446.pdf?pubpdfdload=06%2F836

[16] Fagan, C., Hegewisch, A. and Pillinger, J. (2006), Out of Time: Why Britain needs a new approach to working-time flexibility, TUC.
(http://www.tuc.org.uk/extras/outoftime.pdf)

extend options to men to take up unused 'maternity leave' need to be monitored for take up and consideration given to improving rates of pay for those on leave and providing opportunities to take paid leave on a part-time basis.

Productivity and skilling the workforce

Improving the productivity of the workforce through skills is the third element to the government's employment policy after its 'work first' and 'flexible but fair labour market objectives'. The Leitch (2006) review of skills[17] is part of the preparation for the CSR[4] and certainly represents an ambitious and more comprehensive approach to skill development than previous white papers and policy documents. The objective is stated to be of doubling attainment at most levels by 2020. The focus is both on basic skills and attainment of the minimum level 2 standards (equivalent to good GCSEs) by the vast majority of adults but also a major increase in both level 3 skills (equivalent to A levels) and in level 4 and even 5 skills equivalent to degrees and above. In particular the objective is to increase those with level 4 and above skills from 29% in 2005 to 40% by 2020. This signifies a shift in focus, with greater emphasis on raising the level of skills generated through the training system. This is to be achieved in part through proposals to combine training at work with higher education in new ways. The proposals also contain the long term option of compulsion if the voluntary approach does not work. For those entering the labour market the government appears to have already accepted the recommendation to require young people to stay in full or part-time education and/or workplace training up to age 18. These plans are certainly substantial and ambitious by previous standards but, even if accepted and implemented by the government, a number of barriers to the UK emerging as a high skill economy remain. Some of the policies may also involve some risks for those areas where the UK's reputation for skill development is strongest - that is higher education.

The first problem or barrier to the UK becoming a high skill economy that is not fully addressed is again the behaviour of UK employers. The report focuses on one area of mismatch - that is between the planned supply of skills and employers' demand for skills - and calls for a more demand-led approach. The implicit assumption is made that employers are following 'best practice' with respect to the utilisation of skills within their business processes. Yet there is long standing evidence - reinforced by information from the Workplace Employment Relations Survey - that employers in the UK try to minimise their demand for skill and a very small percentage of the workforce is regarded by employers as skilled, with 50% of workplaces with more than 10 employees regarding their

---

[17] Leitch (2006) Prosperity for all in the global economy - world class skills, Final report of the Leitch Review of Skills December 2006.
http://www.hm-treasury.gov.uk/independent_reviews/leitch_review/review_leitch_index.cfm

share of skilled workers as 25% or less[18]. The consequences for the quality of work and level of service are significant and there is a need not just to respond to employers' demand for skills but also to expand that demand and to work with employers on job redesign that provides more opportunities to utilise skills at the workplace instead of efforts to take skill out of the process. So yes we need to involve employers more, but no we should not allow employers to continue with their skill minimisation strategies.

A related issue is the underutilisation of the skills of large parts of the UK workforce; this is particularly evident in the part-time workforce and the EOC has recently calculated that more than four in five women employed in part-time jobs are working below their potential[19] [20]. The Leitch (2006) report still assumes that the problem is only underdevelopment not underutilisation of skills. This problem particularly applies to women returners and it is disappointing that the policy of developing skills is still geared only to those who are claiming benefits and those who are in work; returners may not be eligible for programmes as the focus is on benefit claimants or those already in employment.

A further barrier to skill development for those lowest down the skill hierarchy is the deep seated prejudice against 'training' among UK employers. There is still evidence to suggest that NVQ level 2 qualifications may be a barrier rather than an assistance in career development[21]. The UK preference for people doing 'proper jobs' needs to be addressed in the new proposals for young people to stay on till 18 in either education or workplace training. Efforts have to be made to ensure that the workplace training option does not stigmatise participants, as has happened with other training initiatives for the young.

The final issue to raise with respect to the Leitch review is the proposals for higher education to be more involved in the delivery of training for adult workers and at the same time for employers to be more involved in deeming what the higher education systems should deliver. This approach is imaginative as it has the possibility of overcoming the negative attitudes of many employers towards training, in comparison to educational qualifications, while at the same time potentially getting employers on side who consider academic qualifications to be unsuitable for their types of jobs and industry. However, there must still be doubts whether degrees learned partly on the job on a part-time basis and as an adult worker will in practice be considered equivalent to degrees earned on a full-time basis straight from school. There are also risks with this policy of

[18] Cully, M., Woodland, S., O'Reilly, A. and Dix, G. (1999) Britain at Work: As Depicted by the 1998 Workplace Employee Relations Survey, London: Routledge.

[19] Darton, D. and Hurrell, K. (2005), People working part-time below their potential, Equal Opportunities Commission September 2005
http://www.eoc.org.uk/PDF/people_working_pt_below_potential.pdf

[20] Grant, L., Yeandle, S. and Buckner, L. (2005), 'Working Below Potential: Women and Part-Time Work', EOC Working Paper Series, No. 40.

[21] Dearden, L., McGranahan,L. and Sianesi, B. (2004), An In-Depth Analysis of the Returns to National Vocational Qualifications Obtained at Level 2, London: Centre for the Economics of Education.

extending degree level qualifications to non standard modes of learning and skills. The UK has a relatively well deserved reputation internationally for delivering high quality academic qualifications on an efficient and timely basis but this reputation may be in danger if too wide a range of qualifications are all labelled degrees. The risks are greater the stronger the influence of employers in determining the content and assessment methods without reference to the quality standards of the higher education institution.

Conclusions

The UK's employment record under new Labour has been good; unemployment rates have been low by comparative standards and employment rates high. The causes of this strong employment record are not, however, to be found in the government's specific employment and labour market policies but instead in the favourable macroeconomic environment, fuelled by expanded public expenditure and UK consumers' apparently unlimited desire for credit. The insistence that employment success can be attributed to the flexible and deregulated labour market has left the government myopic to the fact that the nature of the labour market is one factor in the failure to close the UK's productivity gap. The coherence of the government's approach to attaining its employment, poverty-reduction and productivity objectives would be enhanced if there was more recognition that the current tendency of the UK to generate large numbers of low paid and low quality jobs far from being a strength is in fact a weakness of the UK labour market system.

It is the low quality of these jobs that prevents the welfare to work strategy of the government offering an effective path out of poverty and disadvantage, that leads to a compression of wage differentials and a lack of opportunities for career development for large segments of the population and that leaves workers and their skills underemployed and underutilised. This myopia has resulted in policy being focused almost entirely on the supply side of the labour market, on increasing incentives to work (reinforced by the stick of possible benefit withdrawal), promoting individual investment in training and education and facilitating the reconciliation of work and family through provisions of supply of childcare and opportunities for flexible working. The long term success of each of these policies depends on the development of a labour market where those moving off benefits and into work can find the type of secure employment that acts as a bridge into a career and can help lift a family out of poverty; on employers utilizing the investment in training and education by designing skill in rather than out of jobs; and on women being able to find sufficiently high quality jobs to be able to afford the childcare supplied and to resist being the partner who applies for the flexible and short hours working. The next phase of employment policy needs to focus on improving employers' performance in the labour market. Employers have been allowed to get off scot-free - they are allowed to complain long and hard about the quality of the labour supply while remaining free of any scrutiny of the efforts that they have made to develop employment opportunities designed to motivate staff and to bring out the best in their employees. They have been allowed to walk away from their commitments to secure the incomes of their employees in old age, yet when employers enter into government policy thinking it is primarily as a client to be serviced with no obligations to first of all put their own house in order. The successful introduction of the minimum wage has revealed that there is scope for public policy to change and influence the actions and behaviours of employers - the next phase of employment policy needs to be even bolder in that direction.

15. Sustainable Development Strategy

Joe Ravetz

Introduction

As the UK Sustainable Development (SD) Strategy notes, our civilization is now entering a unique and irreversible experiment with the Earth's climate and resource base[1]. Its central chapter on the 'One Planet Economy' shows that the average UK resident is living on over three times their share of the earth's bio-capacity[2]. Meanwhile, the Treasury-backed Stern Review sets out the most detailed picture yet of the costs of climate change, and the cost-benefit case for tackling it sooner rather than later[3]:

> The overall costs and risks of climate change will be equivalent to losing … up to 20% of GDP or more. In contrast, the costs of action – reducing greenhouse gas emissions to avoid the worst impacts of climate change – can be limited to around 1% of global GDP each year.

The 2007 Comprehensive Spending Review will be aiming to respond to five types of long term trends and challenges[4], of which the last is:

> the increasing pressures on our natural resources and global climate from rapid economic and population growth in the developing world, and sustained demand for fossil fuels in advanced economies.

Each of the other challenges – dependency, international competition, innovation, and terrorism / conflict – is also directly or indirectly related to the challenge of environmental resources and impacts. The 'long term trends' review also flagged up climate, water and resource / waste issues, with key recommendations[5]:

> ensuring the Stern Review forms the basis of relevant considerations in the 2007 CSR together with wider government action over the decade ahead to tackle climate change; and……..ensuring appropriate environmental care,

---

[1] HMG (Her Majesty's Government), (2005), Securing the Future: the UK Sustainable Development Strategy, CM6467, London: TSO

[2] WWF (World Wildlife Fund) 2006: Living Planet Report; Geneva, World Wildlife Fund. available 2006 on www.panda.org

[3] HM Treasury (2006) The Stern Review on the Economics of Climate Change, London, HM Treasury

[4] HM Treasury (2006) Long-term opportunities and challenges for the UK: analysis for the 2007 Comprehensive Spending Review: London, HM Treasury

[5] HM Treasury (2006) Tax and the environment: using economic instruments: London, HM Treasury

alongside maintaining macroeconomic stability and seizing the benefits of globalisation.

The most recent governmental landmark is the Climate Change Draft Bill of March 2007[6]. This contains a set of 'building blocks' for the proposed measures, including:

- Long term targets, to enable more strategic planning and investment.
- Creating a global carbon price, with an aspiration towards a global market.
- Technology & energy efficiency, with a competitiveness and innovation agenda.
- Tackling deforestation: (mainly via international trade and development).
- Adaptation to the unavoidable effects of climate change (mainly via infrastructure and the built environment).

But, as often is the case in politics, it seems there are huge gaps between aspiration and action. In response to the Stern Review's warnings of global economic collapse from climate change, the Budget of March 2007 managed to raise air passenger duty by a mere £5 per passenger, and fuel duty by 2 pence per litre.

Overall, it is clear that the environmental sustainability agenda is centre stage, and that this is seen as not merely a UK but global matter. The question is, how can the government's principal executive strategy, the CSR, respond to this? What are the implications for departmental structures, and for fiscal policy? How far is the government able or willing to re-direct the UK economy to meet the challenge? Is the CSR the best way to do this, and how can it be improved?

This chapter looks firstly at the background, the scale of the challenge, and the goals and targets which might apply. Then it highlights some current methods and tools, and proposes an extended CSR – a form of 'Comprehensive Resource Review' – to help achieve the transformation towards a One Planet Economy[7].

Diagnosis

Responses from the CSR

The CSR 2007 is primarily a tool for national fiscal strategy and the fiscal side of departmental policy – it does not aim to be a blueprint for the wider economy, although it may set aspirations for that. In this context the emerging 'green' agenda is relatively new, and the responses from government are as yet untested and subject to political fortune. A range of possible directions from the CSR 2007 might include:

---

[6] DEFRA 2007: Draft Climate Change Bill: CM7040: London, TSO.

[7] Those interested in being involved in the One Planet Economy Network and its 4 year programme, are invited to register on www.ecologicalbudget.org.uk.

- Environmental taxation: in many sectors there is a case for refinement, targeting and possible increases in taxation or other differential incentives. This is the more conventional response, as set out by the Treasury in 1997, and more suitable for economic analysis[8].
- Further development of markets in pollution, resources and eco-systems. The experience so far of the EU Emissions Trading Systems (ETS) suggests that emissions markets will achieve environmental objectives, only when backed up with strong political direction, to set stringent 'caps' and allocate legacy permits.
- Strategic innovation and 'market transformation' strategies, for sectors, products, technologies, infrastructure and supply chains: generally oriented around 'resource productivity' and the more mainstream agenda for economic competitiveness, as above[9].
- A stronger focus on 'natural capital' resources and assets, with monitoring and valuation systems, and incorporation in both the national accounts and departmental budgeting systems. There is recent experience from the EU and UN, and new research and modelling also enables more detail than before[10] [11]. We focus on this agenda in the second part of the chapter.

There are many questions on each of these. For instance, environmental taxation policy often has multiple objectives, as a combination of revenue raising, behaviour change, and stimulus for innovation[12]. Meanwhile, innovation for environmental technology may be effective, but in most sectors there is underlying demand growth, increased consumer choice and technological complexity, which tends to increase the total throughput of resources. The general theme of 'sustainable consumption and production', despite strong rhetoric from Ministers, still has a problem in finding departmental leverage[13].

---

[8] HM Treasury (2006) Tax and the environment: using economic instruments: London, TSO

[9] Performance and Innovation Unit (2001), Resource Productivity: Making more with less, London: TSO.

[10] United Nations, European Commission, International Monetary Fund, Organisation for Economic Co-operation and Development, World Bank 2003: Handbook of National Accounting: Integrated Environmental and Economic Accounting 2003: New York, UN Statistical Commission, Studies in Methods, Series F, No.61, Rev.1 (ST/ESA/STAT/SER.F/61/Rev.1)

[11] Eurostat 2000: Economy-wide material flow accounts and derived indicators. A methodological guide. Office for Official Publications of the European Community, Luxembourg.

[12] Leicester, A (2006) The UK Tax System and the Environment: London, Institute of Fiscal Studies

[13] Jackson, T. and Michaelis, L. (2003), Policies for Sustainable Consumption, London: Sustainable Development Commission: available on www.sd-commission.gov.uk

Context - underlying themes

At the same time, the SD agenda represents more than environmental protection on a global scale – it involves new kinds of thinking about governance, markets, citizenship, infrastructure and the science base itself.

The background to this is the rapid emergence of the 'greening' of business and of policy: now a powerful electoral issue, but one which is still split between aspirations and practice. Underlying the practical limits and targets for emissions, there are new concepts of citizenship, corporate responsibility, 'contracts' and 'compacts', for instance the state-citizen contract proposed for Defra[14].. We can see several phases in this transition; from the 'end of pipe' approach to fixing pollution, to an environmental management approach for supply chains, to a 'transformation' approach to markets, supply chains and demand side. So what kind of agendas does this transformation involve?

Firstly there is a powerful 'inter-dependency' agenda, in the sense that few issues are isolated problems, rather they are highly inter-connected with few clear boundaries. This implies that the CSR should aim to be more transparent about the links and impacts between one department and another. Then, there is a far-reaching 'values' agenda, in terms of the interactions of social / environmental assets with economic markets and fiscal policies. This implies that the CSR should aim to measure social / environmental values alongside financial values: and then develop policies which **optimize** between economic and environmental values. Thirdly, there is a 'multi-level' and 'multi-lateral' governance agenda: for the environmental and SD theme such 'joined-up' policy is not only desirable but essential. All this raises the question of whether the 'rational management' type of approach to policy analysis can deal effectively with the extended 'actor-networks' which are called for[15].

Context – climate policy/One Planet Economy

At the moment there is a strong policy focus on climate change and carbon emissions policy; clearly this is urgent, but it is often framed as what is arguably an end-of-pipe, *problem focused* agenda. The problem is based on accounting for carbon at the point of emissions; the policy agenda focuses on present or future climate impacts; and the business agenda focuses on energy and emissions technology.

In contrast it can be argued that the One Planet Economy theme, as quoted by the Secretary of State for the Environment, David Miliband, can be more of a *solutions focused* agenda. It uses several types of 'footprint' measures to identify total impacts, both climate and other, and both direct and indirect, all the way from production to consumption. In addition, it focuses on imported goods and

---

[14] Miliband, D (2006): *Open letter to the Prime Minister*, July 2006: available as of March 2007 on www.defra.gov.uk

[15] Carley, M and Christie, I (1998) Managing Sustainable Development, London, Earthscan

their indirect or upstream impacts which are built into the supply chain. This should provide a check on the 'green illusion', in which the UK appears to be more sustainable, simply by displacing its impacts to overseas. Also, it takes on the wider economy, with supply chains from origin to 'end-fate', and with all its social, cultural and political dimensions.

Overall, the One Planet Economy theme looks for pro-active ways to turn the perceived 'costs' of an emissions reduction policy, into the economic and social 'opportunities' of a whole sector, supply chain and market transformation strategy[16]. This should be the ultimate aim of the CSR 2007 in the policy development process.

Context – capital & footprint accounts

The idea that there are different forms of 'capital' is not new, but has re-surfaced as a powerful way to identify and analyse the SD agenda. One analysis looks at '5 capitals', in the form of financial, manufactured, human, social and natural capital[17]. We could say very simply that the financial and manufactured forms are measured and valued in the formal economy, but the last – the 'natural' - is the most endangered by this same economy. For the others – social and human capitals – there are many possible measures, and much which cannot be measured, in terms of well-being and quality of life[18]. Overall, there is a strong case for enlarging the official measures and indicators to look at all forms of capital, and particularly the natural.

Chief among these measures is the 'footprint' – well suited to the One Planet Economy theme, being based on the concept of displacement or impact for others to suffer or deal with. For example, the 'ecological footprint' of a loaf of bread includes the land to grow the wheat, the energy in production and distribution, the materials in packaging, and the office blocks used by advertising and insurance. Three types of footprint have emerged recently which show complementary views:

- **Carbon footprint** – often loosely taken as direct emissions, but specifically identified as the 'upstream' carbon / other climate emissions / other climate impacts, as allocated to final demand categories of consumption[19] [20].

---

[16] Ravetz J (2006): One Planet Economy Network – a Prospectus: Surrey, WWF-UK: available March 2007 on www.ecologicalbudget.org.uk and www.eco-region.org

[17] Porritt J (2005) Capitalism as if the world matters: London, Earthscan

[18] Sustainable Development Commission 2007: Redefining Progress: report on consultation: London, SDC, available 2007 on www.sustainable.gov.uk

[19] Wiedmann, T., Minx, J., Barrett, J., and Wackernagel, M., (2006). Allocating Ecological Footprints to Household Consumption Activities by Using Input-Output Analysis. Ecological Economics Vol 56 (1):28-48

[20] Carbon Trust, 2006: The carbon emissions generated in all that we consume London, Carbon Trust

- **Resource footprint** – generally meaning the primary materials entering the economic system, with results on stock depletion and other environmental impacts[21].
- **Ecological footprint** – a specific definition for the bio-productive land area anywhere in the world required to supply resources or absorb pollution, for the supply chains which meet the 'final demand' needs of consumers[22]. This methodology is highly aggregated with many assumptions, but is now covered by an international standard from the Global Footprint Network (details on www.gfn.org).

This all suggests that one of the first tasks of the CSR and the national accounts which support it, should be to deal in a structured way with the resource flows, footprint and environmental balance accounts in economic, social and environmental terms. This has been demonstrated in the UK with the Mass Balance approach[23], and in Australia with the 'triple bottom line' approach[24]. Each of these can then be disaggregated by regions, by product lines, by social groups, by policy options and by lifestyle choices as far as possible[25]. The diagram overleaf shows simply the relationships between the various footprints, on a supply chain framework.

---

[21] Bringezu, S. and Schütz, H. 2001: Total material resource flows for the United Kingdom. Department of the Environment, Transport and Regions Contract EPG 1/8/62. DETR, London.

[22] Rees W, & Wackernagel M, 1995: Our Ecological Footprint: Reducing Human Impact on the Earth: British Columbia, Gabriola Island , New Society Publishers

[23] Linstead C, Gervais C & Ekins P (2004) Mass Balance: an essential tool for understanding resource flows: London, Forum for the Future

[24] CSIRO Sustainable Eco-systems & University of Sydney, 2005: Balancing Act: a triple bottom line analysis of the Australian Economy. Canberra, AU.

[25] Barrett J, Ravetz J & Bond S: 2006: Counting Consumption: CO_2 emissions, material flows and ecological footprint of the UK by region and devolved country: Surrey, WWF-UK, available March 2007 on www.ecologicalbudget.org.uk

Carbon & ecological footprints

Simplified relationship of climate emissions footprint & ecological land footprint:
exports & imports are not shown.
Source: Ravetz (2007) Pathways to a One Planet Economy: www.ecologicalbudget.org.uk

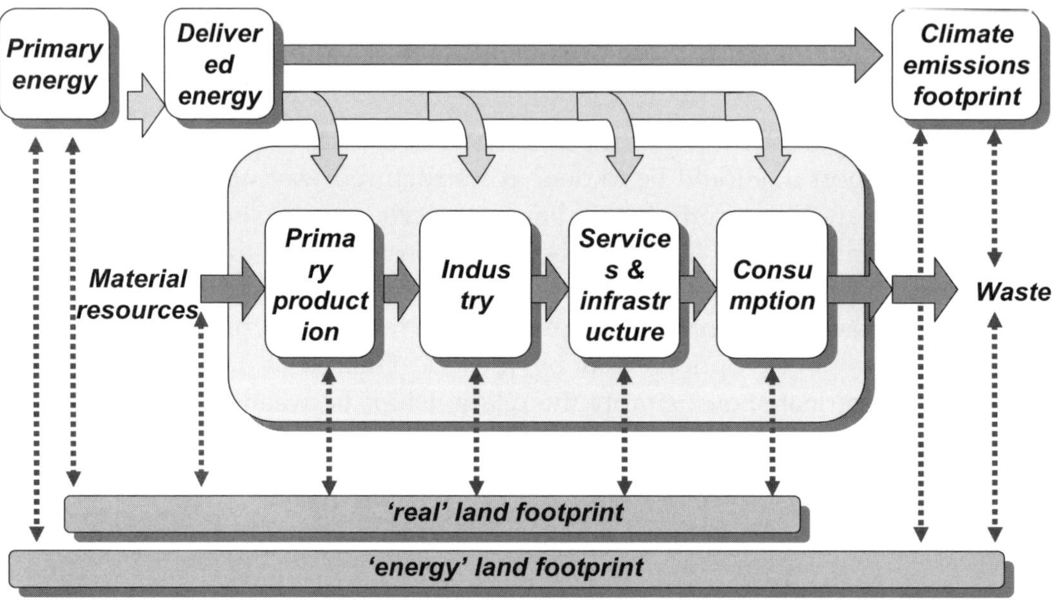

Figure 15.1 Carbon and ecological footprints

Context – UK commitments and actions

At present there is a 'race to the green' between the major parties, and public acceptance of green policies is being pushed to new horizons. However on close inspection many grandiose targets seem rather short of detail, and there is a visible gap between the policy and scientific agendas. From the 'scientific' viewpoint, to avoid 'dangerous' levels of climate change of over 2^0 C, we need to limit atmospheric concentrations of greenhouse gases to less than 450ppmv, with a reduction in global emissions within a decade, and a rapid 80-90% cut in emissions from developed nations by 2030.

From the 'policy' viewpoint, in contrast, we are presented with a less drastic target of 550ppmv, and a 60% emissions cut by 2050. But the scientific assessment is that this would greatly increase the risk of runaway effects on rainforests, desertification, sea level rise, famine, drought and so on. In practice, both causes and effects for both cases are hedged with layers of risk and uncertainty, as explored by the Stern Review[26].

---

[26] HM Treasury: Stern Review on the Economics of Climate Change: London, TSO.

The EU member states as a whole have just committed to a 20% and possibly 30% reduction in climate emissions by the year 2030. One of the main means to achieve this is the EU Emissions Trading Scheme: however the market price of CO_2 allowances has now fallen below \$1 per tonne, which barely covers the paperwork (as of February 2007). The UK is committed in the 2007 Climate Change Draft Bill to meeting its policy target of a 60% reduction in climate emissions by 2050 (excluding international transport): but there are as yet few details. However, recent UK trends are for stable or rising levels of CO_2 domestic emissions, and if the effects of marine transport, air travel and embedded CO_2 emissions are included in the accounts then the increases are much more significant.

When it comes to policy at the local level, many UK cities and regions are now producing ecological footprint accounts in the attempt to deal with their global responsibilities. In practice there is often confusion with carbon accounts and carbon footprint, and there are many gaps between the evidence, the policy levers to respond to it, and the institutions with the capacity for action.[27] For instance, the DCLG has set a target that all new dwellings should be 'carbon neutral' by 2016, but the implications for the industry and the householder are only now being explored[28].

Overall there is a kind of discontinuity, faced with the uncomfortable challenge that 'business as usual' is leading rapidly and visibly towards global collapse. This suggests that a more radical transformation of the economy is called for.

At present there is no single department or policy platform which can deal with such an agenda: but the Treasury and the CSR are about the best that we have.

Challenges – a One Planet contract

There are major challenges for government in the One Planet theme. It cuts across the general model of economic growth, and the general assumption that increased production = increased consumption = increased welfare. In contrast, the One Planet theme highlights the concept of 'decoupling', and the concept of a government-citizenship 'contract', as put by David Miliband in his open letter of July 2006[29]:

> To enable "One Planet living", we need to think about different ways of engaging citizens, businesses and land managers…. I'm developing the idea of

---

[27] Ravetz J, (2000): 'City-Region 2020: integrated planning for a sustainable environment' (with a foreword by the UK Secretary of State for the Environment), London, Earthscan.

[28] DCLG, 2006a: Building A Greener Future: Towards Zero Carbon Development: London, TSO

[29] Miliband, D (2006): Open letter to the Prime Minister, July 2006: available as of March 2007 on www.defra.gov.uk

an 'environmental contract' which sets out the rights and responsibilities of citizens, businesses and government in achieving environmental goals.

This can be expanded into an agenda for new forms of environmental fiscal policy. This goes beyond the conventional forms of environmental taxation with an end-of-pipe approach to pollution abatement. It points towards a 'market transformation' of supply chains, and a 'new institutional economy' which underpins the relationships of suppliers, intermediaries and consumers[30]. Such questions revolve around the concept of 'stakeholding and stewardship', in the context of multi-level governance, and the potential for pro-active roles and responsibilities of government:

- as a **stakeholder, custodian and stake-owner**, in the national and global common resources of climate, biodiversity and so on.
- as **investor and manager** in common resources, through active intervention with taxation and trading systems (just as Keynesian demand management is the basis for macro-economic management).
- as a **standard setter**, so that firms and other organizations will be encouraged and required to be transparent and responsible at all times (through the Operating and Finance Review and similar procedures).
- as an active player through public **procurement and contract specifications** – the prime interface between the public and private sectors.

Such active roles and relationships between state, businesses and citizens will need to be debated in the context of a liberal market democracy, and we do not claim the final answers here. But it is clear that the scale of the challenge is as never before, and some kind of transformation is called for.

Prognosis

It is also clear that the CSR needs to focus other forms of 'capital', than simply financial or manufactured capital. The need and the opportunity for this are now as never before.

One type of capital in particular deserves special attention - the 'natural capital', which is most endangered by climate change and resource use.

Towards an Ecological Budget UK

Could the CSR be extended or accompanied by a parallel 'Comprehensive Resource Review' ('CRR')? As with any strategic planning and budgetting process, this should contain firstly the baseline evidence, with current accounts

---

[30] Jacobs, M (1997) Environmental Valuation, Deliberative Democracy and Public Decision-Making Institutions, In: Foster, J (Ed), Valuing Nature: Economics, Ethics and Environment, London, Routledge

and projections; then an outline of alternative scenarios, options, appraisals, and preferred strategy; and then an implementation plan to achieve it.

Recent research on a national resource accounting system – the Ecological Budget UK database and modelling system[31] provides a starting point to achieve this. These accounts follow the UN 'System of Environment-Economic Accounting'[32], with a framework of core and satellite accounts[33]: and as far as possible they link to the UK indicators for sustainable consumption and production[34]. The accounting framework contains a balance sheet and profit / loss account, just as with the financial accounts of a major business. It also looks at external impacts on the rest of the world, and the costs and benefits of environmental policies and programs. Each of the basic measures of materials, emissions, energy and ecological footprint, can be indexed by economic output, to show some basic measures of resource productivity[35]. The prototype summary UK accounts are shown in the appendix to this chapter.

The result is unique and topical in several ways. Firstly, it shows the total global impact of consumption, not only from resource flow and pollution within the UK, but from the imports of products and materials. On current calculations, over one third of the UK total impact is from imports, which is as yet invisible in the national accounts.

It also shows the indirect or supply chain effects, upstream and downstream of any sector or product – particularly relevant in the service-dominated economy of the UK where, for instance, financial services, which apparently consume only office space, in fact generate large local and global impacts upstream and downstream. Thirdly, the analysis of the data can be pushed forward to show more detail on resource flow and eco-footprint – particularly to show the differences between regions and local authorities, wealthy and poor lifestyles and between business leaders and laggards. With this structure, we can begin to build up a 'One Planet' resource profile of the UK economy, making the following well-founded assumptions:

---

[31] Barrett J, Ravetz J & Bond S: 2006: Counting Consumption: CO_2 emissions, material flows and ecological footprint of the UK by region and devolved country: Surrey, WWF-UK, available March 2007 on www.ecologicalbudget.org.uk

[32] United Nations, European Commission, International Monetary Fund, Organisation for Economic Co-operation and Development, World Bank 2003: Handbook of National Accounting: Integrated Environmental and Economic Accounting 2003: New York, UN Statistical Commission, Studies in Methods, Series F, No.61, Rev.1 (ST/ESA/STAT/SER.F/61/Rev.1)

[33] Pedersen O G & de Haan M (2006): The System of Environmental and Economic Accounts–2003 and the Economic Relevance of Physical Flow Accounting: Journal of Industrial Ecology Vol 10(1-2):19-42

[34] DEFRA (2005): Sustainable Consumption and Production Indicators: a revised basket of 'decoupling' indicators: London, DEFRA, available 2006 on http://www.defra.gov.uk/environment/statistics/scp/index.htm

[35] Performance and Innovation Unit (2001), Resource Productivity: Making more with less, London: TSO.

- The total Ecological Footprint of the UK is 5.4 global hectares per person (gha/cap): compared to the available bio-capacity for the global population of 1.8 gha/cap, the UK exceeds its share by a factor of three.
- The total material resource input is 15.2 tonnes per person per year: of this total, 26% comes directly from imports, 35% goes to capital stocks (new buildings, roads and other infrastructure), 21% goes to export, and 37% ends up as waste.
- The average household directly purchases 2.5 tonnes a year (excluding energy) and throws away a tonne of waste a year; the remainder accumulates in the built environment.
- The overall resource dependency – imports as a proportion of direct material inputs – ranges from 17% in agriculture to 34% in manufacturing.
- The total resource efficiency – material flow per £ output – is 0.34 tonnes per £million.
- The total imported flows – the energy and climate emissions impact embedded in imports – are between 30-60% of the direct flows which are accounted by the UN Framework Convention on Climate Change (subject to further research in progress)
- The overall resource re-investment – the rate of recycling and re-use from total (controlled) waste – is 35%.

Targets for the Comprehensive Resource Review

The key result of the Ecological Budget UK shows that the UK is exploiting the Earth's available resources, as measured in bio-productive land area or 'bio-capacity', at more than three times its 'fair' share, as measured by the ecological footprint in global hectares per capita (gha/cap). This footprint is not a universal catch-all measure, but it does draw attention to the totality of global impacts and limits. By 2050, for example, there is likely to be a 50% increase in world population, to the region of 8-9 billion people. While there may be some additions to bio-capacity through land reclamation and reforestation, there is likely to be further damage from current trends and climate impacts. Therefore a mid-range estimate of change in bio-capacity would be from 1.8 to 1.3 gha/cap in 2050. So, to reduce the *current* UK footprint of 5.5 gha/cap to the 2050 fair share bio-capacity of 1.3 gha/cap would need a 75% or Factor of Four reduction, (after the book of the same name)[36].

Evidently, the transformation of the UK into a One Planet Economy will not happen overnight. But we can define the target rate of change by setting the Factor Four goal at a strategic point such as 2050 (the current horizon for UK climate policy). This equates to a year on year reduction in total resource use of 3.5% per year (starting from 2010), as measured by the Ecological Footprint. By 2020, at this rate of change, the reduction in total Footprint would be about 35%

---

[36] Von Weizsacker E, Lovins A & Lovins H, 1997: Factor Four: doubling resource efficiency, halving resource use: London, Earthscan.

and by 2050 about 75%. If we factor in economic growth at an average of 2.5%, then the required rate of "decoupling" or improvement in the footprint efficiency (Footprint/£GDP) would be a reduction of more than 6% year on year for the next 40 years. This is about twice the rate of decoupling in the recent past, which held resource use more or less level while the economy grew. For comparison, the UK's current target of a 60% cut in climate emissions by 2050, equates to a year on year reduction of 2.25% (starting from 2010). This is a crucial measure, but far from transparent in the DTI Energy Review and supporting papers[37].

These are economy-wide targets for the UK as a whole, beyond the remit of government alone. But if the CRR or CSR is to meet its aspirations, it would aim to facilitate them by targeted fiscal policy, using the full potential of government in public stewardship, enabling, facilitation, procurement, demonstration and so on.

Resource flow restructuring

The shift towards a One Planet Economy will involve restructuring, from an economic base which is heavily dependent on material consumption. This is complex and uncertain, but a 'supply-chain' framework can begin to explore the likely effects, at each stage of production and consumption[38].

This would see a continuous increase in **resource productivity** i.e. the level of added value for producers per unit of resource flows. There is then a counter agenda on the consumption side:

- Shift consumer demand towards low impact products and services.
- Increase social utilization; for instance where cars or equipment could be shared.
- Increase the energy efficiency of products in use, and also the lifetime of the average product, both consumables and durables.
- Increase the rate of re-use, recycling and re-manufacturing, and reduce the waste and emissions leaving the system.
- To achieve all this in a consumer-led market economy will need innovation on the social and cultural dimensions, to increase the 'welfare added' of products, e.g. so that consumers will actively prefer to buy long life, low impact, zero waste products.

This adds up to an increase in the counterpart on the consumption side, what might be called the 'social effectiveness of consumption', or 'consumptivity'. In other words this looks for ways for people to get more satisfaction from less

---

[37] DTI (Dept of Trade & Industry) 2006: UK energy and CO2 emissions projections: Updated Projections to 2020: London, DTI

[38] Ravetz J (2006) Regional innovation & resource productivity – new approaches to analysis and communication. In: Randles S & Green K (Eds) Industrial ecology & spaces of innovation: Aldershot, Ashgate

'stuff' (cetus paribus), and this is also the underlying theme of Sustainable Consumption and Production[39].

Economic & fiscal restructuring

If the flow of money is unchanged, with reducing amounts of 'stuff' entering the system, then the price per unit of stuff would tend to rise. Consequently, there are implications for industrial investment, transport and energy finance, and wider macro-economic balances:

- Energy costs (international) rise – as a direct cost to economy, and/or incentive for innovation and restructuring
- Carbon taxes / quota trading costs rise – the effects depend on redistribution to least cost sectors through subsidy, tax relief or other market trading.
- Material and commodity costs rise – direct cost to economy / incentive for restructuring.
- Energy consumption taxes via product charges, appliance charges, infrastructure charges, domestic / commercial quotas /tariffs.
- Demand side management through ESCO-type partnerships, other micro-incentives.
- Emissions from energy fuel cycle: direct charges: tradeable quotas: combined with direct regulation: combined with incentives and direct support for innovation and industrial evolution.

There are various options for the re-investment of such revenues on a 'fiscal neutrality' basis - i.e. with no change to the overall macro-economic balance of public and private. The current prospects centre on the political acceptability, the redistribution of winners and losers, the unintended side-effects and so on[40]. But behind the details, there are some fundamental questions which revolve around the political and institutional economy, and the contract of rights and responsibilities. When is a tax not a tax? (when it is a charge for services, to be hypothecated and/or reinvested?) When does a market 'fail'? (when intervention is required to meet wider policy objectives?) When is a capital investment counted as a revenue cost? (when the return is beyond the institutional boundary).

With such questions mostly pre-assumed, the current Treasury Budget rounds tend to focus on small changes at the margins, such as airport tax or waste levies, and each of these tends to be controversial. In contrast, the wider agenda of a One Planet Economy would look at the fundamental restructuring of the

---

[39] Sustainable Development Commission 2007: I will if you will: Towards sustainable consumption: London, SDC, available 2007 on www.sustainable.gov.uk

[40] Leicester, A (2006) The UK Tax System and the Environment: London, Institute of Fiscal Studies

economy, and the place of fiscal policy within that[41]. It would take a strategic approach, so that year on year changes would be gradual and amenable to longer term planning by businesses, investors and the public sector.

General principles for a One Planet Economy

To take such questions seriously then raises a more systems-level, holistic vision of a One Planet Economy, and the role of fiscal policy within it. There is no single way to represent such fundamental transformations, or to define a strategy where the One Planet targets are guaranteed. However the Ecological Budget UK programme has at least started to use its tools and methods to define some general principles for a One Planet Economy[42]. The pyramid diagram overleaf shows how 10 principles – not fixed in stone, but general approaches to complex agendas – are overlaid on the supply chain and resource flow framework.

- At the top of the pyramid is the 'ecological budgeting' principle, as the over-arching goal of the One Planet Economy programme: this sets quantitative targets on a strategic basis to enable long term planning.
- Fiscal policy - this assumes a pro-active role of stewardship by the public sector of common resources. This has implications for a wider range of instruments in taxation and spending, to be followed up in the CSR / CRR process.
- Development policy for stabilization and equity: local and regional economies should be resilient to the impacts of economic change and polarization, and empowered to realize their own potential.
- Capital investment and partnerships – on the basis that market transformation involves public-private-third sector partnerships, and that investment needs to combine entrepreneurial risk-taking with a long term view.
- Eco-systems market integration: at the centre are the active links between economic, social and environmental assets: through trading and investment systems, responsive planning, multi-level stewardship, real time monitoring, and multi-lateral decision-making.
- Labour and other stakeholders: surrounding every supply chain is a wider community. The most important of these are the employees, and their stake in the enterprise and in their own development, is paramount.
- Primary industries, trade and overseas development – this looks at the sources for the supply chain, and the imperative for development and empowerment of developing nations.
- Industry and integrated supply chains – addresses the core business activity, and particularly the allocation of responsibilities and incentives along complex supply chains and product lives.

---

[41] Hislop H (2006) Beyond Stern: the environmental challenge for the comprehensive spending review: London, Green Alliance

[42] Ravetz J (2007): Taking the first steps – Pathways to a One Planet Economy: Surrey, WWF-UK: available March 2007 www.ecologicalbudget.org.uk and www.eco-region.org

- Services, infrastructure and asset management: this focuses on the business case for strategic management and investment in assets such as national stocks of buildings, vehicles and so on, together with the human / social capital of the service sector.
- Consumer and social enterprise: finally at the demand side, there is the agenda for more 'sustainable consumption': this can be enabled by community actions, networks, non-profit organizations, other types of social market, lifestyle and cultural shifts.

Each of these principles represents a major component of an complex, inter-dependent economy. They are defined with a series of benchmarks which can start the process of measuring and comparing on a supply chain basis,, applied to each of the 'five capitals', in various levels of time and space.

10 principles for a One Planet Economy

System-level principles to enable benchmarking of a One Planet Economy:
based on the Ecological Budget resource flow / supply chain framework.

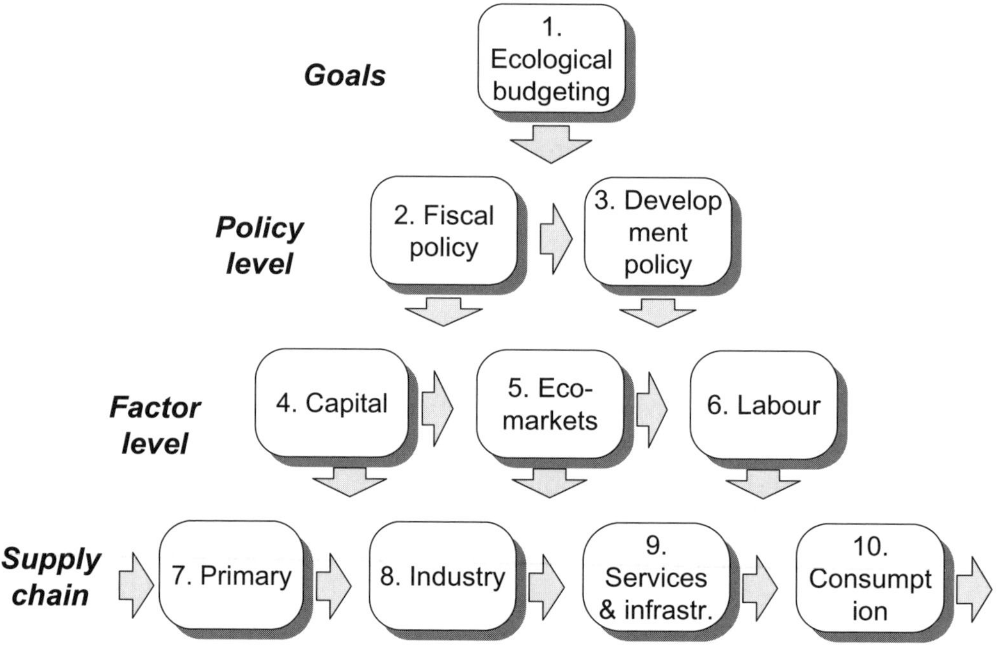

Figure 15.2 10 principles for a One Planet Economy

Implications for the CSR 2007

All the above suggests two basic alternatives for the CSR. For a short term agenda of political and economic stability, it could propose marginal changes to tax, investment, micro-economic differentials, subsidies and so on. For anything beyond it has to face the challenges of the national SD Strategy, the Climate Change Draft Bill, Stern Review, IPCC Fourth Assessment, UN Eco-systems Millennium Assessment, and many others.

This would see the CSR take a more far-reaching review of the longer term directions for the UK economy, with a strategic transformation and restructuring towards the goals of a One Planet Economy. It would involve fiscal policy as a highly pro-active instrument for facilitating a transformation in markets, supply chains, technologies, infrastructure and the demand side. It would involve looking beyond the end-of-pipe approach of current climate emissions policy, to a perspective on the wider economy and all its stakeholders. Underlying this is a new paradigm, already set out by Mr Miliband, on the pro-active role of government in public stewardship of common assets.

To achieve this, if not in 2007 then in the next round, I propose an extension to the CSR 2007 – the 'Comprehensive Resource Review' or CRR. This should set out a business case and investment portfolio for each sector and each government department in the transition towards a One Planet Economy. There is now the beginnings of an evidence base to support this from the Ecological Budget UK, and the One Planet Economy Network (OPEN). Such a CRR may not be simple or easy, but will be essential for the UK to achieve its aspirations.

16. Social enterprise

Rob Paton

Introduction

Social enterprise didn't feature in the last CSR – not even as a footnote. Will it feature this time? More to the point, should it? If so, in which areas of public spending?

To answer these questions requires an understanding of how social enterprises have blossomed since 1997. Ten years ago the term social enterprise was almost unheard of in this country and relatively few people had realised that business could actually be a way to achieve social and environmental goals, rather than simply financial ones. Nowadays, the Government estimates there are over 55,000 social enterprises, or five per cent of all businesses with employees - contributing £8 billion to GDP and turning over £27 billion a year[1].

Social enterprises now compete in a wide range of markets, from health and social care, housing, children's services and transport, to food and farming, environmental services and leisure. Some operate in mainstream commercial markets but for a social purpose (such as the fair-trade coffee company Cafédirect). Others are primarily dependent on public sector contracts (such as CIP, who work with Hounslow Council to deliver affordable leisure services). Many operate in marginal markets where profits are small or non-existent - so they cross-subsidise from other more profitable activities (for example, Unique Social Enterprise run a number of profit-making businesses to sustain the Unique Coffee Bar, a place for disadvantaged young people to come for social, emotional and educational support while enjoying cheap food and drink and free internet access). The social enterprise movement incorporates a diverse range of business models and legal forms, including cooperatives, development trusts, charities with a trading arm and many other forms of social business. Indeed, this extraordinary variety is one of the reasons why social enterprises and their contributions are still so poorly understood.

---

[1] HM Treasury considers social enterprises to be part of the 'third sector', and defines them as demonstrating "independence from the state, a motivation derived from values and social purposes rather than the pursuit of profit, and the re-investment of surpluses principally in pursuit of these values rather than for private distribution." This size estimate comes from the DTI's Annual Business Survey 2005, section 2.14 (www.sbs.gov.uk)

Why Social Enterprise?

Understandably, given the increased attention social enterprise is now receiving from government, some dismiss this as New Labour's latest policy fad. This is inaccurate on at least two counts. First, the encouragement of social enterprise is a policy that has been discretely pursued for a decade, for the most part by a network of what were initially junior and middle ranking ministers (some of whom are now quite senior). Social enterprise 'took off' over the last decade for a complex combination of reasons - but the government has been helping. Indeed, when the histories of the Blair government come to be written, this quiet cultivation of social enterprise may rank as one of its more important achievements. Secondly, this is a development that commands wide and deep cross-party support (indeed, David Cameron recently said: "I want us to be much more ambitious about what we allow social enterprises to do").

The reasons for this broad support are fairly obvious. In terms of modernising public services, both the state and the market (at least as we are used to thinking of them) are as much problems as solutions. Large centralised systems are inherently dysfunctional - this has been understood for years. Most glaringly, *no-one* – least of all government ministers rotated through their posts on a near-annual basis - can run the colossus of the NHS in a way that satisfies professional, patient and taxpayer expectations. But equally, the balloon of neo-liberal hopes has been deflating steadily, punctured by (*inter alia*) difficulties with PFI and the Railtrack fiasco. In many areas of public service, contracting to profit-maximisers embeds problems of incentive misalignment and mistrust. The trouble with New Labour's 'third way' thinking – as Giddens himself acknowledged - was that it was never clear about the organisational form that would underpin it, vesting too much hope in the vagaries of public-private partnerships.

Social enterprises have proved to be a much more robust hybrid; they can, and do, integrate social and economic considerations much more intimately and consistently. Structurally (as independent units), and through their governance arrangements, they provide handles on some of the central issues in public service reform; the need for greater user involvement ('co-production'), greater engagement of professional and other staff; greater 'joining up' of separated services, and, above all, more innovation and variety - hence greater dynamism in the evolution of services to address emerging needs and use new technologies.

The importance of these possibilities is obvious if one looks at the concerns that drive the 2007 Comprehensive Spending Review. These, and the key trends that the Treasury identified as likely to make achievement of the government's goals more difficult over the next decade, read like a roll-call of just those arenas in which social enterprises are active. For example, one trend is an increase in population in conjunction with a decrease in household size, putting pressure on resources and driving a greater need for housing. Housing associations, a well-established form of social enterprise, have to be a large part of the answer. But of course it is not just a matter of throwing up houses – communities have to be created, or re-created, which is where the innovation and added value arises.

TREES, an offshoot of Leicester Housing Association, for example, run a number of projects including the property-focussed social enterprise, Newlife, which had a turnover this year of £6 million. Newlife's objectives vary from area to area but include community development, job creation and skills development. It is, I would argue, a perfect illustration of 'joined up' public action.

Looking after ever-increasing numbers of elderly people, while giving them the respect and comfort they deserve, is another issue on the Treasury's list. With stories of abuse and neglect of those in care frequently making the headlines, this really is a challenge (with ever-increasing layers of supervision and audit part of the problem, rather than the solution). Again health and social care is a field in which social enterprises have a track record in successful 'turnarounds'. The Sandwell Community Caring Trust was formed ten years ago when £1.2m of unsustainable but highly valued care services were transferred from their local council. Apart from achieving significant savings, (an elderly care home run by the council at a cost of £452 per person per week now costs Sandwell just £328 pp/w to run) the 'bottom-up' social enterprise model has had a remarkable effect on staff morale – and consequently on patient care. According to a Sunday Times report on the best 100 companies in Britain to work for in 2006, Sandwell CCT had the happiest employees of all. This new found fulfilment reduced staff absenteeism from 22 days a year to less than one, and staff turnover to four per cent. These factors make a huge difference to elderly people who allow carers into their homes to perform the most intimate of chores.

Climate change and reducing our carbon footprint, is another on the Treasury's list - and another area in which social enterprises are leading the way. From replicable renewable energy schemes (such as Inspire's social franchising method) to intelligent waste management (the award-winning Bulky Bob's, who recycle unwanted furniture to stop it from being dumped in landfills), to Good Energy, the top provider of 100% green electricity, social enterprises are offering real solutions to both our current and future challenges.

However, social enterprises should not be seen as a magic bullet and they sometimes fail. Like any organization they can be run well or badly. Though it is easier to innovate through social enterprise, not all are, or remain, innovative and dynamic, by any means. Crucially, though, if they lose their way, much stronger pressures to be self-correcting are built in to their structure and financing. From a policy perspective, what matters are not particular social enterprises, but having a *system* of social enterprise with a strong presence in all the main fields of public service and social welfare.

The CSR and Social Enterprise - what should the government do?

Social enterprise needs a 'goldilocks' approach – not too hot and not too cold. 'Too hot' would be trying to force the pace with high-profile initiatives, targets to 'drive change' and large sums of money hastily dispensed to an arbitrary ministerial timetable. Social enterprises are not a tap that can be turned on when it suits. That said, 'too cold' would be ignoring the unnecessary obstacles facing social enterprises, and failing to build the infrastructure that is needed to make the most of them. More specifically, three inter-related strands of policy need to be pursued.

The first strand is technical and procedural. In fact, it is mainly a matter of the government making sure its own rules, procedures and support services recognise social enterprises and are appropriate for them. It is not glamorous work – but it matters a great deal. The Social Enterprise Coalition presents the case on these matters to the Office for the Third Sector and progress is being made. For example, the recent decision to provide additional funding to Regional Development Agencies (RDAs) to improve business support for social enterprise, acknowledges a long-standing weakness, but it is one that will take time and further attention to resolve.

A much bigger issue concerns procurement processes. Forty billion pounds is spent by Local Authorities in England each year buying goods, works and services but unfortunately due to the current tendency to move towards ever-larger aggregated contracts, as an apparent result of the Gershon efficiency review, social enterprises, which tend to be small or medium-sized businesses, are often locked out of the market. In some contexts, too, purchasers introduce wholly inappropriate monitoring and claw-back clauses – that would never be used in relation to private companies.

The Government needs to help social enterprises emerge from the public sector by raising awareness of social enterprise models and promoting their uptake while providing appropriate support for groups considering new approaches. All parties agree a big step to promote the use of social enterprises in public service delivery will be to retrain key commissioners and the Government has already pledged to train 2,000 public service commissioners through a National Programme for Third Sector Commissioning. The debate over contract size is still ongoing, but the Government has at least pledged to tackle obstacles to the use of social clauses in public contracts.

In the background to these debates lurks the measurement issue. All parties agree that it is vital now to build an evidence base on the social, economic and environmental value of social enterprise, and to develop better ways of reporting outcomes and impact. But *how* this is done is crucial – since there is a very real risk of stimulating the kind of measurement incontinence that has blighted parts of the public sector. This is a case where the government can do a lot without spending much, by bringing together the relevant expertise and experience – from the sector itself, from within government and from Universities and think-tanks. The results could be much improved official statistics, the sharing of good practice among both social enterprises and commissioners, and support for targeted research.

The second strand of policy concerns the development of the social investment marketplace – in order that more money, on more suitable terms, is available to social enterprise, especially those capable of 'scaling up'. Apart from a general shortage of social finance, the issues here include the lack of familiarity among lenders with the business models of social enterprises (or even their legal forms) leading to inappropriate terms and conditions; a serious gap in the supply of mezzanine finance (the problem of quasi-equity); and, by contrast with conventional capital markets, a still limited ecology of support and advisory services (given that the need is for intermediaries who are fluently multi-lingual across the various worlds of finance, government, business, and community). Historically, too, a strict position (within parts of the movement) regarding acceptable terms of finance has not helped potential social investors and social entrepreneurs reach deals. Hopefully, this block is being overcome – for example, creative use of the LLP form is offering new possibilities for reconciling risk and performance-related returns with social enterprise principles.

The government has listened, and has been taking steps to address these issues. Funds have been set up to provide investment, new legal forms have been created to make it easier for social enterprise to attract finance, Community Investment Tax Relief has been introduced, and a £30 million Community Assets Fund announced at the end of 2006, will, according to chancellor Gordon Brown, "encourage local authorities and the third sector to work together to expand community ownership of community assets". All this is useful. Ten years ago it might have been enough – but what was then a hungry infant is now becoming a voracious adolescent. It is a sign of success that funds counted in tens of millions are no longer sufficient (Steve Wyler, Director of the Development Trusts Association expects the Community Assets Fund to be oversubscribed many times). This is why, currently, all eyes are on the work of The Commission on Unclaimed Assets, established to recommend how the maximum public benefit can be gained from the proceeds of dormant bank accounts. One proposal is for the creation of a Social Investment Bank funded with at least £200 million, and this would be a real advance.

However, a single injection of (more-or-less) public funds will not resolve the finance issue. This is another case where sustained support is needed, taking a number of forms - and the money does not all have to come from the Chancellor. In particular, the government needs to consider how its support – perhaps in loan guarantees – can make it possible for social enterprises to access the burgeoning socially responsible investment funds in the mainstream capital markets. This is an area where developments are happening very fast.

The third strand of Treasury policy must be to encourage a strategic push towards the support and use of social enterprise within those government departments where the possibilities are obvious, but progress to date has been slow. The Department of Health (DoH) is currently the runaway leader – it has set up its own dedicated unit and recently announced a 73 million pound fund for social enterprise. If other parts of government, such as the Department for Communities and Local Government (DCLG), the Department of the Environment, Food and Rural Affairs (DEFRA) and the Department for Work and Pensions (DWP), were to follow in the DoH's pioneering footsteps, the possibilities for innovation would be enormous.

Leave aside other benefits claimed by advocates of social enterprise, cultivating a strong social enterprise sector is a capacity-building investment for future community regeneration and public service provision. Government is fully justified in continuing to support this success story – especially since the direct costs of doing so are quite trivial in terms of the CSR. The CSR is a chance to reconsider *how* the government spends our money, not just *what* it spends our money on. Discussions around the CSR can and should be used to ask questions about the place of social enterprise within the long-term plans of spending departments.

17. Mind the gap: bridging the gender divide

Claire Annesley, Francesca Gains & Kirstein Rummery

Introduction

As Gordon Brown puts the finishing touches to the 2007 Comprehensive Spending Review (CSR) and sets spending targets across Government, the question of gender equality ought to be at the forefront of Treasury thinking. In 2007, despite 10 years of a Labour Government describing itself as 'the most feminist in history'[1], there are still huge gender inequalities in the UK. The recently published Equalities Review, for instance, found that women – partnered or single – with children under eleven are the most disadvantaged in the labour market[2]. Electorally, the importance of addressing issues such as how to value unpaid care, achieving pay equality in the labour market and tackling poverty in old age is as critical as women's votes are crucial to continued electoral success[3]. And, in 2007 as in 1997, 2001 and 2005, there are feminists within the party at all levels working hard to lobby for change in respect of gender policies[4] [5] [6] [7]. At the same time the Treasury faces a new legal Gender Equality Duty which requires all public bodies to promote the equality of men and women. For new father Gordon Brown, questions of how to balance and value the contribution of both paid and unpaid work are likely to be pressing in his personal life as well as being an integral part of New Labour's social justice agenda.

The CSR provides the opportunity to spell out what strategies, investments and reforms in public policy are needed and to set the objectives and targets across Government to tackle gender inequality. In this chapter we argue that while the Government has introduced a range of policies that have a positive impact of women, it does not add up to a comprehensive and successful strategy

---

[1] Times (2005) Gender Pay Gap 'May Never Go' , 5 December

[2] Equalities Review (2007) Fairness and Freedom: The Final Review of the Equalities Review HMSO

[3] Worcester, B. (2005) Women's Support Gave Blair the Edge in The Observer 8 May, 6.

[4] Russell, M. (2005) Women in the Party: The Quiet Revolution in Meg Russell The Building of New Labour. The Politics of a Party Organisation, Basingstoke, Palgrave.

[5] Bright M. (2005) Labour's trouble with women in Observer 20 February (http://observer.guardian.co.uk/focus/story/0,,1418531,00.html accessed 16 June 2005).

[6] Lovecy, J. (2007) Framing claims for women: from 'Old' to 'New' Labour in Annesley, C. Gains, F. and Rummery, K. (2007) Women and New Labour: Engendering Politics and Policy Bristol: Policy Press

[7] Rummery, K. Gains, F. and Annesley, C. (2007) New Labour: Towards an engendered politics and policy? in Annesley, C. Gains, F. and Rummery, K. (2007) Women and New Labour: Engendering Politics and Policy Bristol: Policy Press

to tackle gender inequalities. A successful approach will be one in which: the gender impact of policy is assessed throughout the whole policy process; the true costs of achieving gender equality are budgeted properly; and policy addresses men's behaviour and rights as well as women's.

New Labour and Gender: Pressure for Change

An increased sensitivity towards gender under New Labour was triggered by the electoral imperatives associated with socio-economic change. As women have entered the labour market, they have become more likely to vote for progressive parties rather than conservative ones. As has been widely noted, Labour would have won the 1992 election had it gained the support of women voters and it learnt a valuable lesson from this: that winning the female vote was central to its future electoral campaigns[3]. Inside the party, a shift in politics and policy on gender issues has been pushed by committed feminist, left wing and trade union activists. These groups can in particular claim success in promoting improvements in gender democracy in the party and parliament despite the fact that their campaigns have generally met with ambivalence from the party leadership from Kinnock to Blair[4]. They have, however, found it harder to form a consensus in the party on policy issues[6]. Indeed, progress on gender equality issues has been driven more by the compelling economic imperative than by the electoral pressure for change perceived by party strategists and justice cases made by committed feminists within the party.

Since coming to power in 1997, New Labour has sought to tackle the high levels of social and inequality it inherited, predominantly by getting people back into paid work. As well as developing a commitment to, for example, reducing child poverty, the government has attempted to reduce the degree of gender inequality in British society. This is no mean feat. Gender inequalities permeate all dimensions of British society from the representation of women in political office to the labour market discrimination and disadvantage women face as a consequence, predominantly, of their role in the unpaid caring economy. Getting women into paid employment is not an automatic route to narrowing gender inequalities.

Women's attachment to the labour force is weakened by caring responsibilities for children, the sick, and the elderly. According to the Women's Budget Group, "UK society saves £57 billion a year thanks to unpaid work carried out by people caring for the disabled, ill or elderly relatives"[8]. And this caring work is still, disproportionately, carried out by women; approximately 60% of carers are women. When women do return to paid work, they often struggle to update their skills, obtain jobs that reflect their qualifications or find work that is compatible with their caring responsibilities. This means that women in the UK tend to be concentrated in part-time and low paid sectors and are often over

---

[8] Women's Budget Group (2006c) A Gender Lens on Public Service Agreements (PSAs), September

qualified for the jobs they do. This gendered dynamic to the labour market is at the root of the UK's gender pay gap – one of the highest in the EU. According to the Government's own statistics, women working full time are currently paid, on average, 87.4% of men's hourly pay; while women working part-time are paid 59.8% of men's hourly pay[9].

Women's low pay, in turn, structures the gendered poverty that exists across women's life cycles. It has a proven impact in child poverty, not least because some 53% of lone parent households are classed as poor with 90% of lone parents being women8. What is more, women's involvement in unpaid care coupled with their poor earning capacity in the formal labour market has a significant impact on the gendered investment in pensions. Less than 20% of women qualify for the basic state pension, compared to 98% of men, and one in five single female pensioners lives in poverty. Women pensioners in England receive an average of 57% of men's income, just £97 a week[10].

Getting women into work is central to the Government's commitment to improving gender equality. However, the dilemma for the Government is that the gendered economy is in fact a key driver of women's inequality[11]. What is more, while the Government also hopes that women's economic activity will boost the UK economy's economic performance, productivity and efficiency, it is a factor in the poor productivity of the UK as women, because of caring duties and discrimination, are not able to work to their skill levels and full capacity. The Government's attempts to address issues of gender inequality have by and large taken second priority to its mainstream economic agenda.

Getting 'Gender' on the Agenda

Internal feminist pressure for change had more of an impact on issues of representation and the gender governance machinery than it did on concrete policies to promote gender equality[6]. Following the election of Labour in 1997, a new Women's Unit (WU) was established with the aim of putting "women's interests into the mainstream of government policy" and to "scrutinise legislation to promote sexual equality and with promoting female friendly policies"[12]. The work of the WEU was championed by a new Minister for Women, though this is a portfolio that moves between departments, has few institutional resources and no ministerial salary. In early 1998, the Government adopted a policy of mainstreaming which committed all departments to assess policies for their

---

[9] Women and Equalities Unit. What is the Pay Gap and why does it exist? http://www.womenandequalityunit.gov.uk/pay/pay_facts.htm [accessed 26 March 2007].

[10] BBC (2004) 'Women Losing Out in Retirement' http://news.bbc.co.uk/1/hi/wales/3540679.stm [accessed 06/03/07]

[11] Women's Budget Group (2007) Women's Budget Group Response to the HM Treasury's Pre-Budget Report 2006, February

[12] Squires, J. and Wickham-Jones, M. (2004) New Labour, Gender Mainstreaming and the Women and Equality Unit, British Journal of Politics and International Relations 6(1) 81-98.

impact upon gender and the Women's Unit provided the policy guidelines on departmental implementation[13] [14] [15] [16].

The (renamed) Women and Equality Unit (WEU) subsequently introduced the Gender Equality Public Service Agreement (PSA) as part of the Spending Review of 2002. This is a tool which 'requires the WEU to work with Government Departments to bring about measurable improvements across a range of gender equality indicators, as a contribution to the Government's goals on equalities and social inclusion'[17] [18]. More recently the WEU has developed a public sector duty to promote gender equality, commonly referred to as the Gender Equality Duty (GED). This will come into effect on 07 April 2007. The GED places a legal requirement on public authorities to promote gender equality and eliminate sex discrimination. It diverts the responsibility for demonstrating that men and women are treated fairly to public authorities instead of relying on individuals to make complaints about sex discrimination.

A Scorecard of Achievement

Over the ten years of New Labour's term in office the record of achievement in reducing gender inequality and tackling women's poverty, income disparity and addressing public policy provision in areas of concern to women's lives has been documented in a series of publications from both inside and outside Government[19] [20] [21] [22] [23] [24].

---

[13] Ward, L. (1998) Women given Whitehall Voice, Guardian 19 May

[14] Squires, J and Wickham, Jones, M. (2002) Mainstreaming in Westminster and Whitehall: From Labour's Ministry for Women to the Women and Equality Unit, Parliamentary Affairs 55, 57-70

[15] Veitch, J. (2005) Looking at Gender Mainstreaming in the UK Government, International Feminist Journal of Politics, 7 (4) 600-06.

[16] Women and Equality Unit (2007) What has the Government achieved for Women? www.womenandequalityunit.gov.uk/about/government_women.htm [accessed 06/03/07].

[17] Women and Equalities Unit Gender Equality Public Service Agreement http://www.womenandequalityunit.gov.uk/gender_equality_duty/gender_psa.htm [accessed 26 March 2007].

[18] Women's Budget Group (2006a) Advancing Equality for Men and Women: Government proposals to introduce a public sector duty to promote gender equality, January

[19] Toynbee, P. and Walker, D. (2001) Did Things Get Better? An audit of labour's successes and failures Harmondsworth: Penguin.

[20] Rake, K. (2001) Gender and New Labour's Social Policies in Journal of Social Policy Vol. 30, No 2 pp 209-231

[21] Women and Equality Unit (2003) Delivering on Gender Equality. Supporting the PSA Objective on Gender Equality 2003-2006 WEU/DTI

[22] Women and Equality Unit (2005) Delivering on Gender Equality: A progress report on the Gender Equality Public Service Agreement 2003-2006. Supporting Gender Equality across Government WEU/DTI

Early in the first term, New Labour took several measures aimed at poverty reduction. On top of an overall strategy to get adults into employment, the Government introduced policies to boost the incomes of the poorest workers and families. Although these were not necessarily targeted directly at women, they impacted on women disproportionately because women are poorer at all stages of their lives. The National Minimum Wage (NMW), which benefited 1.5 million of the lowest paid workers, two thirds of whom are women who were amongst the lowest paid workers[25] and the Working Families Tax Credit (now Working Tax Credit) boosts the incomes of low paid families. Parents were given extra support in reconciling work and family life through the National Childcare Strategy, which sought to boost the number of childcare places, as well as the extension of maternity leave and the introduction of paid paternity leave and unpaid parental leave. Many of these policies were further developed over Labour's second and third terms.

These policies were primarily directed at getting adults into employment and reducing poverty. While some of New Labour's initiatives had a direct and positive impact on women, it was not a gender equality strategy and the impact on women and men was differentiated. Indeed the impact on women was also very varied with differential impacts on working women and non working women, disabled women, those caring, those in partnerships and those with secure income and those in low paid jobs[7]. In terms of policies specifically addressing gender inequality, there is evidence that over New Labour's three terms, the gender policy machinery is having an impact. Firstly in raising awareness of issues around gender inequality across Government. Secondly in using the PSA target setting processes to institutionalise a gender focus on departmental policy activity.

Although gender mainstreaming initiatives of the WU received patchy support from the Prime Minister's Office, indicating the low political saliency of this agenda, one critical intervention by the Women's Unit was to become involved, although at a late stage in ensuring equality issues were included in the first set of Treasury public spending agreements[15]. Overall, the literature suggests that the women's policy machinery and the policy of mainstreaming at this time had only variable success. The impact on policy has been strongest where the concerns of the Women's Unit and New Labour in general have coincided and in Departments headed by sympathetic Ministers[26]. In the second term, the renamed Women and Equality Unit, working under the Minister for Women, Patricia Hewitt in the Department for Trade and Industry (DTI) began to shape

---

[23] Women's Budget Group (2006b) Women Budget Group's Response to HM Treasury's Budget 2006, May

[24] Annesley, C. Gains, F. and Rummery, K. (eds) (2007) Women and New Labour: Engendering Politics and Policy Bristol: Policy Press

[25] Triesman, D. (2002) Women in Politics after Estelle, The Guardian 31 October, p. 23

[26] Durose, C. and Gains, F. (eds) Engendering the Machinery of Governance in Annesley, C. Gains, F. and Rummery, K. (2007) Women and New Labour: Engendering Politics and Policy Bristol: Policy Press

the policy making agenda[12][15][26]. Responsibility for mainstreaming passed back to individual departments but the WEU retained a role in monitoring achievement of mainstreaming targets. Although when the 2002 PSA targets were published there was disappointment that there was not more explicit gender awareness.[12] But the WEU was able to strengthen the second round of PSA set in 2003[15].

For the first time, the DTI set a gender equality public service agreement to take stock of the achievement of other departments in meeting their targets. The PSA aimed to "bring about measurable improvements in gender equality across a range of indicators as part of the Government's objectives on equality and social inclusion"[21]. This PSA and the reporting and accountability it created is described as 'the most powerful gender mainstreaming tool'[15] and an "excellent initiative aiming to give focus to this key area and to tackle gender inequality across government"[8]. Targets set by departments and monitored by the WEU included better representation of women on public bodies, in the senior civil service and in the science and technology industry; increases in usage of Government sponsored business support services; DTI employees reporting satisfaction with their work life balance; working with the Equal Opportunities Commission to ensure large employers undertake pay reviews; the creation of new childcare places and taking action to reduce domestic violence[22].

By the third Labour term, there are signs that gendered awareness has become more embedded into Treasury thinking[27]. Inside Government, the WEU has undeniably been central. It is likely that the WEU will join the Commission on Equality and Human Rights when it replaces the separate Equal Opportunities Commission, Disability Rights Commission and the Commission for Race and Equality in October 2007[12][28]. It remains to be seen if moving the WEU out of its departmental home and away from the centre of the machinery of governance will inhibit or enhance oversight of the application of the Gender Equality Duty. Outside Government, the work of the Women's Budget Group has been absolutely critical[29]. This group of academics, non-governmental-organisation representatives and trade unions have sought to work with the Treasury to identify 'where are the resources going and what is their impact on gender equality'[30].

Perhaps the most striking example of gender aware policy making is the new pensions policy which explicitly sets out to address through public policy instruments gendered inequality in accessing state pensions. For the first time, women are given pensions credits for time spent in unpaid caring work when

---

[27] HM Treasury/DTI (2004) Gender Analysis of Expenditure Project. Final Report London: The Stationery Office

[28] http://www.cehr.org.uk accessed 3 May 2007

[29] Himmelweit, S. (2005) Making Policy-Makers More Gender Aware: Experiences and Reflections from the Women's Budget Group in the United Kingdom in Journal of Politics and Policy Vol. 27, No. 1/2pp. 109-22

[30] Women's Budget Group http://www.wbg.org.uk/index.htm [accessed 26 March 2007].

they could not build up their own pension rights[31] [32]. While this is a step in the right direction in terms of recognising the value of unpaid care work for promoting gender equality, it does not fully compensate women for potential loss of earnings during periods of care and while it helps future female pensioners, it does not help those who are poor today.

However in the Treasury's review of trends and challenges which should inform the investments and reforms required in the CSR, a gender awareness is conspicuous by its absence[33]. The document notes falling fertility rates and that more women are entering the workforce but does not address gendered disparities in the social and economic circumstances of men and women nor the potential consequences and implications for public finances. And in the third term, the huge fiscal difficulty of dealing with gender inequality is emerging when looking at the impact on local authorities who are required to equalise pay between male and female employees. The move is expected to boost women's pay and will add 4% to wage bills and cost authorities £3 billion cost in back pay[34]. There is still much for New Labour to do on the gender equalities front.

A Brown Budget for Gender

Looking to the forthcoming CSR there are good reasons to be optimistic about the possibilities for setting CSR objectives and targets which act to address the gender inequalities outlined above. Firstly there is administrative machinery in place and growing experience of setting, monitoring and delivering PSA targets to address gender inequalities. Secondly there is the new Gender Equality Duty which places a legal requirement on public bodies to promote the equality of men and women. Thirdly the activism and expertise of key actors in and around Government will continue to inform and fight for policies to address the relative poverty of women and their restricted life chances. In particular the Women's Budget Group combines both technical expertise and realism in how is seeks to work with the Treasury. Sadly there are also reasons to be pessimistic about the degree to which addressing gender inequalities will be adopted despite the

---

[31] Pension Commission (Turner Report). (2006) A New Pension Settlement for the Twenty First Century: The Second Report of the Pensions Commission, London: The Stationery Office

[32] Rummery, K. (2007) Caring, Citizenship and New Labour: Dilemmas and contradictions for disabled and older women in Annesley, C. Gains, F. and Rummery, K. (2007) Women and New Labour: Engendering Politics and Policy Bristol: Policy Press

[33] HM Treasury (2006) Cm 6889 Releasing the resources to meet the challenges ahead: value for money in the 2007 Comprehensive Spending Review, London: The Stationery Office

[34] Local Government Employers Report, November 2006 Unblocking the route to equal pay in local government www.lge/aio/60274 [accessed 8 March 2007]

pressing legal, administrative and electoral imperatives facing a Brown administration. So what is holding New Labour back?

Firstly, achieving gender equality in the labour market comes with a cost which could impact on other areas of public spending. Recognising the real value of the contribution that women make in the unpaid caring economy also has significant financial implications be it in the form of compensating women for this work or in the sense of providing an affordable alternative of comparable quality.

- In order to accurately assess the gendered implications of policy reform the Treasury should adopt gender budgeting and ensure gender analysis is incorporated into allocating and tracking public revenue and spending.

Secondly as the Women's Budget Group continues to point out, the Government has succeeded in introducing isolated policies which are certainly of benefit to women, but it falls short of developing an overarching and comprehensive strategy for promoting gender equality policies which complement and reinforce each other across the breadth of its economic and social policy. While the Gender PSA goes some way in achieving this, the WBG's suspicion is that it is constructed to pre-existing and achievable targets, rather than being the product of strategic planning on the part of Government[18].

- A more strategic approach which assesses the gender implications of policy from design, through implementation and to evaluation is required.

Finally, achieving gender equality is not solely about the status and situation of women; it also requires the Government to tackle the status and behaviour of men. However, New Labour is reluctant to do so, as the recent reforms of maternity and paternity leave clearly illustrate. Here the Government openly advocated gender equality regarding the care of young children but it fell short of providing men with equal and independent rights to take paid leave to care for a young child. Such gendered discrepancies in rights reinforce the traditional perceptions of roles in public and private life and in turn perpetuate gender inequality.

- The CSR should endorse future gendered policy developments which overtly address men's rights and behaviour as well as women's.

If Brown wants to win a fourth Labour term of office, addressing the gender gap, and being seen to address the gender gap, will be a critical in terms of winning women's votes as it was in 1997, 2002 and 2005. Certainly Cameron's Conservatives appear to be positioning themselves to appeal to this half of the UK population in setting work life balance issues high on the Conservative party policy agenda. Cameron is on the record in asserting he is committed to being a good parent even if achieving the highest office of state and will seek to be able to put his children to bed at least one night a week[35]. For us, this does not represent achieving the kind of work life balance which men will need to engage

---

[35] Cooke, R. (2007) Balancing Act, Observer 11 February.

with if gendered inequalities are to be addressed. However we can only hope that having two fathers with young children both vying to appeal to women's votes, will serve to ramp up the pressure for serious gender targets across Government.

18. eGovernment: terminology and scope

Peter Kawalek

Introduction

Various labels are now used to describe government spending on information and communications technology (ICT) renewal. Most obviously, the term eGovernment has been used and is associated with the use of new technologies such as the internet and websites. Latterly, the term 'transformation' has been promoted, notably by the Cabinet Office. Although precise definitions are not available, 'transformation' is concerned with creating and anticipating the future through changes to services, rather than just the addition of technology to those services.

In making this distinction, between adding technology to services (i.e. sustaining them), and changing services (i.e. introducing new models and disrupting old models), parallels are drawn with current thinking on organisational innovation. Studies show that different change strategies are needed for changes that sustain an existing model, vis-à-vis changes that introduce a new model. This point will be explored in greater detail later in this chapter. Throughout the debate over ICT there are problems with the use of alternative terminology, as the ICT industry at large is famously bedevilled by jargon.

In central and local government, the pursuit of 100% electronic access targets has been seen as the primary focus of eGovernment (in local government this was manifest as BVPI 157). The evidence is that these targets led to electronic channels of communications (websites and call-centres) being added to services, rather than these services being remodelled in a more fundamental way. From this arises the need for a radical level of change as expressed through the term 'transformation.'

Opportunities for Transformation

The essential role of new ICT is to alter the economics of organisation and thereby create opportunities for different models of organisation. This allows both cost and quality improvements to take place. In society at large, there are many examples of how new ICT allows different models of business. The internet companies such as Amazon, eBay and Google are the most obvious. Increasingly, attention has also turned to the entertainment and media industries as traditional models have been challenged by a new internet and download culture. Even exalted names like the BBC, ITV, MTV and CBS are confronting the most profound challenges of their existence. Elsewhere, traditional 'bricks and mortar' companies like Tesco have also been radically altered by new ICT, particularly as supply-chains have developed as global networks. Traditional sectors such as retail and manufacturing now offer considerable evidence as to how ICT is altering the economics of organisation.

For some time a number of sources have speculated that government would be included among sectors that are most profoundly affected by the opportunities of new ICT. This is because a very substantial proportion of its activity is concerned with administration (e.g. customer records, applications, procedural reports) and such activity is amenable to cost and quality benefits brought by the use of digital media. However, many sources (including specialist magazines like BusinessWeek, academic journals, government reports such as Cabinet Office[1]), have warned of the government sector's poor record with ICT projects and change management more generally.

Today the government stands surrounded by cross-currents. ICT may enable its transformation, but it has not in the past been effective in its deployment of ICT. Later in this section it will be shown that the change strategies currently employed by the government will not resolve these cross-currents.

Will There Be A Radical New World of Government?

Examples from other sectors are relevant because they are subject to the same economic costs as government. These costs of organising can be understood through the economic notion of 'transaction costs,' which is associated with the canonical studies of Coase and then later, Williamson[2]. The concept encapsulates all cost associated with the procurement of some service or good. Therefore, transaction costs are made up of search and analysis costs as well as price. It has been shown that ICT can radically diminish transaction costs[3]. This simple principle underpins the effective development of call centres, e-commerce and many 'internal' ICT applications. For example, with e-Bay it is now feasible in total transaction cost terms to purchase items (e.g. mundane household items) that previously would have been cost-inefficient to procure.

At the same time, new ICT is impacting greatly on modern culture with the internet in particular being the vehicle for social change. The impacts are again well documented in the media with the rise of MySpace, You Tube and self-publishing through blogs etc. In a short period of time this will mean that the Government is recruiting from a labour market whose younger members have different cultural experiences and expectations. For example, they will have grown up spending more time on the internet than watching TV. They will expect to be able to quickly retrieve information on a global scale (e.g. what is happening on climate change in California, or Norway). And they will be more

---

[1] Cabinet Office, (2000) Successful IT: Modernising Government in Action, Cabinet Office, UK.

[2] Willamson OE, (1981) The Economics of Organization: The Transaction Cost Approach, American Journal of Sociology, 1981

[3] Downes, L., Mui., C, (1998), Unleashing the Killer App., Harvard Business School Press.

skilled in the use of wiki, blog and video than they will in conventional report writing.

It is already possible to conceive of a radically altered world of ICT-enabled government. To take one example, we might ask how the Electronic Social Care Record (ESCR) will impact on social services. It is feasible that it could be used to allow centralised social work offices to be replaced by many, small offices. These might be, for example, above charity shops or similar accommodation on high streets. Work practices might likewise be altered, with staff using the offices when they need to (e.g. to meet colleagues or clients), but also carrying out mobile-working or home-based working. This is all possible because ICT means that staff no longer have to sit near to their records (usually contained in filing cabinets in their centralised office), as the information can be made available wherever they are located. In this way, ICT can be used to promote the ideals of 'New Localism.'

As well as being a vehicle for affecting the location of services, ICT can be a vehicle that supports new models of service provision. It is suggested above that new social work offices could be located above charity shops or in similar accommodation. Extending this, the ICT also makes it feasible that the charities could employ the social workers, as the information is again wholly transferable. Therefore there is no practical reason why staff, already working to the standards of a professional body, need to be employed by the local authority. Other agencies like national charities or corporations could also offer services. In this way, ICT can be used to promote the ideals of 'choice.'

Extending this point, social workers might prefer not to be employed at all, but may organise through self-employment, co-operatives and similar models. Social work practices might be established on a basis that is analogous to General Practice in the NHS. A new world of social enterprise might open up. Again this is possible because there are much lower costs of transferring information between agencies (i.e. the local authority and any other agency can easily share client records subject only to the approval of that client).

As well as affecting the location, provider and mode of social-work services, ICT can be used as a vehicle to change the processes themselves. For example, the procurement of specialist care services, managed care, youth homes and so forth could be managed by new, centralised booking agencies. These would be similar to the way in which Expedia, LastMinute and the East London Lettings Company act as intermediaries between many different providers and their customer base.

Social workers could be given web and telephone access to databases and advisors on care provision. The economies of scale involved in such organisations show that ICT can be used to promote the aims of 'Gershon.'

In this illustrative example, new ICT has been shown to be capable of addressing the challenges of the New Localism, Choice and Gershon agendas. Throughout, the principle is that ICT be used to change the way in which services are provided. The details of the examples are not the main issue (e.g. whether charities would want to provide social care, or whether social workers would like to be self-employed). The illustrative example serves to illustrate the potential of ICT to enable changes to organisational models.

In the example, the large and hitherto monolithic organisation of social care could be replaced by a network of many smaller providers acting with common standards. The network utilizes common information and has a common administrative infrastructure. It is both more local and more central. Government now becomes networked. The example challenges and changes organisational structure.

Many base assumptions are challenged and rethought in this illustrative example and yet the ESCR, upon which it is based, is no more than today's technology. Future technology may enable more radical permutations and new staff but may have a more radical interpretation of what is desirable.

Moreover, this is only an example. What is true of social services is true of many other public services. Many new permutations are possible. For example, why should the environmental services of a local authority stop at its borders? Why shouldn't a truck cross a boundary to pick-up fly-tipping or bulky waste? With information sent to the cab of the truck, and seamlessly between accounting departments, it is possible that authorities could use each other's resources in order to best optimise services. Similarly, why should the trucks belong to the council at all? What if it were to encourage some local provision by independent contractors? It is possible to do this in this and many other service areas.

The Reality

It is difficult to reliably calculate government spending on eGovernment. For example, it has been reported that local government planned to spend £3.1 billion up to 2005/6 (with central government input to this being £675 million). However, it is difficult to be certain that the larger figure excludes 'routine' IT spending. However, across the sector, central and local, it is clear that spending has already been substantial. Government aims for 'transformation' are to be met by further resources, supporting new projects. Typically, funds are given to, or managed by, the institutions concerned in order that they can take on the additional costs of changing their operations. Within each institution further decisions are made about how to allocate change resources, usually with some combination of operational and ICT management picking up both the resources and the responsibility.

The lesson from current studies is that if ICT is to be used to facilitate new organisational structures, then an appropriate change strategy needs to be adopted. This is the argument concerned with sustaining versus radical innovation. The basic message is that sustaining change can be entrusted to the organisational structures that will deploy it. The usual change management disciplines then follow (stakeholder involvement, excellent communication, project management etc.) However, where change is intended to develop new structures (i.e. it is disruptive), then alternative change strategies are needed. Typically these rely on new, empowered and well-resourced teams creating pilots for the design of the service. The creation of this separate change team is the key change management requirement. In some circumstances this separate team will develop and become responsible for the delivery of the new service, not just its design.

However, this distinction between sustaining change and the creation of new models (disruptive change of winners and losers) is not reflected in the way that government sets-up and resources its change initiatives. Instead, the sustaining model prevails in all cases. This means that resources are given to the very structures that are the target of the reform. In this, government unwittingly strengthens what it wishes to reconstruct.

When funding is allocated in this conventional way, typically what follows is that a conventional change management route is used to try to induce an appetite for radical change (i.e. stakeholder involvement, excellent communication, project management etc.) This actually makes bold change less likely as it submits it to a committee-review process and the reservations of many stakeholders. At best, people are asked to 'buy-in' to something that they cannot envisage. Moreover, in any contest for further resources (e.g. money or people's time), the status quo is likely to prevail over the disruptive future.

Therefore, increased government spending does not resolve the cross-currents surrounding ICT projects (i.e. that they are pushed towards more radical ends but are still subject to the limitations that have afflicted previous government ICT projects). Instead, attention must be given to the direction of this spending and its alliance with the required change strategy for the project being undertaken.

In theoretical terms, the position is that radical change programmes have a strong bottom-up, cellular element that meets a vague but sufficiently aspirational overall vision. Many of the above examples conform to this principle e.g. the creation of Amazon, eBay, Google, MySpace and YouTube were all small, cellular initiatives that grew as their success was proven. Moreover, even in a corporate example like Tesco, many radical initiatives are constructed outside of the mainstream of the organisation (its successful internet commerce initiative was created in such a way). The history of successful innovation offers up many more examples of this kind of approach, including the invention of the PC itself (by IBM), the creation of the world-wide web (at CERN) and the development of TCP/IP at the Defense Advanced Research Projects Agency. Other examples include a number of banking services (e.g. Egg and Smile, or more radically, Zopa at www.zopa.com) as well as innovations in pharmaceuticals and public utilities (e.g Ecotricity).Government does normally sponsor this kind of exploratory change model and instead seeks to impose a sustaining change strategy upon disruptive innovation.

Failure to adopt appropriate change strategies will mute the impact of new technology. Government will spend more on IT and fail more. There will be some successes but commentators will not view it as 'transformation.' It will be more of the same.

19. Government regulation and small firms

Francis Chittenden & Tim Ambler

Reviewing UK government approaches to deregulation over the last 20 years (1987-2006), a recent report[1] concluded that despite the good intentions of both Conservative and Labour governments, these initiatives have been largely unsuccessful. This is unsurprising since regulation is one of the three main levers of government, alongside taxation and government spending.

Ministers rely on regulation to influence events and deliver commitments made to the various groups they believe will shape electoral opinions, such as consumers or trade unions. Such behaviour is consistent with the 'economic theory of regulation'[2] where, indirectly, favours are granted by government to particular interest groups in return for sustained political support.

Regulatory Impact Assessment

In an attempt to make civil servants and ministers more accountable for their regulatory activities the present government introduced Regulatory Impact Assessments (RIAs) in 1998. RIAs were defined[3] as:

a policy tool, which assesses the impact, in terms of costs, benefits and risks of any proposed regulation.......if used early enough, an RIA helps policy makers to think through consequences of proposals, improving the quality of advice to Ministers and encouraging informed public debate.

The 2000 RIA guidance stated (page 11, para 6.1) that "There is an expectation that benefits will almost always exceed costs" and Ministers must sign the RIA to specifically confirm "that the benefits justify the costs".

However, several studies have concluded that the RIA system has become a 'tick box' exercise that many civil servants feel obliged to complete in order to facilitate the passage of new regulations. Ministers do not appear to be constrained by the declaration even though few RIAs present adequate evidence of the benefits that might accrue[4]. Thus, to date, RIAs do not:

---

[1] Ambler T and Chittenden F (2007), Deregulation or Déjà Vu? UK Deregulation Initiatives 1987/2006, published by the British Chambers of Commerce, London, p. 31.

[2] Stigler George J. (1971), The Theory of Economic Regulation, Bell Journal of Economics and Management Science, 21.

[3] Cabinet Office, Regulatory Impact Unit (2000), Good Policy Making: A Guide to Regulatory Impact Assessments.

[4] NAO (2006), Evaluation of Regulatory Impact Assessments 2005–06, Report by the Comptroller and Auditor General (HC 1305 Session 2005–06); Ambler, T, Chittenden, F, and Ahuja, K (2006), Regulators: Box Tickers or Burdens Busters? London, British Chambers of Commerce; Ambler, T, Chittenden, F, and Hwang, C, (2005), Regulation: Another Form of Taxation London, British Chambers of Commerce; Ambler, T, Chittenden, F, and Obodovski, M, (2004), Are Regulators Raising Their Game? UK

1. Challenge the need for new regulations.
2. Substantively improve the new regulations to make them less burdensome and/or more effective.
3. Create the mechanism for review and revision, or rescission, of regulations at a later date.

Consequently the regulatory burden on business has risen rapidly in the last decade[5] leading the government's Better Regulation Task Force to estimate that the cost of regulation to the UK economy amounts to approximately £100bn per annum[6], equivalent to 10-12% of gross domestic product.

Today a significant proportion of regulatory costs result from Brussels[7]. Unfortunately the EU Impact Assessment system is in the early stages of development and currently represents a method of enhanced communication about proposed regulations rather than a system of assessment of likely impacts[8], since these remain largely unmeasured.

Democratic Control

The failure of Impact Assessment systems might be less damaging if UK Parliament exercised tighter control over regulatory activities. However, unlike the careful scrutiny to which government taxation and spending plans are subjected, most new regulations pass into law with little detailed scrutiny, for a number of reasons:

1. At least 60% of new regulations are enacted by Statutory Instruments and, despite the fact that SIs fall within the remit of several parliamentary committees few are ever challenged[9].

2. Regulatory impact assessments are frequently lengthy and turgid documents, consequently few MPs commit the time necessary to understand and dissect them.

3. In addition the poor quality of most RIAs is acknowledged by MPs and this further convinces them of the futility of devoting time to their examination.

Regulatory Impact Assessments in 2002/3 London, British Chambers of Commerce; Ambler, T, Chittenden, F, and Shamutkova, M, (2003), Do Regulators Play By the Rules? An Audit of UK Regulatory Impact Assessments London, British Chambers of Commerce.

[5] As evidenced by the British Chambers of Commerce 'Burdens Barometer' that lists all Regulations that create a net burden on business in excess of £15m per annum. As of June 2007 the total stands at almost £56bn.

[6] Better Regulation Task Force (2005) Regulation - Less is More, March, p.12.

[7] The British Chambers of Commerce 2007 Burdens Barometer shows that 72.5% of the costs to business arise from EU laws.

[8] Radaelli CM, (2004), The diffusion of regulatory impact analysis – Best practice or lesson-drawing? European Journal of Political Research, 43.

[9] Ambler T, Chittenden F and Xiao D (2007), The Burden of Regulation: Who's looking out for us? , London, British Chambers of Commerce, April, pp27.

The explanations expressed in points two and three above are based upon discussions with a small number of MPs. However, the Better Regulation Executive's current proposal that RIAs should have a single page summary on the front is presumably designed to partially address this issue. The National Audit Office is currently investigating the extent to which RIAs inform the parliamentary process, so a more complete picture will emerge later in 2007.

Lax parliamentary control of regulation is not unique to the UK and has been remarked upon by the OECD who observed[10] in 1997 that:

> regulatory costs are the least controlled and least accountable amongst government costs. Many governments have no idea how much of their national wealth they are spending through regulation.

In 2005 the UK followed the Dutch lead and introduced a mechanism to assess the 'Administrative Burdens' of regulation. The logic being that whilst parliament may have voted for the policy costs of a regulation (e.g. additional holiday pay necessary for staff to receive four weeks paid leave) they did not fully countenance the resulting additional administrative costs (e.g, the extra cost of maintaining records to show that staff have been given four weeks holiday). Administrative costs are strongly redistributive in their incidence since small organisations face fixed costs that mean that administration is much more expensive than for larger organisations. Thus small businesses incur the majority of Administrative Burdens in the economy and small firms have articulate representative organisations that, as predicted by the economic theory of regulation cited above, ministers need to respond to.

In fact there is evidence[11] to suggest that small firms face higher costs in respect of both the administration and policy consequences of regulation, although this is not well understood by civil servants or Ministers. Evidence of this lack of understanding may be seen from the fact that only a tiny minority[12] of RIAs identify additional costs of regulation for small firms even where regulations have a large impact on business.

Some of the reasons why small firms incur higher policy costs of regulation, as well as higher administrative costs are as follows:

1. There are fixed costs associated with most regulatory change e.g. searching for and assessing the appropriateness of new equipment to comply with a regulation (such as the 'Work at Height' rules). Small businesses have fewer economies of scale over which to spread these costs.

2. For similar reasons, new equipment and assets tend to be more expensive for small operators per unit of output. Small firms also tend to have to acquire multi-purpose equipment as they have to compete on the basis of flexibility and service.

---

[10] Quoted in Regulation - Less is More, BRTF (2005) p12.

[11] Chittenden F, Kauser S and Poutziouris P (2002), The Regulatory Burdens of Small Firms: A Literature Review, Sheffield, The Small Business Service.

[12] Just 8% of RIAs issued in 2005/6.

3. Small firms incur higher costs of capital than larger businesses. Thus all forms of investment expenditure are more expensive for smaller firms.

4. Small firms do not have in house regulatory expertise such as a health and safety officer. Consequently new regulations require the attention of the owners to understand and make decisions about the appropriate response. Thus regulatory change constrains or exhausts the supply of general management talent more quickly in small firms than in larger businesses.

5. If the owners feel unable to cope with the additional volume or complexity of regulatory work they will have to recruit external advisers, often consultants, who will probably be relatively expensive. Consultants may also exhibit a tendency to advise clients to over-comply, at the margin, in order to reduce the professional indemnity risks that consultants face.

6. Because small firms' profits are smaller and more volatile than large firms, small businesses are less likely to be able to offset the costs of regulation against tax. Even in years when the costs can be used to reduce tax charges, the applicable tax rate will tend to be lower than for large firms. Thus small business owners incur a higher proportion of the net costs of regulation than do larger companies.

7. Finally, small scale of operations means that human and physical assets are less easily divisible than in larger firms. For example, where a small business with two machines that are utilised 24 hours per day faces a 10% reduction in output, because regulations require that certain potentially toxic substances have to be removed from the manufacturing process, it will have to purchase a new machine that can only be operated at 20% capacity in the short-term. A company with 20 machines will simply purchase two new items of plant both of which can immediately operate at full capacity.

Poor democratic and administrative accountability with respect to regulation, as described above, and the re-distributive effects of regulation means that there is both an opportunity and a need for the Comprehensive Spending Review to play a role in ensuring delivery against the government's commitment to reduce the burden of regulation on the economy.

The Administrative Burdens Reduction Exercise[13] that is currently underway could be given additional momentum if the Comprehensive Spending Review were to link future departmental funding to performance against regulatory simplification plan targets. This link could be created by introducing an 'Administrative Burdens Reduction Incentive', described here.

---

[13] For further information go to:
http://www.cabinetoffice.gov.uk/regulation/reform/simplifying/index.asp

Administrative Burdens Reduction Incentive

The Administrative Burdens Reduction Incentive (ABRI) would be applied to all departments of government that impose regulations on businesses. The objective would be to make government departments bear the financial burden of imposing regulations on small firms and so improve government accountability. For practical reasons the scheme would be introduced gradually and could work like this:

1. Since the Cabinet Office, HMRC and the Financial Services Authority have determined that the administrative cost of regulations incurred by business amount to over £30bn this should be used as the initial benchmark.

2. The Treasury could advance this sum of money to the relevant government departments each year (as if they were going to pass it on as compensation to the private sector).

3. As no compensation arrangements exist the Treasury would then impose a levy of the same amount of money (as under 2) on those government departments, so that in year one neither they nor the Treasury are any worse off. Thus there are no immediate implications for government spending.

4. In year two, steps two and three above would again take place, except that the amount advanced under two would be 6%[14] less than in the previous year, thus imposing a net cost on the government department, known as the Administrative Burdens Reduction Incentive. This cost would fall on the department's operating budget and would not be allowed to alter either the revenue targets or spending plans of the department (so that they could not pass the cost back to the Treasury by the back door).

5. As a result of the 'Administrative Burdens Reduction Incentive or ABRI', the only way that the government department could avoid suffering a fall in its income would be if the Administrative Burden imposed on small firms were to fall at the same rate (or faster) than the 6% 'ABRI'. In the short-term, performance against targets would be monitored by the National Audit Office that has already been charged with monitoring implementation of the Administrative Burdens Reduction Exercise.

6. After, say two or three years of applying this system to Administrative Burdens the Reduction Incentive would also be applied to policy costs, which would require a further data collection exercise.

Introducing the Administrative Burdens Reduction Incentive would recognise that, as an important lever of government, regulation is akin to a form of taxation. Many regulations place responsibilities on business but the benefits

---

[14] The 6% figure is calculated on the basis that this is the compound rate of reduction necessary to reduce Administrative Burdens by approximately 25% over 5 years. 25% is the Government's current target.

flow to others, frequently government and consumers, and this is a form of redistribution that is similar to one of the impacts of taxation[15]. Hence, regulation is a form of taxation but, as we have argued, without central and rigorous control by a designated ministry and without proper scrutiny by Parliament that largely ignores RIAs and SIs. Introducing the Administrative Burdens Reduction Incentive as part of the Comprehensive Spending Review would place the Treasury in control of regulation and so improve the accountability of government to Parliament.

---

[15] Ambler, T, Chittenden, F, and Hwang, C (2005), Regulation: Another Form of Taxation? London, British Chambers of Commerce.

20. Using the private sector to finance capital expenditure: the evidence

Jean Shaoul

Introduction

A key question is how to finance the urgently needed refurbishment, renewal and expansion of Britain's transport, healthcare, education, prisons and other public infrastructure. In 1997, the incoming Labour government took up with some zeal the private financing of public infrastructure via the Private Finance Initiative (PFI), begun in 1992 by the Conservatives, and made it the cornerstone of its modernisation agenda. By December 2006, there were nearly 800 signed deals with a capital value of £55bn[1]. While the total amount of revenue expenditure committed for the next 30-years is unclear, since the Treasury reports it after assumptions about the Corporation Tax yield[2], it is taking an increasing amount of the key denominator. That is the annually managed public expenditure still spent 'in house', which is itself falling due to different forms of outsourcing, thereby constraining the flexibility of future budgets.

Originally justified as providing the capital investment that the public sector could not afford, the government later claimed that PFI would deliver greater value for money (VFM) over the life of the projects due to the private sector's greater efficiency and innovation and the transfer of some of the financial risks (and costs) to the private sector. More recently, the government has justified PFI on the basis that it delivers assets to time and budget[3]. The shifting rationale may imply that, like the various justifications given for the war against and occupation of Iraq, the promises are something of a chimera. Under the PFI, the public sector procures both the services and the underlying services and in return pays an annual fee to cover both elements for 30-years.

Independent and empirical research into how PFI is working in practice shows that it is both costly, inflexible, creates liabilities for the taxpayers and must lead to some combination of higher taxes, cuts in service provision and user charges. While the government claims that PFI has led to the largest building programme in the history of the NHS, the first wave of PFI hospitals were so

---

[1] http://www.hm-treasury.gov.uk/documents/public_private_partnerships/ppp_pfi_stats.cfm, accessed 12/12/2006

[2] Treasury (2003) 'PFI Meeting the Challenge', HM Treasury, London

[3] Treasury (2003) 'PFI Meeting the Challenge', HM Treasury, London

costly that they led to cuts of up to 30% in bed provision[4]. The schools programme has led to similar closures and rationalisations[5], increasing children's journey length.

The purpose of this chapter is to review the outcomes in terms of the cost, including the cost of risk transfer, and hence value for money, and consider some of the wider implications of this policy for service delivery and control of public expenditure. The chapter first, by way of background, explains the control of the policy. It then reviews the evidence of how it is working in practice and finally draws some conclusions.

The control of PFI

A PFI project, to proceed, must demonstrate that it is affordable and likely to deliver value for money (VFM)[6]. VFM is demonstrated by identifying and discounting the whole life costs of the project as financed under conventional procurement methods and compared against the costs of the PFI option. The scheme with the lowest cost is assumed to offer the greater VFM. The comparison also includes the costs of some of the risks associated with the construction and management of the asset and delivery of services. Since some of the risks are to be transferred to the private sector, the PFI option will – it is argued - provide greater VFM than a publicly financed alternative where the public sector bears all the risks.

But several points should be noted. First, the VFM case is necessarily based on *estimates* of future costs and operates only at the point of procurement. Second, risk transfer is the crucial element in delivering whole life economy since under PFI private sector borrowing, transactions costs and the requirements for profits necessarily generate higher costs than conventional public procurement. Thirdly, the public sector retains the ultimate responsibility for essential and often statutory services for which there is usually no alternative. Fourthly, government commitment to the policy means that the revenue streams are assured as the capital markets recognise[7]. Thus the ability to transfer risk in practice remains very limited as the rescue of failed PFI/PPP projects such as National Air Traffic Services, the Channel Tunnel Rail Link, the Royal Armouries Museum, etc. demonstrate. Finally, major hospital and IT schemes have attracted only one qualified bidder, which means that the corporations are now in a position to exert the monopoly power that undermines the VFM argument and thus to

---

[4] Gaffney, D., Pollock, A. M., Price, D., Shaoul, J., NHS Capital Expenditure and the Private Finance Initiative - Expansion or Contraction? British Medical Journal, Vol. 319, 1999, pp48-51.

[5] Glasgow and North Tyneside schools programme, to cite but two examples

[6] Treasury (1997) Step by Step Guide to the PFI Procurement Process, HM Treasury, London

[7] Standard and Poor's (2003). Public Finance/Infrastructure Finance: Credit Survey of the UK Private Finance Initiative and Public-Private Partnerships, Standard and Poor's, London.

control the direction of future policy in ways that privilege the few at the expense of the many.

But neither the appraisal methodology nor the control process is neutral. Firstly, this highly technical VFM appraisal methodology, established by the Treasury, has been extensively critiqued. It is not neutral but is itself biased in favour of the private sector option and has important wealth distributional implications[8]. Secondly, under conditions where private finance is the only game in town, then as the National Audit Office (NAO) has acknowledged, there are incentives to ensure that the case favours the private option[9]. Thirdly, the key government department, the Treasury, both champions and controls the PFI process. The Treasury's Projects division was initially established in 1997 with a two year life, largely with staff on secondment from the private sector. This was later reconstituted as a Public Private Partnership, Partnerships UK (PUK), whose mission is to help the public sector deliver: fast and efficient development and procurement of PPPs; strong PPPs that build stable relationships with the private sector; savings in development costs; and better value for money[10]. Some 51% of the shares are held by private sector institutions, including financial services companies that have been involved in the financing of PFI projects, and others that have PFI contracts. Furthermore, the majority of the board members come from the private sector, with the public sector represented by only two non-executive directors and the public interest represented through an Advisory Council. The structure, ownership and control of PUK are important because they set the PFI agenda and reflect the conflict between policy promotion and policy control acknowledged by government[11]. Fourthly, the project and the case is managed by the Treasury, the Departmental Private Finance Units, Partnerships UK or 4Ps, all of whom are largely staffed by private sector secondees from firms with a vested interest in the policy. This means that the control process is dominated by parties which have a vested interest in the policy's expansion[12].

The government claims that PFI represents VFM, but this is largely based upon the business case used to support the use of private finance. But this is hardly an independent assessment as we have shown above. While the National Audit Office did not itself carry out independent assessments either before (with the exception of London Underground) or after financial close, it did scrutinise various projects and in many cases criticised various aspects of the way the

---

[8]Shaoul, J. A critical financial appraisal of the private finance initiative: selecting a financing method or reallocating wealth? Critical Perspectives on Accounting, Vol 16, 2005, pp441-471.

[9] As quoted in an interview Financial Times 5/6/02

[10] Partnerships UK (2003) What is Partnerships UK, http://www.partnershipsuk.org.uk/puk/index.htm, accessed 12/12/06

[11] Timms, S. (2001) Public Private Partnership, Private Finance Initiative, Keynote Address by the Financial Secretary to the Treasury to Global Summit, Cape Town, December 6th

[12] Craig, D., (2006) Plundering the public sector, Constable, London

business case had been compiled[13] [14] [15] [16]. While the government has commissioned several surveys of PFI[17] [18] that purport to show that PFI represents VFM, these have been carried out by financial consultants with a vested interest in the policy, and have been comprehensively critiqued elsewhere[19] [20]. But in the final analysis, these all rest upon *expectations* or *estimates* of future VFM over the life of the project.

Post implementation evaluation of PFI

There are a wide variety of sources - NAO reports, academic and other commentaries, including evidence gleaned as 'snippets' from the press - to show how PFI is working in practice.

    1.   Building to time and budget

The government claims that PFI projects have been built to budget and on time. This is based on two surveys by the NAO[21] [22], which were surveys and consultations with project managers and were not backed up with any data on cost and time overruns, another study cited by the NAO[23] and a Treasury report[24], both of which contained neither data nor methodology. A fifth report[25] contained so many flaws in the study design and methodology that the results are uninterpretable[26]. While the NAO reported that the aims of PFI had generally

---

[13] National Audit Office (1997) The Skye Bridge, Report of Comptroller and Auditor General, HC 5, Session 1997-98, The Stationery Office, London.

[14] National Audit Office (1998) The Private Finance Initiative: The First Four Design, Build, Finance and Operate Roads Contracts, Report of Comptroller and Auditor General, HC 476, Session 1997-98, The Stationery Office, London.

[15] National Audit Office (1999) The PFI Contract for the New Dartford and Gravesham Hospital, Report of Comptroller and Auditor General, HC 423, Session 1998-99, The Stationery Office, London.

[16] National Audit Office, (2000) The Financial Analysis for the London Underground Public Private Partnership, Report of Comptroller and Auditor General, HC 54, Session 2000 - 2001, The Stationery Office, London.

[17] Arthur Andersen and Enterprise LSE, (2000) Value for Money Drivers in the Private Finance Initiative, Report commissioned by the Treasury Taskforce, January. Available from the Treasury's website: treasury-projects.gov.uk/series_1/andersen.

[18] PwC (2001) Public Private Partnerships: a clearer view, PwC, London

[19] Pollock, A., and Vickers, N. (2000) Private Pie in the Sky, Public Finance, April 14th, pp22-23.

[20] Shaoul, J., Stafford, A., Stapleton, P. Partnerships and the role of financial advisors: private control over public policy, Policy and Politics, forthcoming

[21] National Audit Office (2003) PFI: Construction Performance, Report of Comptroller and Auditor General, HC 371, Session 2002-03, The Stationery Office, London.

[22] National Audit Office (2001) Modernising construction. Report of Comptroller and Auditor General, HC , Session 200, The Stationery Office, London.

[23] Agile Construction Initiative (1999) Benchmarking stage two study.

[24] Treasury (2003) PFI Meeting the Challenge, HM Treasury, London

[25] Mott MacDonald (2002) Review of large scale procurement, Mott MacDonald, London

[26] Pollock, A., Price, D., Player, S (2005) The private finance initiative: a policy built on sand, Unison, London.

been met in the construction and design of the 11 hospitals built to date, this must be qualified by the widespread criticism of at least one hospital (it has corridors too narrow to permit more than one trolley) and problems in other hospitals. Other more strategic criticisms have been made of their design[27][28]. In the context of schools, the Audit Commission's review of PFI schools found that PFI did not guarantee better buildings despite their higher cost[29]. Most of the additional cost of private over public finance is justified in terms of risk transfer, largely construction not operational risk. This raises several points. First, it begs the question why conventional contracts cannot be written in such a way as to ensure that the contractor builds to time and budget. Second, why the cost of risk transfer is so high given that after completion of the construction phase, the companies have been able to refinance their deals. Third, these refinancing deals carry with them the potential, as in the case of the refinancing of Fazakerley prison[30], for the companies to increase their profits in ways that serve to increase the risk to the public sector and lengthen the contract period[31][32].

2. Penalties to incentive operational performance

Although there have been numerous adverse press reports in the UK of poor service delivery in hospitals under the contract, some of which are documented in evidence to the Health Select Committee[33], there have been few deductions and these have been small[34]. There have been similar press reports of concerns about poor performance in schools projects. In many cases, the original contract negotiation team has moved on making it difficult to know the assumptions and intentions underlying the contract. Monitoring has turned out to be more costly than anticipated, performance indicators have been difficult to operationalise,

---

[27] Worthington, J. (2002). 2020 Vision: Our Future Healthcare Environments, Report of the Building Futures Group, The Stationery Office, London.

[28] Appleby, J., and Coote, A. (2002) Five Year Health Check: A Review of Health Policy 1997-2002, The Kings Fund, London.

[29] Audit Commission (2003) PFI in Schools: The quality and cost of buildings and services provided by early private finance initiative schemes, Audit Commission, London

[30] Because the private sector's debt repayment profile is restructured, the public sector could find itself exposed to additional termination liabilities, should the contract be terminated for any reason. This increased exposure would occur when the private sector had received most of the benefits and be facing additional costs associated with long term maintenance, thereby tempting the private sector in adverse circumstances to cut and run.

[31]National Audit Office (2000) The Refinancing of the Fazakerley PFI Prison Contract, Report of Comptroller and Auditor General, HC 584, Session 1999-2000, The Stationery Office, London.

[32] National Audit Office (2002) PFI Refinancing Update, Report of Comptroller and Auditor General, HC 1288, Session 2001-02, The Stationery Office, London.

[33] Health Select Committee (2002) The role of the private sector in the NHS, HC 308, Session 2001-02, the Stationery Office, London

[34] Standard and Poor's (2003). Public Finance/Infrastructure Finance: Credit Survey of the UK Private Finance Initiative and Public-Private Partnerships, Standard and Poor's, London.

due to the subjective nature of the outcome, and contracts changes have been time consuming and complex[35].

3. Prisons

In the case of criminal justice contracts, court service projects have escalated in price, refuting the claim that PFI contracts deliver fixed prices[36]. HMP Altcourse at Fazakerley, the first PFI prison, was controversial from the start because of its poor planning, lack of scrutiny of costs, a flawed savings assessment, operational performance failures and lastly the refinancing scandal that saw the private sector refinance the deal in a way that generated extra £11m for itself while at the same time increasing the risk to the public sector[37]. A report on prison performance noted that prisoners were confined to their rooms for longer periods and that their cells contained 'substantial ligature points' that 'rendered the cells unfit for use at all'[38]. The NAO reported that operational performance against contract had been mixed[39]. But PFI contracts, even when 'successful', have hidden costs to the rest of the public sector. Centre for Public Services[40] found that the private sector paid lower wages to its prison staff than did the public sector and some of its workforce were paid such low wages that they qualified for working family tax credits, in effect a low wage subvention by the state to the private sector.

4. IT projects

PFI has been conspicuously unsuccessful in IT projects. But these failures are important because they demonstrate the fallacy of risk transfer argument: risk was transferred in unanticipated ways. Consider just two of the most well known IT project failures. When the Passport Agency's new system was rolled out before being adequately tested, prospective travellers experienced such delays in receiving their passports that they went in person to collect them, resulting in the passport equivalent of a run on the bank and more than 500 missing their travel dates. While the Passport Agency largely waived the penalties in the interests of partnership, the £12.6m resultant costs to hire extra staff led to an increase in the passport fee[41]. The much vaunted risk transfer was therefore not from the public

---

[35] Edwards, P., Shaoul, J., Stafford, A. and Arblaster, L. (2004) Evaluating the operation of PIF in roads and hospitals, Research report no 84, ACCA, London

[36] Centre for Public Services (2002) Privatising justice: the impact of the Private Finance Initiative in the Criminal Justice System, Report, Sheffield.

[37] National Audit Office (2000) The Refinancing of the Fazakerley PFI Prison Contract, Report of Comptroller and Auditor General, HC 584, Session 1999-2000, The Stationery Office, London.

[38] Chief Inspector of Prisons for England and Wales (2000) HM Prison Altcourse, Report of a Full Inspection 1-10 November 1999, Home Office, London

[39] National Audit Office (2003) The Operational Performance of Prisons, Report of Comptroller and Auditor General, HC 700, Session 2002-03, The Stationary Office, London.

[40] Centre for Public Services (2002) Privatising justice: the impact of the Private Finance Initiative in the Criminal Justice System, Report, Sheffield.

[41] National Audit Office (1999) The Passport Delays of Summer 1999, Report of Comptroller and Auditor General, HC 812, Session 1998-99, The Stationery Office, London.

sector to the private sector but to the public as individuals. The Contributions Agency's NIRS2 system was late and poorly tested. This led to incorrect and lost records, late and wrong welfare payments, additional costs to both the Contributions and the Benefits Agencies and an estimated £5bn in 'lost' taxes to the Inland Revenue as a result of the incorrect and lost records since recipients could not be or were under assessed for tax. This shows that when things go wrong, costs may be diffused well beyond the purchasing agency. Again, the limited penalties were waived, and when there was a need to renegotiate the contract, the Agency found that it was locked in due to the private contractor owning the copyright on the software[42]. Indeed, the outcomes of IT projects in the benefits recording and payments systems, the criminal justice system and other administrative services have been so poor that even the government has had to admit that PFI may not be the best means of procuring IT services[43] and PFI for IT has now been abandoned.

5.   Financial cost of PFI in hospitals

A study of the first 13 operational or partly operational PFI hospitals as of 2002, which had capital costs of about £1.4bn, combined annual PFI payments of about £230m and total payments of about £6bn over the 30 year life of the projects, found that in a number of cases, the actual payments to the private sector turned out to be considerably higher than originally estimated, as much as 36% for the QEII Greenwich and 34% for South Manchester in 2003[44]. While this may be due to volume increases, inflation, contract changes and failure to identify and/or specify the requirements in sufficient detail, e.g., the failure to specify marmalade for patients' breakfast led to an increased charge, such contract drift suggests, at the very least, that the total cost of PFI is likely to be very much more than the £6bn predicted at financial close.

The hospital Trusts' cost of capital, including the capital element of PFI and capital charges on their remaining assets, rose from about 6% of income pre-PFI to 12% income post PFI in 2003, in aggregate £140m, more than half the cost of PFI, even though the new hospitals have up to 30% fewer beds than the ones they replace. While the Trusts received a general increase in funding as well as in some cases a specific increase to cover some of the extra costs of PFI, one third was eaten up by the increased cost of PFI. Six of the 13 Trusts had a very substantial deficit, much higher than the national average. Four of these six were paying higher charges than stated in their full business cases. The QEII Greenwich Trust's auditors[45] declared that it was technically insolvent and it was locked into a PFI deal that added £9m to its annual costs over and above that built under conventional public procurement. Without government support, its long term financial situation was insoluble.

---

[42]Edwards, P. and Shaoul, J. (2003) Partnerships: for better, for worse? Accounting, Auditing and Accountability Journal, Vol.16, No.3, pp.397-421.

[43] Treasury (2003) PFI Meeting the Challenge, HM Treasury, London

[44] Edwards, P., Shaoul, J., Stafford, A. and Arblaster, L. (2004) Evaluating the operation of PIF in roads and hospitals, research report no 84, ACCA, London

[45] PWC (2005) Queen Elizabeth hospital NHS Trusts: Public interest report, PWC, London

The private sector companies, special purpose vehicles (SPV) or consortia organised as brass plate companies, operate in a complex and opaque web of subcontracting to their sister companies that increases the costs and complexity of monitoring and enforcing the contract, and makes it impossible to assess the parent companies' total returns. After paying interest on their debt, which was higher than the total construction cost and rising, of about 8%, the SPVs reported a post tax return on shareholders' funds of 104% in 2002. The SPVs' high effective cost of capital (£123m) means that the annual risk premium, the difference between public and private sector interest[46], was £62m, equivalent to 26% of income received from the Trusts. It is unclear whether this represents VFM or indeed whether VFM can indeed be measured *ex post facto*. But irrespective of whether £62m a year represents VFM, this analysis raises questions about the affordability of PFI in practice, and future service provision, an issue which the emphasis on VFM downplays.

6.   Financial cost of PFI in transport

While the use of private finance in roads has been deemed a 'success', this was and is a consequence of very high payments to the private sector. A study[47] of the first eight DBFO contracts signed by the Highways Agency and paid for on the basis of shadow tolls are costing about £210m a year, or 6bn over 30-years, found that the payments in just three years for which information is publicly available was £618m, more than the £590m cost of construction, refuting the claim that the government could not afford the capital cost. After paying interest on their debt, which was higher than the total construction cost, of about 9%, the SPVs reported a post tax return on shareholders' funds of 29% in 2002. The annual risk premium was about £56m or about half the cost of capital (£103m) and one third of the income received from the Agency in 2002. With annual operation and maintenance costs of about £50-60m a year, or £1.8bn in total, this means that after paying interest on debt (about £1.8bn), itself more expensive than public debt, the Agency is paying nearly £1.8bn (out of a total of £6bn) for the major maintenance and private sector profits, a high price for risk transfer. Thus 'success' comes at the expense of affordability, value for money and service cuts elsewhere.

The Skye Bridge has proved similarly expensive. The contract was terminated at the end of 2004, after total contributions from the state and road users totalled nearly £90m for a £24m bridge (with the £14m cost of the approach roads paid by the state). PFI has not been without problems in transport as the collapse of the National Air Traffic Services PPP and the Channel Tunnel Rail Link, and recent press reports of problems on the London Underground PPP demonstrate.

---

[46] As defined by the National Audit Office

[47] Shaoul, J., Stafford, A, Stapleton P. (2006) Highway Robbery? A financial evaluation of Design Build Finance and Operate in UK roads, Transport Reviews, Vol 26, No 3, pp257-274

Conclusion

These results are not a purely British phenomenon, as the evidence on the hospital sector in Australia[48] [49] [50], and privately financed roads in Spain[51] shows. There too the outcomes were inconsistent with the claims. At best, PFI has turned out to be very expensive with the inevitable consequences for service provision, taxes and user charges, not just today but for a long time to come. These projects may burden government with hidden subsidies, diversion of income streams and revenue guarantees whose impact on public finance may not become apparent for many years. When things go wrong, and this is not infrequent, the costs are diffused throughout the public sector and onto the public at large, a travesty of risk transfer.

The question that must be faced is: who will bear the costs? For example, in the context of hospitals: are extra funds to be diverted to the Trusts with PFI hospitals either from elsewhere within the local healthcare economy, at the expense of primary care and other hospitals in the area, or from the rest of the NHS budget, at the expense of the whole system, with all the consequent implications for access to and equity in healthcare provision?

The logic of PFI/PPP is that the government has established the pre-conditions for a financially driven system of public services for sectors that require planning rather than competition. This has never been provided for more than a small fraction of the population on a 'for profit' basis because they were not commercially viable. At the very least, PFI creates budget inflexibilities that increase the pressure on public services to cut their largest and controllable cost: the jobs, working conditions and pay of their staff, and thus access to quality services. In other words, PFI heralds an emerging conflict both between capital and labour at the point of production in public services and between the government and the public at large over the reduction in the social wage: access to welfare services. Any rational government would take note of such independent and impartial evidence and at the very least dampen some of the excess enthusiasm it's shown for a scheme that clearly has dangerous pitfalls.

---

[48]Senate Community Affairs References Committee (2000). Healing our Hospitals, Commonwealth of Australia, Canberra.

[49] Auditor General Western Australia (1997). Private Care for Public Patients: the Joondalup Health Campus, Report No 9, Perth, Australia.

[50]New South Wales Auditor General (1996), Report for 1996; Volume I, NSW Parliament, Sydney.

[51] Acerete, J.B., Shaoul, J.., and Stafford, A. (2006) Taking its toll: the cost of privately financed roads in Spain, paper presented at the fourth international conference on accounting, auditing and management in public sector reforms, Siena, Italy.

21. Choice in public services

Ian Greener & Ann Mahon

Increasing choice is a central part of Labour's attempts to reform public services in the UK[1]. This chapter explores the factors driving these reforms and compares choice scenarios across a range of public services. Despite the apparently common label of 'increasing choice', experiences are often remarkably different between and indeed within, different public sector organisations. The final section of this paper introduces a framework, derived from Herbert Simon's work, to explore the implications of these differences and to suggest contexts where choice may be more readily implemented.

Choice in theory

The rationale for increasing choice in public services relates to both demand and supply. On the demand side, the driver for increasing choice is often presented as a response to wider societal changes and particularly the rise of "consumerism"[2] [3]. There is a wide body of thought suggesting that as society gets more affluent, people become more discerning and demanding in their consumption of goods and services and less willing to defer to the "expertise" of professionals. Public services, traditionally associated with producer rather than consumer values[4], are no longer an exception to this change, with users demanding better services and higher standards. In these terms, choice reforms are an inevitable consequence of social change[5].

On the supply side, choice reforms are justified on the grounds that, by turning formerly passive and deferential service users into active and demanding consumers[6], public service providers have to be more responsive to their needs. If they are not, they risk losing the funding attached to service provision to new entrants from the private and not-for-profit sectors, or to other public service

---

[1] Minister of State for Department of Health, Minister of State for Local and Regional Government, Minister of State for School Standards. The Case for User Choice in Public Services, Public Administration Select Committee into Choice, Voice and Public Services, London. 2005

[2] Aldridge A. Consumption. Oxford: Polity. 2003

[3] Paterson M. Consumption and Everyday Life. London: Taylor and Francis. 2006

[4] Jordan B. Public Services and the Service Economy: Individualism and the Choice Agenda. Journal of Social Policy, 2005.35, 143-62

[5] Secretary of State for Health. The NHS Plan: A Plan for Investment, A Plan for Reform. London: HMSO 2000

[6] Le Grand J. Motivation, Agency and Public Policy: Of Knights, Knaves, Pawns and Queens. Oxford: Oxford University Press. 2003

providers now positioned as competitors[7]. Choice is thus a driver for improving the performance of public sector organisations.

An abstract model of choice then, works by giving the public a greater say in the delivery of the public services they are receiving, at the same time forcing up standards as public organisations are forced to compete for the funding which they formerly took for granted. How this plays out in practice varies significantly from service to service.

Choice in practice

There are a range of sociological and cultural factors that impact upon whether people wish to have and wish to exercise choice in public services as well as some important questions about the impact of choice when it is available particularly on equity and efficiency. It is outside the scope of this chapter to offer a comprehensive review of choice and how it is experienced across the full range of public services. The aim here is to outline examples of choice reforms in education, health, social care and housing. At one end of a scale, it might be argued that there are public service areas where choice reforms are now tried-and-tested, and seem to work relatively straightforwardly, but there are other areas where there are significant problems. The analysis that follows aims to shed some light on this argument by working through services along this spectrum.

Choice in education

In **primary education**, parents in urban and suburban areas are increasingly used to receiving data concerning local school performance from their local education authority, visiting potential schools, talking to other parents to find out where they are sending their children, working out from their own experience what they think makes a good school, and finally making a choice of where to send their child. There are capacity limitations – with good schools often having limited places, but because of the large number of public providers of primary education, it is relatively unusual to find parents who have not managed to find a place for their child in a school they feel happy with.

In **secondary education**, the choice process appears broadly similar to primary education, but problems are more frequent with around one child in ten not getting a place in at least one of the schools their parents have chosen. This seems like a small number, but when multiplied across the country, leads to a lot of unhappy parents and children, often distributed disproportionately across the

---

[7] Deakin N, Walsh K, The Enabling State: The Role of Markets and Contracts. Public Administration, 1996.74, 33-48

most vulnerable groups in society because there are fewer high-performing schools close to where they live[8].

In both primary and secondary education choice is greater for those with higher incomes, greater access to information and the willingness and means to travel. Pupils from more deprived background therefore are less likely to benefit from choice compared to their more affluent peers.

In **higher education**, students may theoretically apply to any University they wish, but Universities, because of their capacity limitations, effectively select from student applications according to their projected qualifications. This means that the Universities perceived to be the best often end up educating the most gifted students, and student choice plays a relatively small part, as students end up going to institutions that either suit them in terms of travel, or which reflect their educational achievements rather than their preferences.

Choice in health and social care

In **social care**, especially in the area of personal care, perhaps the most radical reforms in the UK welfare state are taking place, with service users being offered the right to hold individual budgets for their own care – known as direct payments. This involves a needs assessment and allocation of funds to purchase services for themselves, according to that assessment. Because social care has had considerable private sector involvement for a number of years, and because these reforms allow users to purchase care from friends and family, a wide variety of potential choices open up, but it may be more difficult for some users than for others, depending upon the nature of their illness or disability and the availability of support.

Historically patient choice in **healthcare** has been a low priority – certainly compared to its place in social care and education, but it is currently a key policy theme in relation to patient choice of hospital and particularly for elective surgery. Recent evidence based on the London Patient Choice Project and some other small pilots implemented during 2002-2003 suggest that choice is more enthusiastically embraced when patients face long waiting lists[9]. Fotaki et al's review confirms findings from earlier empirical studies[10] of the centrality of healthcare professionals in affecting choice. Key messages to emerge from Fotaki et al's review are that patients are not currently sufficiently informed to make choices, patients do benefit from participating in choices about their treatment and that patients want information about choices of treatment, but they do not

---

[8] Ball S, Bowe R, Gewirtz S. Circuits of schooling: a sociological exploration of parental choice of school in social class contexts. The Sociological Review, 1995.43, 52-78

[9] Fotaki M et al (2005) Patient choice and the organisation and delivery of health services: scoping review, University of Manchester.

[10] Mahon A et al (1993) Factors that influence general practitioners' choice of hospital when referring patients for elective surgery. British Journal of General Practitioners, 43: 272-276

always want responsibility for choosing their treatment or care. As such, there are questions about potential inequalities resulting from wider choice, but also general questions to be answered about exactly how patients are meant to make informed choices where decisions are as complex as they often are in this area[11][12].

Choice in housing

In **housing** constraints are greater still. In the allocation of social housing, a number of local experiments have led to local authorities attempting to offer their tenants greater choices, but there appears to be also a considerable degree of chance involved as, if a potential tenant rejects a property offered to them, they may end up being put on the bottom of a waiting list for available homes. Choice can be reduced to whether or not to take a particular property rather than between available properties.

In addition to this, users of public services always theoretically have an alternative choice – they can contract with the private sector themselves, but this option will only be available to those with the resources to avail themselves of it, and this inevitably results in at least some inequality between social groups.

Making sense of choice

The brief and necessarily selective review of choice in the public sector suggests a range of choice scenarios. Under what circumstances is choice to be more easily implemented? When does choice work for users and when is it less effective? To consider these questions the choice scenarios described above can be mapped to a framework derived from Herbert Simon's work on decision-making.

Herbert Simon was one of the clearest writers on decision-making, and his work is the inspiration behind the public research institute named after him at Manchester University. Simon (1960) suggested decision-making processes have four stages[13]. First there is intelligence during which information about the decision is gathered. Next there is the design stage where information is structured and prioritised. Stage three involves making a choice based upon the preceding stages and finally, in the fourth stage, choice is implemented if the resources required to make it happen are in place. Applying this framework across the services we have covered produces insightful results as shown in Table 21.1.

---

[11] Greener I. Who Choosing What? The evolution of 'choice' in the NHS, and its implications for New Labour. In Social Policy Review 15, ed. C Bochel, N Ellison, M Powell, pp. 49-68. Bristol: Policy Press. 2003

[12] Greener I. The Role of the Patient in Healthcare Reform: Customer, Consumer or Creator? In Future health organisations and systems, ed. S Dawson, C Sausmann, pp. 227-45. Basingstoke: Palgrave. 2005

[13] Simon H. New Science of Management Decision. New York: Harper and Row. 1960

Table 21.1 Choice processes in public services according to Simon's model

Service Stage of decision making	Primary education	Secondary education	Higher education	Social care	Healthcare	Housing
Intelligence	Easy	Easy	Easy	Difficult	Difficult	Easy
Design	Easy	Easy	Moderate	Difficult	Moderate	Easy
Choice	Easy	Easy	Moderate	Easy	Easy	Easy
Implementation	Easy	Moderate	Moderate	Moderate	Moderate	Difficult

Using this framework it appears that in primary education, it is relatively easy to collect together the relevant information, structure to make a choice and to implement that choice. Local authorities already provide league tables, and process parental choices, most of which result in parents getting a school they appear happy with. The position is similar with secondary education and higher education, although implementation of choices in these areas may be more difficult than in primary education.

In social care, it is easy to make choices if you have a budget to spend in the form of direct payment, but possibly more difficult to identify the best provider of care, and to implement decisions. In healthcare it is relatively easy to make a choice from four possible referral providers, but, as in social care, it is not clear exactly how you are meant to choose between them and there remains a degree of dependence upon professional support and advice. Finally, in housing you are presented with simple choices, but won't necessarily be able to implement what you choose.

Implications of this analysis

The implications of this analysis are that there are some services and choice scenarios where it is very difficult for users to make choices unassisted (social care, healthcare) and which require some professional input and help. In these situations support is needed, especially amongst the most vulnerable and deprived, before choices can drive policy in the way envisaged by the government.

In areas where it is possible to access, understand and to organise the information available (education), choice is far more likely to drive service improvement, but good providers often run up against capacity problems likely to lead to frustration on the part of users choosing these services but not receiving them. As such, it would make sense to allow popular providers to expand their capacity, but this is often a complex and disruptive process with dire implications for unpopular providers.

Finally, there are other public services where there is a lack of information, a lack of ability to understand it, a lack of choice and an inability to implement choice. One possible candidate for this unenviable status is that of rail travel, where choices about travel are often based on when it is to be taken rather than the facilities on offer, and structural limits on infrastructure limit choice so much as to make it meaningless.

Conclusion

In all, choice means very different things in different public services. The application of a framework derived from Simon's work allows us to distinguish between different choice scenarios and contexts. The analysis presented here is not intended to be definitive or complete – it is offered as a framework to guide further debate and discussion in this challenging policy area.

22. Public sector pay

Damian Grimshaw

Introduction

Public sector pay is an important tool for securing the effective allocation of people in the labour market into public sector jobs. For public sector managers, it also needs to meet worker expectations of fair reward to foster their commitment and cooperation at work. And public sector pay contributes significantly to meeting broader governmental goals of equity, both in reducing the incidence of low pay and in closing the gender pay gap.

These multiple functions and objectives of public sector pay mean that there are inevitably conflicting demands on the direction of policy reform. In this short commentary, three key issues are highlighted. In each case, the current state of play is reviewed and considerations for reform are identified. The key issues are as follows:

- Managing pay settlements
- Local pay flexibility
- Pay equity

Managing pay settlements

Since Labour came to power in 1997, public sector workers have experienced fluctuating fortunes with regard to the size of annual pay settlements, both in relation to settlements earned in the private sector and between public sector occupational groups. Gordon Brown famously held back settlements during 1997-1999 when public expenditures were frozen at pre-Labour limits, but subsequently put in place a sustained policy of public sector pay catch-up. However, this particular era has now ended and over the last 12 months we have heard familiar Treasury concerns that generous pay rises may overheat the economy and require tough measures of belt-tightening. Treasury evidence to Pay Review Bodies in 2006 requested them, 'to remain vigilant to the risk of higher pay settlements feeding into higher service sector inflation'[1] – a position that has been repeated again and again by Gordon Brown:

> And we will take no risks with inflation at home. The public sector pay settlements will show settlements averaging just 2.25 per cent – combining fairness in pay, with more for nurses, with vigilance and discipline in the fight against inflation[2].

---

[1] HM Treasury, Inflation evidence for Pay Review Body recommendations, 13/07/06.
[2] Gordon Brown's 2006 Budget speech, 22/03/06.

> The overall awards come within the inflation target of 1.9% demonstrating our total determination to maintain discipline and stability and continue with an 11th year of sustained economic growth[3].

Unsurprisingly, the new pressure has met with alarm from trade unions and professional associations, as well as from the six heads of pay review bodies[4]. But also as a matter of equity and consideration of market forces, the new insistence that public sector pay settlements be tied to the inflation target (currently 1.9% by the Treasury's preferred consumer price increase measure) is unrealistic (and highly risky) for three reasons. First, it holds pay rises below the actual increase in cost of living, resulting in a cut in real pay. The March estimate for the consumer price increase is 2.7% and the more generally used index – the retail price increase – stands at 4.2%. Workers who receive a real wage cut may reasonably assume this reflects a decline in productivity, but this is obviously difficult to square against improved performance indicators in hospitals, schools, etc. Second it generates a widening gap between public and private sector pay, with private sector pay settlements during 2007 expected to average slightly higher than the RPI increase of 4.2%. Like the late 1990s, as the gap widens we can expect to see recruitment difficulties for teachers and nurses as private sector jobs become relatively attractive to graduates seeking employment. And third, it exacerbates the widening gap between public sector salaries and house prices, sustaining the difficulties of newly recruited public sector workers in buying a first house.

A further problem with exerting such strong pressure to tighten belts is that those groups with less wage bargaining power, less public visibility, or less political capital, are more likely to suffer significant falls in their real wage income. A clear example of this was the very low settlement during 2006-07 (just 1.6%) for prison officers. By contrast, most NHS staff won a 2.5% rise and senior civil servants a 3.25% settlement. In part, such differences reflect one of the peculiarities of the UK public sector pay system – it is fragmented and lacks the coordination of pay settlements characteristic of France or Germany. In the UK, different groups are represented in different ways, with pay determined by pay review bodies, centralised collective bargaining and decentralised wage-setting – each offering different scenarios for government, employer and employee bodies to reach agreement. But there is another explanation for fragmented pay settlements – that those groups closer to the political machinery seem to be enjoying more luck, as evident by the above-average settlements won during 2006-07 in the Foreign Office (4.06%), the Home Office and Cabinet Office (3.5%), the Department for Environment, Food and Rural Affairs (3.6%) and Work and Pensions and Crown Estates (3%)[4].

While it is clearly the proper role of the Treasury to provide a steer to wage negotiators regarding the inflationary outlook, the decision to cut real wages during a period of continuing house price inflation (that is not being fuelled by

---

[3] Gordon Brown's statement cited on the BBC website, 01.03.07, Anger at public sector pay offer (news.bbc.co.uk/1/hi/uk_politics/6408061.stm).

[4] David Hencke Public sector row over Brown's 2% pay limit (The Guardian, 18/08/06).

public sector workers) is wrong. Also, more ought to be done to coordinate pay settlements to provide all public sector workers with a common-held perception of their value in the delivery of public services. What is needed is a new determination to coordinate pay rises across different areas of the public sector workforce, with special concern to protect those with less political visibility and weaker wage bargaining power.

Local pay flexibility

Two important achievements of the New Labour government have been to reinstate a commitment to national pay frameworks both in the NHS and local government. The long period of experimentation with local pay bargaining under previous Conservative governments demonstrated the limitations of this approach. A range of studies suggest that local pay practices potentially decouple economically deprived areas from more prosperous areas; reduce the transparency of wage information needed for effective and balanced wage bargaining; conflict with centralised control over spending; build in rigidities at the aggregate level in the functioning of the labour market; and have limited ability to strengthen links between pay and performance[5].

The new harmonised frameworks for NHS workers and local government workers represent a significant shift in approach and underline a commitment to a fair and coordinated approach (see below for further consideration of pay equity effects). Nevertheless, pressures for some form of local flexibility are back on the drawing board. One pressure derives from the Lyons review that evaluated the merits of public sector relocation. As well as cheaper estates costs, the review argued that relocation into 'less overheated labour markets' would offer the chance to improve recruitment and retention without driving up labour costs. The argument is that, especially for junior grades, public sector national pay frameworks offer more generous pay than comparable private sector jobs in locations outside of London[6]. It follows that downward flexibility in pay frameworks is needed to capitalise on the potential for local pay differences. As illustrated in the Lyons review:

> Failure to align public sector pay closer to local rates could undermine any positive effect [of the geographical dispersal of government jobs][7].

As a means to reduce public spending such a strategy has an obvious appeal to officials within the Treasury. Indeed, Larry Elliott, economics columnist for The Guardian claims that Brown is pushing for "the break-up of national pay bargaining"[8]. Moreover, such a strategy has an intuitive appeal to managers in public sector organisations since it provides them with the tools to respond to

---

[5] See, for example, D. Marsden and R. Richardson (1994) Performing for pay, British Journal of Industrial Relations, D. Grimshaw (2000) The problem with pay flexiblity, International Journal of HRM.

[6] Lyons review: Independent Review of Public Sector Relocation (p.22).

[7] Ibid. p.31.

[8] Larry Elliott, The Guardian 06/06/06.

cost and other local factors that influence ease of recruitment and retention without the need to uprate pay for all workers nationally.

However, the lessons learned from local pay experiments in the late 1980s and early 1990s need to be remembered, as noted above. Also, studies of large private sector employers, such as retailers and banks, show that local pay flexibility is not necessarily applied; in fact many large chains apply a national pay structure for their organisational branches[9]. And the most recent warning derives from the comprehensive research conducted by Bob Elliott and colleagues at the University of Aberdeen. Their ESRC-funded study shows that a move towards more regional and local pay flexibility presents local public bodies with a trade-off between equity and efficiency, since while they may accrue cost savings by matching public sector pay structures with local private sector pay, inequalities in pay among public sector workers would widen considerably[10]. They find that changes in public sector pay to match private sector pay would increase inter-decile pay differentials for men in the public sector from 2.11 to 2.4 and for women from 2.00 to 2.33 (op cit: 531).

Pay equity

The public sector has a strong record in generating relatively high levels of pay equity, compared to the private sector, in terms of both a low incidence of low paid work and a narrow gender pay gap. Table 22.1 demonstrates the relatively high earnings for women compared to men in the public sector: in 2005, women in full-time jobs earned on average 87% of men's pay in the public sector but just 78% in the private sector; women in part-time jobs earned on average 66% of men's pay in the public sector and just 55% in the private sector.

Table 22.1 The gender pay ratio within the public and private sectors, 1997, 2001 and 2005

	Female full-time pay as % of male full-timers within each sector		Female part-time pay as % of male full-timers within each sector	
	Public sector	Private sector	Public sector	Private sector
1997	86.8	74.2	63.2	52.9
2001	87.6	76.0	64.4	52.5
2005	86.6	77.8	66.2	55.3

Note: gross hourly average earnings, including overtime.

Source: Annual Survey of Hours and Earnings (own calculations).

---

[9] Arrowsmith, J. and Sisson, K. (1999) Pay and working time: towards organisation-based systems?, British Journal of Industrial Relations, 37: 51-76.

[10] Devolved government and public sector pay reform: considerations of equity and efficiency, Regional Studies, 39 (4): 519-539.

The combination of women's over-representation among the public sector workforce and the relatively narrow gender pay gap means that the public sector makes an important contribution to aggregate trends in the gender pay gap. One study suggests that more than 75% of the narrowing of the aggregate gender pay gap during 1986-1995 was due to a combination of the narrow gender pay gap within the public sector and the relatively high pay of female public sector workers compared to female private sector workers[11]. However, the public sector's relatively strong record on pay equity today faces some conflicting pressures, which policy needs to address.

Market testing and low pay

A first issue concerns trends at the bottom of the wage structure. The present government has continued past policies introduced by Conservative governments to market-test many public sector activities undertaken by low wage workers, most of whom are women employed in part-time jobs. The result is a continuous regime of belt-tightening for workers employed as cleaners, caterers, estates, security and others in public hospitals, schools and local authorities, with some working for private sector firms and others employed by the public sector. Much of the policy debate (and trade union campaigns) has focused on problems of a two-tier workforce in those private firms that protect terms and conditions for outsourced public sector workers but establish worse conditions for new recruits. The government's new 'two-tier code' has now made this impossible in the NHS and local authorities, but this needs to be extended right across the public sector to provide universal protection. However, the larger issue is the continued drive to market-test activities involving low wage work. Many studies show that this has led to a deterioration in the quality of these jobs, involving intensification of work, loss of control over working time schedules, worse pay and weaker autonomy in the job. It is time to learn from this evidence and design new policies that serve a new objective to improve the quality of services by enhancing the quality of these jobs, in place of the old mantra of hoping that market competition would automatically generate efficiency and quality improvements.

Evidence from earnings data gives some indication of how market testing of low wage jobs undertaken by female part-time workers has reduced the benefits of working in the public sector. Figure 22.1a shows that in 2005 the lowest paid female part-timers (lowest decile, D1) earned 15% more by working in the public sector than in the private sector. But those earning the average wage earned a premium of 33% and the highest paid decile earned a 54% premium. Moreover, the public sector wage premium for men and women in low wage full-time jobs is significantly higher, reflecting in large part their greater shelter from policies of

---

[11] Grimshaw, D. (2000) Public sector employment, wage inequality and the gender pay ratio in the UK, International Review of Applied Economics, 14 (4): 427-448.

market testing; for women the wage premium amounts to 31% and for men, 26% (figures 22.1b and 22.1c).

In the NHS, there is likely to be some positive change following enforcement of the two-tier code and the implementation of the Agenda for Change pay agreement, which has significantly boosted basic rates of pay for low wage workers. However, without a coordinated roll-out of this type of approach it is likely that the large number of women in low wage, part-time jobs will become an institutionalised feature of UK public services. This needs to be addressed in order to diffuse a common notion of public sector ethos and common expectations about what it is to work in a public services job, thereby encouraging teamwork and cooperation among different workforce groups. Moreover, a change of policy regarding market testing will contribute enormously to the recommendations of the Women and Work Commission[12] to develop initiatives to improve the quality of part-time work.

Figure 22.1 Trends in nominal pay in the public and private sectors for low paid, average and high paid workers 1997–2005.

Low paid are represented by the lowest decile wage, D1

High paid are represented by the highest decile wage, D9

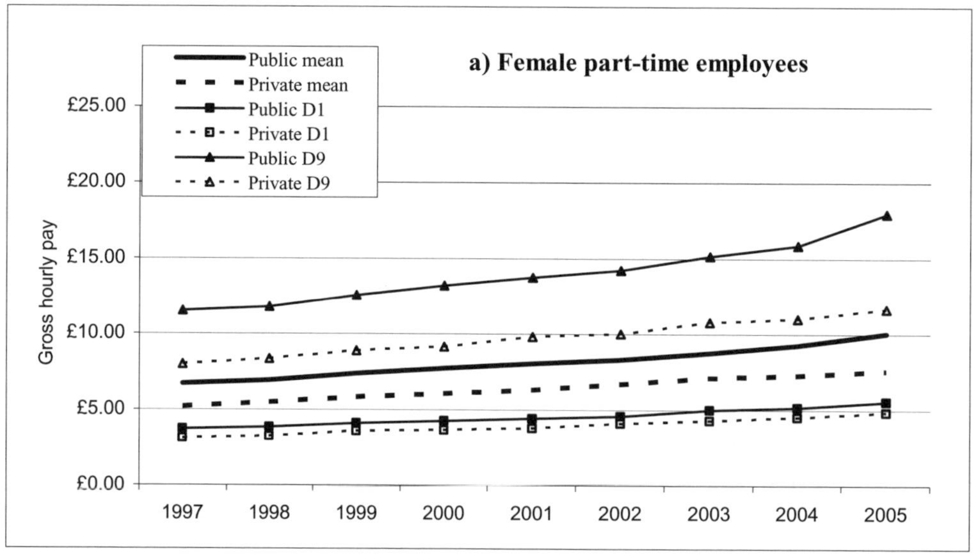

[12] Women and Work Commission (2006) Shaping a Fairer Future, pages 33-39.

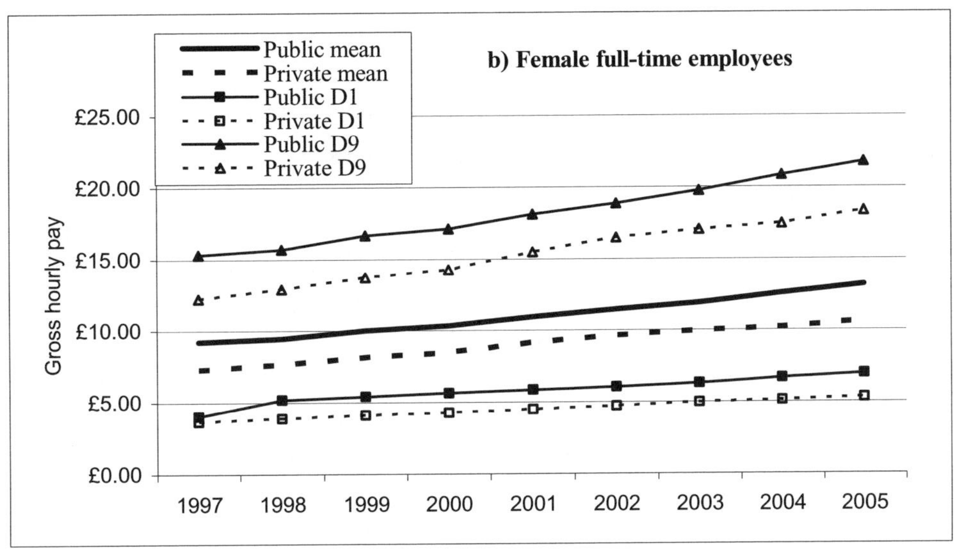

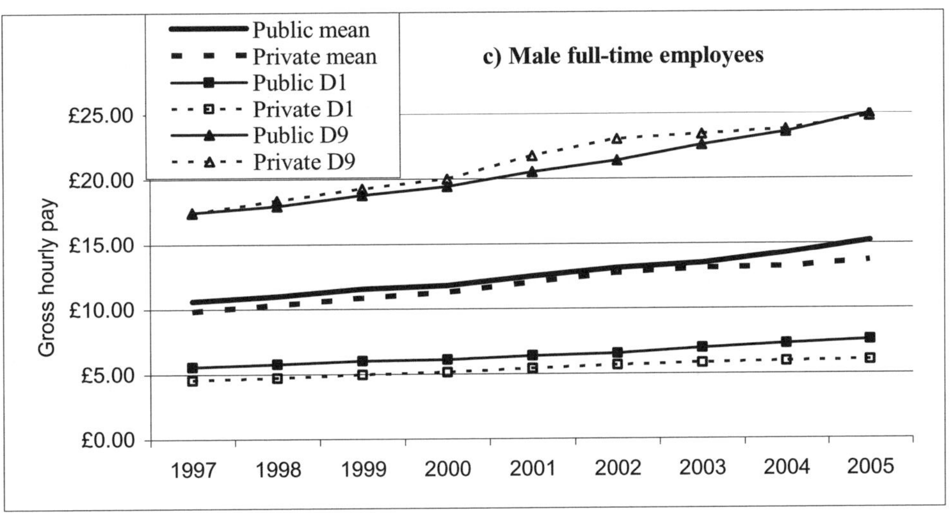

Source: Annual Survey of Hours and Earnings, own calculations.

Sex segregation

A major factor underpinning the remaining gender pay gap in the public sector is sex segregation, both vertical, within occupations (the so-called glass ceiling), and horizontal across occupations (occupational crowding), with women less likely to be represented among higher paid, high status jobs. There are many positive examples of policy reform which address this problem. For example, traditionally different groups of public sector workers – often segregated by sex – were covered by different systems of wage-setting. This resulted in different rates of pay and bonuses, often reflecting stereotypical notions of skills associated with women's and men's jobs, as well as differences in bargaining strength. But now local government workers are covered under a single, harmonised agreement (the Single Status Job Evaluation scheme) to embed equal pay principles into pay and job structures. And NHS workers are covered by a similar type of job evaluation scheme which incorporates equal value principles.

A further positive development is the new Public Sector duty on Gender Equality (the Gender Duty), enforced from April 2007, which requires all public authorities to promote gender equality and to reduce sex discrimination both in the way services are delivered and in the organisation of employment. Sex segregation ought to be addressed through proper application of this Duty in several ways: interrogation of how flexible working benefits male and female employees; consideration of how to improve the gender balance among new recruits; and identification of problems concerning the return rate of employees from maternity leave. Proper monitoring of the application of the Gender duty is required, as well as a budget for additional monies where needed to implement improved policy and practice within public authorities.

Equal pay reviews

The Women and Work Commission failed to reach a consensus on the important policy issue of whether or not to require organisations to complete an annual equal pay review; it therefore did not make a recommendation in its 2006 report. Instead, in its summing up of the pros and cons of making reviews compulsory, the Commission makes a strong case for the government, as public sector employer, to lead the way:

> Best practice in the public sector would make a difference to the nearly 40 per cent of women employees who work in public sector jobs spread across the country. Best practice in the public sector can also influence better practice in the private sector. ... The government must put its house in order ... all public sector employers must be at the forefront of implementing good practice in their treatment of women[13].

---

[13] Women and Work Commission (op. cit.: 89-90).

Moreover, the report recommends the Treasury "should ask public sector employers to account for their progress on equal pay during the Comprehensive Spending Review" and for the proposed Public Sector Pay Committee to ensure all new pay systems are "at the forefront of good practice on equal pay."[14] The new Gender Duty (see above) responds to this recommendation by requiring public authorities to investigate pay gaps between men and women doing the same job or jobs of similar value.

However, it is unlikely that private sector employers will voluntarily follow the 'best practice' demonstrated by the public sector. The evidence on equal pay reviews to date is illustrative. After an initial surge of activity following campaigns by government, the EOC and trade unions, during 2003-05 there has been negligible progress. The most recent survey reveals that 33% of public sector large organisations and 34% of private sector large organisations had completed a review by 2005[15]. The Gender Duty ought to improve completion rates for the public sector, and Government therefore should meet its Public Service Agreement target for 45% of large organisations to complete an equal pay review by 2008. But what will provide the spark for private sector employers?

The need for compulsory pay reviews for all large organisations, both public and private, ought to be established. A first stage should be to monitor application of the Gender Duty and to evaluate progress in addressing obstacles to gender equality at work including: obstacles to women's career progression; discrimination in entry rates of pay; the absence of equal value between male-dominated and female-dominated jobs requiring equivalent skills and expertise; unequal access to training; and difficulties in balancing work and family life. It is very likely that the evidence will highlight the advantages of a more equitable workplace for quality of working life and quality of services provision. A second stage should then consider the appropriate form of legislation to ensure all large organisations in the private sector also benefit from improved gender equality through conducting an annual equal pay review.

---

[14] Women and Work Commission (op. cit.: 92).

[15] Adams, L., Carter, K. and Schäfer, S. (2006) Equal pay reviews survey 2005, EOC Working Paper Series No.42.

Strategic Priority 2003[i]	Strategic Priority 2006[ii]	PSA Target 2002[iii]	PSA Target 2004[iv]
A world safer from global terrorism and weapons of mass destruction.	Making the world safer from global terrorism and weapons of mass destruction.	PSA 1 – International terrorism and the proliferation of WMD.	PSA 1 – Weapons of mass destruction PSA 2 – International terrorism
Protection of the UK from illegal immigration, drug trafficking and other international crime.	Reducing the harm to the UK from international crime, including drug trafficking, people smuggling and money laundering.		
An international system based on the rule of law, which is better able to resolve disputes and prevent conflicts.	Preventing and resolving conflict through a strong international system.	PSA2 – Reduce tension in South Asia, the Middle East, Balkans and elsewhere PSA 4 – Improve effectiveness of the UK contribution to conflict prevention and management	PSA 3 – Conflict prevention PSA 5 – European security
An effective EU in a secure neighbourhood.	Building an effective and globally competitive EU in a secure neighbourhood.	PSA 3 – Strengthen European security PSA 8 – A modern, reformed, and enlarged EU	PSA 4 – Effective EU PSA 5 – European security
Promotion of UK economic interests in an open and expanding global economy.	Supporting the UK economy and business through an open and expanding global economy, science and innovation and secure energy supplies.	PSA 5 – Deliver measurable improvement in the business performance of UKTI's customers PSA 6 – Secure agreement by 2005 to a significant reduction in trade barriers	PSA 6 – UK Trade & Investment
Security of UK and global energy supplies.	Achieving climate security by promoting a faster transition to a sustainable, low–carbon global economy.		
Sustainable development, underpinned by democracy, good governance and human rights.	Promoting sustainable development and poverty reduction underpinned by human rights, democracy, good governance and protection of the environment.	PSA 7 – Make globalisation work for sustainable development in the UK and internationally (and particularly in Africa)	PSA 7 – Engaging with the Islamic world PSA 8 – Sustainable development

Strategic Priority 2003[i]	Strategic Priority 2006[ii]	PSA Target 2002[iii]	PSA Target 2004[iv]
	Managing migration and combating illegal immigration.		PSA 9 – Entry clearance performance targets
	Delivering high quality support for British nationals abroad, in normal times and in crises.	PSA 10 – Effective and efficient consular and entry clearance services	PSA 9 – Entry clearance performance targets
Security and good governance of the UK's Overseas Territories.	Ensuring the security and good governance of the UK's Overseas Territories.	PSA 11 – Improvement in the governance, environment and security of the overseas territories, and more diversified economic development	
		PSA 9 – Effective advice on, support for, and delivery of Government objectives across the full range of the UK's international interests	
		PSA 12 – Improve value for money across the full range of FCO, BBC World Service and British Council activities	

[i] Foreign & Commonwealth Office, *UK International Priorities: a strategy for the FCO*, Foreign & Commonwealth Office, 2003
[ii] Foreign & Commonwealth Office, *FCO Departmental Report 2006/07,* 2007
[iii] Foreign & Commonwealth Office, *FCO Departmental Report 2006*, 2006
[iv] Foreign & Commonwealth Office, *FCO Departmental Report 2006*, 2006